A BLESSING OVER ASHES

A BLESSING OVER ASHES

The Remarkable

Odyssey of My

Unlikely Brother

ADAM FIFIELD

Perennial

An Imprint of HarperCollins*Publishers*

First Perennial edition published 2001.

Designed by Kellan Peck

The Library of Congress has catalogued the hardcover edition as follows:
Fifield, Adam
   A blessing over ashes: the remarkable odyssey of my unlikely brother / Adam Fifield—1st ed.
   p. cm.
   ISBN 0-380-97680-3 (hardcover : alk. paper)
   1. Saut, Soeuth. 2. Fifield, Adam. 3. Cambodia—Description and travel. 4. Political refugees—Cambodia. 5. Political refugees—United States. 6. Cambodian Americans—Biography. I. Title.

   E184.K45 S284 2000
   959.604'2'092—dc21   99-043965

ISBN 0-380-80049-7 (pbk.)

01 02 03 04 05 QW 10 9 8 7 6 5 4 3 2 1

TO MY BROTHERS

ACKNOWLEDGMENTS

If I thanked everyone who contributed to this book, the acknowledgments section would be longer than the first chapter. So to those of you I don't mention, my apologies.

I called my brother, Soeuth, in early 1996 to propose a feature article about him for the *Village Voice*. The article, due to a change in editors, never ran. Now more than four years later, the hundreds—perhaps thousands—of hours we spent together exhuming his past, turning over his memories, have paid off. Here is something solid, veritable—a book. So thank you, Soeuth, for taking my midnight calls when you had to get up at six A.M., for all those weekends I crashed on your couch and drank your beer, and for letting me pry without limits into your life.

The same goes for my little brother Dave, my mother and father, my grandfather, Ken Fifield, and my mother's parents, Albert and Priscilla Pearson. Parts of their lives are on display here, too. They have been inordinately patient, gracious, and informative. Without them, this book would be a lot slimmer and a lot duller.

Soeuth's wife, my sister-in-law, Mai, also put up with my often invasive interviews without refusing to answer one single question. Thank you, Mai.

My girlfriend, Kathleen Powers, did not have to undergo one of my interviews, but she did have to listen night after night for two full years as I fretted ad nauseam over the fate of my book.

She gave me unconditional support and love. Thank you, Kath—you lead me through the tunnel.

I would never have assumed that I had what it took to write a book without the encouragement of Samuel G. Freedman. He is a mentor, friend, and guardian angel. He read an early draft of the article I wrote, persuaded me to turn it into a book, introduced me to my wonderful agent—Tina Bennett—line-edited my first draft, and gave me enough confidence to believe in myself and my book when I doubted both. He also introduced me to my girlfriend. Without Sam, I would not have two of the most important things in my life. There is no way to adequately thank you, Sam.

Tina Bennett is, I truly believe, a Super Agent. A tireless and devoted advocate and advisor, she stuck with me through four editors and was in my corner whenever I needed her. She, too, line-edited many parts of this book.

Thanks to all the dedicated editors who worked on this book: Rachel Klayman for buying the project; Hamilton Cain for giving me such an insightful, incisive and exacting edit; Kelly Notaras; Krista Stroever; and to Tia Maggini and Jennifer Hershey for smoothly shepherding *A Blessing Over Ashes* through its final stages.

As for the dozens of other people I interviewed and consulted, my appreciation goes in particular to Bi Hoang, Phun (Johnny) Phon, Tom Fisher, Bob Silverstein, Hubert Wagner, Mark Johnson, Doc Seubert, Carol Lee Lane, James Riopeel, Mickey Holler, Joe Piper, Jerry Rule, Crystal Rule, Joseph Donnelly, Thane Sandburg, Louise Sandburg, Walter Miller, Wiltrud Miller, Thel Sar, Samkhann Khoeun, Somaly Sophuok, Sophy Theam, and most of all, the members of Soeuth's Cambodian family. Some of you are characters, others sources—all precious parts of the fabric of this story.

I also owe thanks to friends who helped me out in one way or another: Wayne Barrett, Gary Crosse, Andria Chin, Evan, Robert and Joli Halper, Anne Burgan, Eric Wolf, Dierdre Hussey, David Littlefield, and Meala and Bopha Chan. Thank you, all.

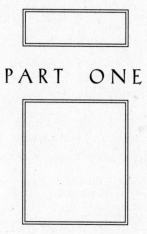

PART ONE

My new brother, Soeuth Saut, arrived on a snow-blurred night, a few weeks after the Christmas of 1983. We waited for him in our front room with soda, potato chips and a bright red-and-yellow banner, reading "WELCOME SOOTHE!" which my little brother, Dave, and I had drawn with magic markers. Mom had set our family photo album out on the coffee table, next to the soda and chips. Dave and I sat at opposite ends of the couch, Mom and Dad in chairs. No one said anything. Outside, the wind funneled steadily at the side of our house, and I could feel, on the back of my neck, cold spurts of breeze from gaps between the windowpanes Dad hadn't caulked up yet. Dad seemed to be thinking of other things; his hands were folded in his lap, his eyes aimed sideways at the door, his Adam's apple sharp and still. Dave examined his distorted reflection in a Christmas-tree ornament ball, while Frisbee, our dog, twitched in her sleep at Dave's feet. Mom let out sturdy, expectant sighs, hoping someone else would be the first to puncture the silence.

Mom had informed us, while pouring the chips into her wooden salad bowl, that our new brother had taken his father's first name as his last name because he didn't remember what his real last name was. When we had asked if he would take our last name, she had said that would be up to him. She had also assured us that he wouldn't be coming to us straight from the other side of the world. He had been living for a little while with another family here in town, who were strict Germans from whom he had run away. I hadn't asked Mom how she knew he wouldn't run away from us.

When tires finally crunched over the gravel in our driveway, Frisbee barked herself awake, Dave lifted his gaze lingeringly from the Christmas-tree ornament and I cracked my knuckles. Mom smiled at each of us individually, swiveling her head around the room.

A car door clicked quietly, carefully shut, and then another one was shut with equal care. Footsteps thudded slowly up the garage stairway outside. With almost choreographed precision, Dad stood up suddenly, plunged both hands deep into his change-heavy pockets and drew a long breath. Before he could exhale, there were three small, quick knocks at the door.

Dad opened the door and then unlatched the screen door and smiled his doctor smile out the doorway. "Come in," he said. He took a few steps back and jingled the change in his pockets. As if lured, somehow, by the jingling of the change, a small figure shuffled in, followed by a tall, dark-haired man. The man was smiling under his mustache, or trying to; our new brother was not. The boy was short and scrawny, with shiny, copper-colored skin. We could see only the bottom half of his face—the hyphen of a little mouth, the slope of a nose—because the shadow of a baseball-cap visor eclipsed his eyes and forehead. His big blue parka swallowed him and made his legs look like a bird's. His arms clutched his sides so that he seemed straitjacketed against us. Though his eyes were hidden, his gaze was trained in the direction of the radiator, whose wheezing was the only sound in the room.

The man, whom we would come to know as Mr. Silverstein, held onto the straps of a rumpled duffel bag that dangled at his knees and contained all of this boy's possessions. After a moment, Mr. Silverstein gently set down the duffel bag, placed his hands on the boy's shoulders and said, "Well, here he is."

We all said, "Hi."

Dad rocked on his heels and raised his eyebrows, and Mom said, "We're very happy to have you in our home."

The boy said nothing.

After a few seconds swelled into an awkward silence, Mom stumbled over and hugged him. He hugged back weakly, hands hanging limp from reluctant arms. When she stepped away from him, he stood shivering, as if Mom were ice-cold to the touch. I could see his eyes now, which stared intently at the floor. I supposed he could peer right through it, burrowing through the wood, the pipes, the concrete, the rich layers of Champlain Valley loam and all that lay beneath them, until he was able to see clear to the other side of the world.

When he finally looked up, hard eyes fixed me from beneath the visor of his baseball cap. Eyes that tell you someone is bigger and older than the body he is trapped in. But then his eyes darted to the floor again. He stole a few more glances at Dave and me, but never once looked at Mom and Dad, even when they spoke to him.

The red-and-yellow welcome banner hung uselessly on the wall. He didn't look very welcome. He didn't cast one peek toward our family photo album. He didn't eat any chips.

We ushered him through the house, showed him his room, and when we came back downstairs, Mom pointed out some board games, probably Monopoly and Scrabble, that we had set out on the dining room table. His eyes scanned the games and then flew up to Mr. Silverstein for an explanation, and Mr. Silverstein smiled and squeezed his shoulder. It was only later I would understand that Mr. Silverstein, a lanky Jewish man with a ponytail, was one of the few adults in the world who hadn't betrayed or abandoned him in some way. At that moment he was this boy's only connection to the world.

We did not sit down to play board games. Our new brother and Mr. Silverstein stood on one side of the dining room table, and we stood on the other side. As Mom told Mr. Silverstein about our horses and the rope swing out at the river and downhill skiing, the table felt like some kind of barrier designed to keep us from each other. The boy had taken off his baseball cap and now clutched it to himself with both hands, and the light from the dining room chandelier shone on his dark, downcast face. Mr. Silverstein kept his big-knuckled hand on the boy's shoulder. Each time I sneaked a glimpse at my new brother, I knew I was risking that hard stare—but his head hung still, like a hat on a stand. One thought pulsed in my head: that this was a big mistake, that this boy didn't belong with us, that he didn't belong anywhere.

Eventually, Mr. Silverstein clasped his hands together and pivoted sharply toward the kitchen, as if a pot on the stove had started to boil over. He said, "I think it's time I get going." He bent down and whispered to Soeuth, and Soeuth nodded. Standing up, Mr. Silverstein raised his eyebrows at all of us, and we smiled, trying to look up at him and not at this stranger in our house.

Mr. Silverstein squeezed the boy's shoulder again, quickly, then made his way toward the kitchen. Mom followed him. The sound of Mr. Silverstein's pant legs swishing as he walked away made our dining room suddenly big and quiet. Silhouetted by the incandescent light of the kitchen, Mom and Mr. Silverstein shook hands. He handed her a wrinkled manila envelope, which she tucked under her arm. I imagined that the envelope contained deeply encoded secrets, warnings about this boy's fearsome, otherworldly, ninja powers. Then Mr. Silverstein put on his coat, and Mom walked him to the back-porch door.

Dave, Dad and I were left alone with the new boy. Dad laced his fingers together and rocked on his heels. Dave and I mimicked him. Our new brother stood still.

"Well, boys," Dad finally said. "How 'bout some ice cream?"

Dave and I nodded. "Sounds good, Dad," we mumbled in unison.

But when Dad went into the kitchen to open the freezer, our new brother scuttled up the stairs and shut himself in his room. We ate our ice cream without him.

*   *   *

That night I listened carefully for any sounds coming from Soeuth's room, which was across the hall from mine, but heard nothing. I was worried, because I hadn't had a chance to warn him about the ghosts. That was the only problem with our house—it was full of ghosts. Built a few decades before the Civil War, it was a big, drafty farmhouse with a lot of history in it, our neighbor, Farmer Seeley, had said. After all, a lot of farming families had lived in it—and most of them had died in it, too. Farmer Seeley had paid a visit one afternoon in the fall to give Mom a quart of his fancy-grade maple syrup. He sat at our kitchen table in his overalls, sipping coffee and picking flecks of hay out of his knotted beard. The funerals were held over where you got your dining room table, he had informed us. They used to lay up the body right where you put your Thanksgiving turkey, he had added with a wink at Dave and me. Every night that next week when all the lights were shut off, I began to hear clicks and clacks and breathing noises from the unoccupied room across the hall from my own, and I came to appreciate Farmer Seeley's wink as of the most serious sort.

So Dave and I had stayed out of that room, except to help Mom prepare it for the new boy. We vacuumed the rug, wiped dead flies off the windowsills, broomed cobwebs off the ceiling corners, made up the bed. I put one of my old teddy bears on the bed, even though I knew he might be too old for it. Mom tacked up a poster of some place in Asia, maybe China or Thailand—a waterfall, cascading between bright green palm trees—which clashed with the tawdry wallpaper, bright pink and yellow flowers set against jaundiced green. We put a chair and a table in the corner; other than that, the room was bare. We didn't know how he would want it.

We sat in Mom's high-backed wicker chairs, our eyes flickering with the dinner candles, and waited for Soeuth. Mom asked Dad about his new hours, and he said he had more time on the week-ends but would be on call more. Then he loosened his belt and swiveled toward me and Dave and said, *don't ever think of being doctors, boys, ever.* We both nodded and mumbled, *yes, Dad,* and Dave tore apart his napkin, carefully arranging its shreds in a wreath around his plate. Just after Mom touched her chin to her chest and just before she was about to announce that she would look for Soeuth, we heard the barely audible brush of his sneakers on the carpeted stairs.

He came in slowly, staring down, taking care with each step. In the candlelight, he looked like a tiny ascetic figure moving through the dim hall of a monastery. He slid slowly, cautiously, into his chair. As Mom explained different strategies for eating baked potatoes and pork chops and Dad demonstrated, Soeuth kept his eyes on his plate.

After Mom brought out the ice cream for dessert and assigned me and Dave to clear the table, she and Dad stood on each side of Soeuth behind his chair and showed him our family photo album. As he studied the red-eyed, flushed faces of our relatives, his face bore the honed concentration of someone searching for suspects in a police lineup.

"That's Grandpa Ken!" Mom exclaimed with a jolting cheerfulness. It was a photo of our guffawing grandpa holding a diapered, drooling Dave. Soeuth regarded the photo obediently and then averted his eyes back to his place mat.

"He's my father," Dad explained.

"This is Adam when he was two," Mom said. The photo showed me standing inside a toilet bowl, naked, squeezing a big gob of toothpaste into my mouth. Soeuth seemed puzzled.

"This is my father." Mom flipped to a stark black-and-white photo of Grandpa Al when he was captain of the Tufts football team, cradling the ball, frowning toughly. When she had first shown me that photo, I remember thinking Grandpa Al looked like a mobster in football gear. Soeuth gave the photo a cursory, dead-eyed glance.

Dad put away the photo album, and Mom served the ice cream. Soeuth didn't touch his, didn't even lift his spoon. Once the rest of us finished, he slipped out of his chair and slunk up to his room. When Soeuth's door squealed shut upstairs, Dave stared at me inquiringly. I shrugged back. In the ensuing silence, Dave began slurping spoonfuls of chocolate syrup, until Mom took the Hershey's squeeze bottle away.

Soeuth made barely a sound during his first few weeks with us, spending most of his time shut up in his room. I wondered what we had done wrong, why the very sight of us either seemed to mortify him, paralyze him or send him packing. Was it indifference? Fear? Or was this whole thing a trick? Was he planning to awake in the murky hours of the night, sneak into our rooms, slit our throats and then cook us up on some giant spit he'd whittled?

One night, after everyone else had gone to bed, I asked Dad, who had put on his Buddy Holly glasses to read the *Journal of the American Medical Association,* if he could show me where Soeuth's country was in the encyclopedia. He nodded, stood up and selected the C–Ch volume from our *World Book Encyclopedia* collection, which Mom had bought for us after I turned eleven the year before. He cracked the book about halfway and flipped toward the front. When he found the page he wanted, he chewed his lower lip thoughtfully and said, "Hmmm," and closed the C–Ch book and returned it to the shelf. He then snatched the J–K book, flipped to the right page, handed me the book and said, "There it is, Addie. I'm going to go brush my teeth. Then, in a few minutes, I think you should brush yours, too."

He removed his glasses, rubbed his eyes and went upstairs. I set the book in my lap, hoping I could pick up a few useful clues about this place on the other side of the world called Kampuchea, which was pronounced *kam-poo-CHEE-uh* and was also, confusingly, called Cambodia, according to the *World Book* authors. But I didn't read the profile; I didn't have time for that. I looked at the two black-and-white photos. One showed a few thatched huts perched on stilts on the shore of what the photo caption said was the Tonle Sap lake. The caption said something about floods, and I thought about how we get floods, too, here in the Champlain Valley; maybe a flood would make Soeuth feel more at home. In the next photo there was a man walking down an empty city street, and behind him there was a truck with a lot of people crowded on top of it, some sitting on the hood, waving flags. The unsmiling man in front of the truck had a gun and was smoking a cigarette and appeared to be walking very fast. I thought about how brave this photographer must have been to stand there and take this picture. Everyone else in the photo also looked very serious, like they all were getting ready to do something big and violent and maybe against the law, and I figured that these must be the bad guys with the fancy French name that Mom had told us about. I slapped the encyclopedia shut and set it on the coffee table and ran upstairs to brush my teeth and go to bed.

The next day, Saturday, Soeuth came down from his room for lunch, wrapped in a blanket. Standing silently by the antique chinaware case in the dining room, he watched Dave and me jam curls of bologna into our mouths at the kitchen table. The only sound was that of the mustard threading out of the squeeze bottle. When we were down to the last slice, Mom strolled into the kitchen, smiling brightly, noticed Soeuth and said: "Well, hello, sweetheart—how did you sleep?"

He didn't answer.

She walked over to him and patted him on the head. He jerked away from her and ran behind the table. His eyes accused her sharply from behind a dining room chair.

"Soeuth?" She was dumbfounded. "Honey, what's wrong?"

He ran up to his room.

Mom called Mr. Silverstein. After she got off the phone, she told us she had made a big mistake.

"Boys . . ." Her voice was raspy and faint, her eyes red. "In Soeuth's country, it's very bad manners to pat someone on the head."

We stared at her wordlessly.

"Boys . . ." She laced her fingers together tightly. "Remember . . . don't touch Soeuth on the head."

Mr. Silverstein would become our liaison to Soeuth's culture. He visited every few weeks and taught us what we should and shouldn't do to be sensitive to the customs and taboos of Cambodia. When Mr. Silverstein spoke, his words were carefully hewed. Whenever he said the word "culture," masterfully rounding and then hinging its two syllables together, I felt in the presence of a great, mysterious wisdom. Most of the time, Mom was the conduit for this wisdom, and we would imbibe it secondhand.

I was enthralled, at first, with this idea of "culture." The word furnished my imagination with outlandish, exquisite things— chanted rituals, brightly colored beads, mortars and pestles, voodoo dolls and funny accents—things that made one unique, things I knew we Fifields could never have. The visitors who had stayed with us before Soeuth, from places like Ecuador and Belgium and Indonesia, all had "culture," too, but it wasn't until Soeuth's arrival that the concept of a set of age-old traditions and beliefs made me realize that growing up with white middle-class parents in the whitest state in America pretty much guaranteed you a culture-free existence.

After another talk with Mr. Silverstein, Mom explained to us why she should never have touched Soeuth on the head. Cambodians believe that your head is the seat of your soul, she said. I pictured Soeuth's soul caged up in his skull, a gnomish old man in a rocking chair with a broom ready at his side, in case of a ceiling disturbance, to bang all around the inside of his head and make one hell of a racket.

It is common in Cambodia, Mr. Silverstein told Mom, for boys to hold hands, just like boys do high fives here. Everybody calls each other brother and sister in Cambodia, even if no one is related—I tried this at school and received some chilly stares in return. And Cambodians really hate to lose face, we learned, and for the longest time I imagined Soeuth's face to be some sort of detachable plate, loosely screwed to his head, that could pop off at any time. Mom clarified that losing face meant being made to look wrong or stupid in front of other people, and so I was careful not to correct Soeuth on anything. She was also instructed never to include Soeuth in a photograph with three people together, she told us, because many Cambodians believe that an untimely death or disaster will befall the shortest person in the photo or the one in the middle.

To me, the photo rule made perfect sense. By the time I reached ten, I harbored a store of superstitions. I would go out of my way not to step on cracks in sidewalks, even crooked hairline cracks, fearing that one misstep could put Mom in the hospital in traction. I developed a compulsion to perfectly align the coffee table coasters with the table corners. If, while walking along Creek Road, I saw a pebble or a hunk of gravel that cast a long shadow on the road, I would kick it aside; on some days, when the gravel shadows were as numerous as dandelions in a field, it took me half an hour to walk three hundred yards.

I knew there were certain unspoken rules some of us had to live by—those of us shouldered with the awareness of the delicate balance between good and evil, between chaos and order, and the tiny things that could upset those balances. But Soeuth, it seemed to me, was paralyzed by such an awareness, spending most of his waking hours shut off from interaction.

We tried giving him things. Dave was always knocking on Soeuth's door, taking food up to his room. It would be a few seconds before the door whined slowly open, and Soeuth's eyes peered out of the darkness.

"Hey, Suit," Dave would say; he still couldn't get his name right, still couldn't say it like soot in a chimney. "Hey, Suit, I got some fruit roll-ups. Here. Take some." Dave would hold up the box with both hands, like he was offering something coveted and expensive, and string a big smile across his face. Soeuth would look impassively at the fruit roll-ups and then shake his head, as if we were snake-oil salesmen, and shut the door.

We showed him Space Invaders on the Atari. He sat quietly on the floor next to us, watching as we each racked up our best scores to date. When it was his turn, he handled the joystick carefully, weighing it in his hands, and then proceeded to swiftly double my score. His eyes never left the screen, as if he were exploding the spaceships by force of will alone. As he played, his hands fluttered like butterfly wings; his body was still. When his game was over, he rose without saying a word and went back to his room.

Dave and I squatted in front of the Atari, his sudden absence like a ringing in our ears.

"What the heck?" Dave was pouting and absently pounding his joystick on the carpet. "We're just trying to make things . . . homey for him."

"I know, Dave," I said, prying the joystick loose from his fist. "But maybe he's never felt homey before."

"I guess he hasn't really had a home for a while."

"And his parents got killed," I noted.

Dave nodded and said, "Yup." Then he added, "That must be sad."

We sat there on the floor, Dave thumping a beanbag with a loose fist.

We tried to devise other ways of breaking through to him. I suggested we ask him to play Star Wars, but of course he had never seen the movie, so that was no good. Maybe we could build a snowman, Dave proposed. So we asked him, but he shook his head in three or four quick jerks, like he had been hit with a temporary bout of palsy, and left the room. They probably had no snow in Cambodia, we figured: winter in Vermont would be tough. I thought he might like hide-and-seek, since Mom had said that he had to hide from the bad guys in Cambodia. But Dave nixed that idea, too, saying that he would probably just hide in his room once we started playing and never come out. So we gave up.

There were a few times when Soeuth woke up at night shaking and sweating. On one of those nights, I heard my parents' voices floating into my room. My door was opened a crack, and I could see Mom and Dad both kneeling down beside him in the hallway; he was sitting in the squeaky rocking chair, cocooned in a blanket, his face ossified by some nightmare.

"What's wrong, dear? You can tell us," Mom said in her tranquil voice.

Soeuth rocked very slowly back and forth without answering or looking up.

Dad tried. "Hey, Soeuth, we want to help you," he said in his doctor voice. "This is your house, too, and we want you to feel comfortable in it."

He just sat there stunned, his brow furrowed, the outline of his skull hard and prominent.

"Please, Soeuth, we want to help you," Mom insisted.

He kept rocking, his jaw locked. But then his eyes flickered, and his mouth bunched into a frown. He said it like it was the natural answer anyone should have expected: "Ghos."

Mom and Dad glanced at each other.

"Ghosts?" Mom said. "Are you worried about ghosts?"

He nodded.

"Dear, you don't need to worry about that," she said like she was an expert on ghosts, which she wasn't. "We don't allow ghosts in our house."

"Ghos," he said again, his word hanging in the air like the

echo of a distant gunshot. His eyes traced the wall above the staircase, as if there were some pattern in the wallpaper only he could see. "Ghos . . . Mom, Dad, ghos."

It was the most I had ever heard him say. His voice was low and gravelly, not the voice of a kid.

Mom's face narrowed, registering this new information. "Your parents' ghosts?"

He nodded.

She didn't have an answer for that. "Dear, no matter whose ghost it is, they can't hurt you. Okay? . . . You can sleep with us, in our room—there are no ghosts there, just Frisbee."

He shook his head.

Mom smiled her sorry smile. "Okay, Soeuth. You can always change your mind."

My parents went back to bed.

Later, on the recommendation of Mr. Silverstein, Soeuth and Mom built a funeral shrine on a foldout card table in the southwest corner of his room. Mom fixed four sandalwood incense sticks in wooden incense holders, two at each end of the table, and, behind the pairs of incense holders, set two small porcelain vases, each containing a nosegay of daisies and carnations. In the middle of the table, she placed a small wooden salad bowl in which Soeuth arranged an offering of grapes and bananas. Behind the salad bowl, Soeuth set a jade Buddha that Mom's missionary friend had given to him. The hope was that the somber, straight-backed Buddha, the fresh fruit and the warm, diplomatic smell of the incense would appease Soeuth's parents' ghosts.

When I first saw the shrine, I was mesmerized. Strands of incense smoke swirled and knotted together at the ceiling, high over the Buddha's head, and, although no larger than sunflower seeds, the Buddha's deep-carved eyes reeled me into the room. I put my hands together under my chin—the action seemed appropriate—and prepared to issue a special entreaty to the Buddha. I would ask him, since he was hopefully already taking care of Soeuth's parents' ghosts, if he wouldn't mind making peace with the other ghosts in the house as well. It was probably nothing to him either way, I figured. Just as I was about to make my request, it occurred to me that the ghosts could swarm in here at any minute and that I could end up as wide-eyed and slack-faced as Soeuth.

"Addie . . . ?" Mom's voice wafted up the stairs, unfastening me from the stare of the Buddha. "Your father could use some help stacking wood."

The shrine seemed to work. A few days after it was built, the hauntings ceased. His parents' ghosts had gone back to Cambodia or some other place, I supposed, and apparently so had all the other ghosts, because I heard not one mysterious click or clack in the house after that. I laughed to myself when I thought about the bewildered spirits of old Vermont farmers now trapped in a Cambodian jungle.

I asked Mom if I could have a Buddha figure like the one Soeuth had. Not only would my shrine keep ghosts away, it would summon spirits from the afterworld and then act as a sort of spook dispatching center, sending them into the homes of certain deserving individuals. My offerings would be a plate of Oreos and a bag of Cheetos, and maybe a Twinkie or two. I would put the Buddha in the middle, my Luke Skywalker action figure on the right and Chewbacca on the left. A shrine with those three, especially the Buddha with his deep, galactic eyes, would inspire, I assumed, respect from even the most ill-tempered otherworldly entities. But Mom said that it would hurt Soeuth's feelings if I had a Buddha figure, because Buddha was like Jesus to Soeuth, Buddha was the son of God on the other side of the world. But Jesus didn't seem as invulnerable and mighty as Buddha, with his weary eyes and thin, beat-up body. Since the only Jesus I could find was a baby in a cradle glued to Mom's antique nativity scene, I gave up on the idea.

When February finally thawed into March, Dave suggested we all three go out to build a fort in the woods. I thought it was a good idea, but maybe still a little unrealistic. Until now, Soeuth had ventured outside only to go to school. Mom had always made Dave and me ride the bus, but since Soeuth's arrival, she had driven us all to school every morning. I never saw Soeuth in school that year, because he was a year ahead of me, in seventh grade, and attended classes in a different building. When he returned home from school, he would often wrap himself in a blanket and lie on the floor, less than a foot from the crackling drone of the wood stove.

One day, after school, Soeuth didn't come inside with Dave and me. After a few minutes, we went outside and found him curled in the fetal position on the picnic table under the maples in our backyard. Mom tried to talk to him, but he wouldn't speak or move. With his body balled up tight, his eyes open and unblinking, Soeuth reminded me of the birds I had found on the pool patio, stunned after a batting around by one of our cats. We didn't know what to do, so we left him alone. At some point he must have sneaked inside and crept up to his room, because when we went back out to check on him a half hour or so later, he was gone.

On an afternoon a few days later, when Dave and I were climbing one of the knotty old maples in our backyard, Soeuth plodded down the back-porch stairs and stood slouched under the hood of his sweatshirt. He was staring at the soggy gray grass at his feet and occasionally sneaking glances at us. Suddenly, he scurried up the tree like Tarzan, as though its branches were helping him, hoisting him up. He said not a word as he climbed past us, gliding through the leaves, his hands barely connecting with the branches. He was the most agile tree climber I had ever seen. And he didn't seem afraid of falling, his feet swinging loosely under him, as if the distance between him and the ground were five feet, not twenty-five. Dave and I stopped climbing and sat on our sturdy lower branches, safe and dumbfounded.

When the sun began to sink into the mountains, Mom called out that dinner was ready. "Bo-oys . . ." she yelled, the word knifing like a boomerang toward us. Finally she yelled that if we didn't climb down right away and eat our dinner, we wouldn't get any. So Dave and I obeyed. But Soeuth stayed in the tree. When we went back out to fetch him, he was cowering in a thicket of branches, his arms locked tight around the tree's trunk, tears glistening on his cheeks. Mom and Dad tried to coax him down, but he eyed them warily like a treed muskrat and wouldn't budge. They both stood there a while at the bottom of the tree, in the sunset's amber glow, hands on their hips, heads craned up so that their Adam's apples poked out—as if watching for the blink of a UFO on the horizon. Dave and I were sitting on the porch steps, flicking pebbles into Mom's flower bed. It occurred to me that we could leave Soeuth's dinner at the base of the tree to lure him down, but just as I was about to suggest this, Mom and Dad trudged back to the house. "C'mon, boys." Dad's voice was hoarse, defeated. "Let's go in." Later that night, well into dark, he climbed down. But we wouldn't see him until the next day.

When I rambled down the stairs in the morning, humming the James Bond theme song, I spotted Soeuth and Mom sitting at opposite ends of the kitchen table. The sight of him stopped my humming.

"Morning, Addie!" Mom chirped. "Have some Cheerios! Dave's already eaten breakfast."

As I opened the cabinet, I glanced over at the table, and his eyes met mine in a jarring moment. My gaze shunted to the cabinet and, for a minute or two, I absently read the ingredients on the Cheerios box.

"Do you want to talk about it?" Mom asked, her voice as soft and buttery as I've ever heard it.

Soeuth's chair squeaked for an answer.

"We can talk about it later if you want."

There was a short, sputtery sigh. "Sometime," he whispered, his voice sandpaper on old wood. "In Kambudja . . ." Then he stopped. It was painful for him to speak.

"It's okay," Mom said. "It's okay, Soeuth. You can tell me."

I carefully extracted the box of Cheerios and padded at a funeral pace over to the counter. I eased the refrigerator door open. As I dribbled the milk over the bowl, I stole a few peeks at the table. He was slumped over, staring into a cup of soda.

His shoulders caved in toward his chest, like somebody had tried to fold him up and put him in a box. At this point, he shuffled loudly in his seat and said, "If I bad . . . no food."

Mom stood up from her chair and knelt down beside him and rested her hand on his shoulder. He did not move away from her but kept staring into the soda. He said, "No food . . . scare die."

Then he looked up at her. "No food . . . run 'way."

Mom blinked, speechless. Then, at some point, she told him he could eat whatever, whenever, he wanted.

But he didn't eat much anyway. At dinner, he slouched in his chair, trying, it seemed, to duck the often haphazard back-and-forth of family conversation. He would study his plate, as though he were peering through an invisible microscope, scrutinizing the molecular makeup of his mashed potatoes. The only food he ate a lot of was rice. Mom would always fix him a bowl of rice to go with whatever else we were having for dinner. He would eat it for breakfast, too. I hated rice. It seemed pointless and reminded me of maggots and was not something you asked for; I much preferred macaroni and cheese or chocolate pudding or Steak-ums. But Soeuth's face would darken at the sight of these and other Fifield family staples.

One Saturday morning, while Dave and I poked around with willow-tree twigs for garter snakes in the weeds that speared up around the horse barn, I suggested to Dave that we invite Soeuth to the river to cast our lines in for some bass and rainbow trout. He agreed that it was a good idea. That afternoon I made the proposition.

Soeuth's eyes betrayed no recognition when I brandished a fishing pole and tackle box and said: "Let's go fishin'!" I held the pole high over my head so that the bait hook dangled before his eyes. "You know, you put a worm on here." I went to pinch the hook between thumb and forefinger, to show him the barb that kept the fish from sliding off, and ended up pricking myself. A ladybug-sized bead of blood formed on the tip of my thumb.

Wringing my hand, I tried not to grimace. "And then," I continued, "when you drop the hook in the water, a fish bites it."

"Feesh?" he said. He knew what a fish was; it was one of the words Mom had taught him or he had learned in school.

"Oh, yeah. Gargantuan ones! Taller than you! Hell—taller than me!" So I proceeded to relay a Farmer Seeley fishing story. Sitting on a shelf of limestone out by the river one day, minding his own business, Farmer Seeley sees a log, six feet long or so, riding on the current, scraping along pebbles in a shallow patch of river. He doesn't think much of it, just reels his line out of its path. Then the log, all of a sudden, starts swimming, squiggling itself over a sandbar. "By Jesus!" Farmer Seeley says to himself and then sits up straight and lets out his line. The log fish nips at it for a while, until finally the hook catches him, and Farmer Seeley has a fight on his hands. He and that fish are wrestling like a barn dog and a bobcat. He reels at it, and it pulls back, and he nearly loses his footing a few times and curses the damned, ornery fish, wishing then that he'd gone to the river that day with his twelve-gauge, not his fishing pole. Eventually, the fish twitches a few times and then goes fairly limp, and Farmer Seeley pulls it in. It was a northern pike just shy of six feet—the kind of mean-tempered fish that could clip a few fingers. When he slits it open to clean it, he finds an extra bonus inside its belly: a ten-inch-long rainbow trout, nearly undigested.

Soeuth wasn't as impressed as I had hoped, but his eyes glittered as he thought about it. Finally he said, "Wheh de feesh?"

"The river!" I answered. "The river, out back!"

On Sunday afternoon after church—Soeuth had started coming to church with us and would sit next to Dave and me in the pew, hunched over in a question-mark-like shape, his eyes burning some unspoken, other-side-of-the-world prayer into the hymnals on the seat back—Dave and I set out the poles and tackle on the pool patio. Dave propped our fishing poles, gunmetal-gray and pea-green rods with foam grips, against the side of the house. We scooped out the contents of our bait box and laid them out on the table like jewelry at a yard sale. There were red and white float bobbers, nylon leaders, hooks, snap swivels, bass casting lead sinkers and a whole assortment of bug and minnow lures. But we were mostly worm fishermen, in the tradition of Grandpa Ken, and also had a Campbell's soup can full of night crawlers we had collected from Mom's garden the night before.

Since we figured Soeuth had never been fishing before, we set aside Dad's lucky pole, a sleek, jet-black rod with an aluminum casting reel and cork grip, for him. Dave and I always fought over this pole whenever we fished off Grandpa Ken's dock on Lake St. Catherine, but today we both agreed that the newcomer should have the advantage. When he shuffled onto the pool patio, I thrust the lucky pole at him and said: "Here you go, it's the best one we got, and we saved it just for you." His gaze slid up and down the pole a few times before his lips pursed and his face wrinkled distastefully.

Our new brother went to the river that day armed with only a towel and Mom's green plastic colander. We squeezed under the barbed-wire fence on the north side of the barn to avoid the stench of the sewer pond. Soeuth tagged behind Dave and me as we plodded sloppily through the cow pasture, lugging our gear, tromping out a matted path through weeds and thistles. We had shed our shoes and socks and rolled up our pant legs for this excursion, and by the time we reached the East Middlebury River, the spaces in between our toes had caked up with mud and mustard-brown muck from cow paddies.

When Dave and I cast our lines, Soeuth scampered off around a bend in the river.

"Where the hell's he going?"

"I don't know," said Dave distractedly, letting out his line. "Current picks up down there, though. A lot harder to fish."

After a half hour, Dave's line got tangled with mine, and he started complaining of a hitch in his reel. Neither of us had yet felt the slightest tug on our lines. We both cursed, muttering that the fish must have swum clear to Canada, when Soeuth came trotting around the bend, his towel slung over his shoulders, proudly holding out Mom's colander before him. He set the colander on a wet knob of sand, and we both gasped when we saw that it was brimming with a shiny heap of crayfish, trout and bass.

He crouched carefully on the bank, perched on the balls of his feet, his hands hanging over his knees. His eyes plumbed the quiet water, skimming the shallow, sandy bottom. Then his arm was a blur, shooting down in a sudden splash. When he rose to his feet, a crayfish was pinched between his thumb and forefinger. He dropped the twitching, muddy critter into the colander and looked up for approval.

Dave said, "Wow."

As Dave and I volleyed a few "holy shit" glances, Soeuth reached into his pocket and plucked out a crouton. He sank back into a crouch and raked his fingers through the sand until he found a golf-ball-sized rock. He flipped the crouton into a spot of water mottled by the shade of cattails. He waited, squatting on the bank, rolling the rock in his palm, until a rainbow trout wiggled up and went to pecking at the crouton. His eyes fixed on the trout. He raised his arm and winged the rock. Plunk! The fish rolled belly-up, stunned by Soeuth's rock. Tenderly, he fetched his prize and cradled the slick trout, soothing away the last few seconds of its life. In that moment, as this mysterious boy stood before us and made everything go quiet, I felt a sense that, for the first time in my life, I was attached to the world.

Soeuth prowled the banks, eyes darting at movement in the murky water, arms floating weightlessly at his sides, hands steady and waiting to strike. When his eyes caught something, he dropped down and hugged the bank, his hands like hounds sniffing for a hint of prey.

Soon we were slinking along the banks and tributaries after him, eyes honed for movement, hands poised and ready to snatch our prey. When he slid into the water, his feet padded over the sharp riverbed stones at a steady pace; Dave and I followed cautiously, flinching at every step.

That spring, crayfishing became a ritual. Each day after school the three of us would gather up our towels and catch containers (which included the colander, a salad bowl and Mom's brownie tin) and head for the banks of the East Middlebury River. It wasn't like normal fishing, because a pole was useless—you mostly had to catch them with your hands or some other way. Dave and Soeuth built a miniature trap to snare crayfish—modeled after a lobster trap Dave had bought at Seaweed Charlie's in Maine. And Soeuth developed a method where he would hold out a towel at the mouth of a tributary, and Dave would run toward him thrashing through the water, scaring schools of fish into it.

But we didn't so much care for other fish anymore. If Soeuth dumped out the take from his towel on the bank and there were a few trout and baby pike jiggling around with the crayfish, we'd usually throw the trout and pike back. There was one baby pike Soeuth didn't throw back, because it was frisky and you could tell it was teething. He put it in a plastic Ziploc bag, and when he, Dave and I took a walk past the cemetery and to the Seeley Farm, Bonnie and Anna Seeley were out saddling up their Arabians in the yard. They had met Soeuth before and sauntered over and said hi and their horses snorted and Soeuth wordlessly handed the Ziploc bag with the baby pike in it to Bonnie, who accepted it with a smile. Bonnie said she was going to put the baby pike in her fish tank and maybe it would make friends with her goldfish. But the next morning when she went to feed the fish, she discovered that all the fish, except the baby pike, were gone and the baby pike's belly was fat, like it was pregnant. Dave and I laughed after Mom told us this story, but Soeuth didn't.

It wasn't long before the kitchen was full of crayfish. We would line up the catch containers on the counter, and if we weren't careful, a few of the critters would hop out and twitch until they fell to the floor, where they would likely be snatched up and ferried away by one of our six cats. Those we didn't eat were stored in the freezer, where, more often than not, they could survive for a few days. Mom once opened the freezer and shrieked upon seeing a dozen or so of the little, blood-brown crayfish overtaking the ice cream and the frozen peas. Later, Soeuth would smear Mom's frying pan with butter and toss a few of them into it and they would dance to the sizzling music until it cooked them dead. Then you'd just dab them in more butter and eat them like miniature lobsters—except that you ate them whole. We must have eaten hundreds of them. We had crayfish soup, crayfish sandwiches, even a crayfish casserole.

As we all sat on the riverbank one afternoon, I bet Soeuth a dollar he wouldn't eat a crayfish live. Dave and I often dared each other to eat nauseating concoctions we had thought up, like ice cream with ketchup or chocolate pudding with relish, or milk mixed with pickle juice. After I had made the proposition and Soeuth had nodded his acceptance and I was sure there was no way I could lose—I had already decided that I would buy a Reggie Jackson baseball card from my friend Jeff with my earnings—Soeuth reached into the colander and held up one of the squirming critters so Dave and I could see it. He then casually popped it in his mouth, its antennae wriggling between his teeth. As he crunched on its still writhing shell, Dave laughed until he fell to the ground. Soeuth laughed, too. It was the first time we had seen him laugh.

He told us then that when he was in Cambodia, he'd eat just about anything.

"Only we get one cup rice," he said, dropping rocks into the colander. "So we go find animal. Feesh, snake, rat, leezard. Find what keep us survive."

"Rats!" Dave shrieked. "Gross!"

"No," Soeuth said seriously. "Rat the best. Rat is fat. Good meat. Put on stick. Cook."

"What else did you eat?" I asked.

He frowned, remembering, and then said succinctly: "Bug." He made a loop with his thumb and forefinger and slipped it over his other forefinger and squeezed the second knuckle. "Bug like this."

"A roach?"

"I don't know roach." He smiled. "Bug beeg and . . . ?" He flapped his arms.

"Wings?"

He nodded. "Bug fly, good meat."

Dave stared at Soeuth, a hybrid look of disgust and intrigue on his face. We were all silent for a moment.

"No crayfeesh Kambudja," Soeuth finally said, popping another live one in his mouth. "If crayfeesh Kambudja, eat crayfeesh all time."

He swallowed with one hard gulp and went to picking bits of shell out of his teeth and then we all three rose and walked side by side through the field back to the house.

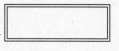

PART TWO

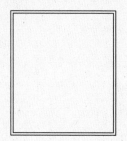

In the summer of 1976, when I was four and spending my days in the sandbox or on the swing set or chasing my dog, Oscar, around the yard, Soeuth was seven and a child slave in Pol Pot's Cambodia. For twelve, sometimes fourteen, hours a day, he planted rice seedlings along muddy rows of flooded fields. As he worked, carefully spacing the seedlings six inches apart, he would often study his reflection in the water, training his face not to betray what he felt. All around him were acres and acres of other children, boys and girls, barefoot and bent toward the earth, shuffling along their rows, pushing their seedlings into the soupy water, sustained by a weary, collective rhythm of fear. The rainy season in Cambodia lasts from May to October, and so, that summer, the children worked many days in the rain. If it was not raining, the sun baked their backs and necks. Rain or not, their lower backs would flare with pain, from bending over all day, but if they stopped and stood up to stretch, they were whipped. Soeuth was whipped many times.

They worked, ate and slept in the same clothes. Soeuth had one shirt and one pair of pants and, like most everyone else, no shoes. Since it rained so often, mud clung to his clothes, and when the mud dried, it made the clothes stiff and coarse. The clothes were never washed.

This first camp where Soeuth was sent was called Wat Slar Gram. It was a Buddhist temple that had been taken over by the

Communists. There was a high, serrated pagoda in the center of the temple grounds and other buildings, sheds and huts and such, scattered around it.

When he first arrived at Wat Slar Gram, Soeuth, along with thousands of other children, slept outside in a cement courtyard. On many nights, the rain was torrential, and everyone would lie awake in puddles, shivering and curled against the cold.

After a few weeks, Soeuth and a group of other children were allowed to sleep in a hut on camp grounds. It was a civilian hut, near the temple, that had been claimed by the Communists. Perched on stilts and made of bamboo and leaves and plywood, it resembled the hut his father had built after his family's first home, a sturdy three-room hut, had been burned down. The Communists must have decided not to burn down this hut, Soeuth figured, because it was shabby and had only one room. He slept on the plywood floor of the shabby hut with ten other boys, since girls and boys slept separately. He was glad that he could sleep under a roof, glad to escape the rain, but for the first few weeks many of the other boys had whimpered in the night, and it was hard to sleep. Sometimes, after he had finally fallen asleep, a series of gunshots outside would startle him awake.

The children were summoned at 5 A.M. each morning with a whistle. They were not served breakfast. They stood in a line to be counted and then marched, single file, off to work. At 5 or 6 P.M. most evenings, they heard the whistle again and came in from their work to line up in the canteen, a large, open-air shed where they were each served a small, flat bowl of watery rice gruel. They sat in circles on the ground or in the mud, heads bowed, and slurped the gruel with spoons.

Once a week, after dinner, they were divided into small groups and herded into nearby huts or bigger brick buildings that had formerly housed the monks. The children sat cross-legged on the floor, pressed knee to knee, their tiny postures rigid with atten-tion. The light of evening filtered through the windows and cracks in the walls, suffusing the room with a tangerine-hued softness. Soeuth felt small during these meetings because he was only seven, and most of the other children were at least ten and were taller.

They watched and listened to the adult who stood at the front of the room. He wore a black shirt and pants and a red-and-white checkered *khrama*, like all the leaders, and spoke in a flat, somber voice. His eyes were heavy with purpose.

"You must forget your families," the unsmiling adult with the *khrama* would begin. His words were evenly, individually, uttered. "You must forget your religion. You must think now only of Angka. Nothing has come before now, and you must forget your past. Angka is your family now. Angka will take care of you. You must kick all the rich people for Angka. You must smash the heads of the rich people for Angka. You must work for the glorious revolution. You must make your country better than before."

The children stared and listened at these meetings, motionless, as the unsmiling adult with the *khrama* spoke. The speech was usually the same, the omnipresence and omnipotence of the giant, faceless god called Angka emphasized with hypnotic repetition. Sometimes the unsmiling adult with the *khrama* would lead the children in a chant or song pledging allegiance to the glorious revolution of Angka. It was hard to know what anyone really thought about Angka—because you couldn't speak anything other than your allegiance to it—but after several of these meetings, many of the children seemed to have been swayed, by the speeches and chants, that Angka was indeed their god and their keeper and that their families, their homes and their Lord Buddha were all mere illusions of an invented past.

Soeuth wasn't sure whether he believed in Angka, but guessed that he could maybe forget his father, if he really needed to. It would be very hard, though, to forget his mother and grandmother and brother and sisters. His grandmother most of all. She had always been the nicest to him, giving him coconuts and sugarcane and letting him sleep next to her. He loved her very much. She was small and gentle and her face had deep, kindly fissures in it and her eyes crinkled when she smiled.

But he tried not to think about her too much, because he

knew that missing your family was considered a crime, just like stealing—a crime for which you could be whipped, or worse.

A boy from Soeuth's village, Gee, slept in the same hut and often worked alongside Soeuth in the fields. One night Gee suggested that the two of them escape the camp and journey home together to see their families, just for a few days. Tall, bucktoothed and long-limbed, Gee was a few years older and seemed quite brave and reasonably trustworthy. Do not worry, he told Soeuth; just do what I say and you'll be okay.

The rice seedlings the children had planted that summer had grown into a vast lime-green sea of waist-high plants that would now provide good cover for their escape, Gee said. The boys' village, Asrolaub, was only a few miles from the camp, Gee noted, so it shouldn't take them more than a half day or so to get there and see their families and have a good meal. Soeuth agreed to go with Gee. He hoped his family was still alive.

When I became old enough to comprehend the concept of good versus evil—an awareness informed, in great part, by *Star Wars*, *The Hobbit*, *Bonanza*, the *Conan* paperbacks and routine skirmishes with bullies at school—I conjured an otherworldly me, the opposite of the stuttering, flat-footed four-eyes. He still wore bifocal glasses, like mine, but was as strong as a hundred Percheron workhorses and wielded a luminous, double-edged silver sword—the kind that Conan had, and sharp enough to slice clean through an engine block—with a two-handed, leather-bound hilt. He had buffalo-hide boots, a simple flap of hide to keep his nether regions covered and an Adam Cartwright-style cowboy hat. The brightness of his sword and his own glorious aura required that his bifocals be custom-tinted like state trooper shades.

Whenever we went shopping with Mom at the Grand Union, I would wander down the aisles, hoping for the linoleum floor to crack open beneath me and send me hurtling toward Extinction Land, an imagined plane where my invincible, otherworldly self was often charged with saving helpless, large-breasted women in diaphanous silk shawls. A barren realm pocked with craters of steaming excrement, domed by an oppressive, urine-colored sky and filled with fossils, Extinction Land was a place, I fancied, too perilous for Luke Skywalker or Adam Cartwright or even Conan. My most common savior scenario began with me standing at the mouth of a cave, the only safe haven in all of Extinction Land.

My delicate charges cowered close behind me as the Lord of
Extinction Land approached. Wearing a hockey jersey with the
numbers 666 embroidered on the front, the Lord of Extinction
Land was a stitched-together Frankenstein of all the bullies who
had ever tripped me up or broken my glasses or spit loogies into
my hair. He sat atop a creaky carriage assembled from the ribs
and tusks of extinct mastodons and drawn by the reanimated
skeletons of some kind of giant, Cujo-like dog. A cloud of flies
buzzed around him.

"I have come for them," the Lord of Extinction Land
croaked.

I trained my eyes on his and said stonily: "Beware my sword!
This is the Cave of Safety—the face of evil can only wither upon
entering here." (I loved the word "wither," and ever since Mom
had taught me that word while showing me sickly tomato plants
in the garden, I tried to incorporate it into all my savior
scenarios.)

I grasped the hilt of my sword and swung the bright blade
into the air, and a sudden flash of white heat fell upon the Lord
of Extinction Land—as if the great door of Heaven itself had
been flung open before him—and he shrank into a tangle of
stitches as the busty, helpless women cheered.

The scene contracted at this point, wavering for a few seconds
and then vanishing entirely. I would awake to the lumpy white
surface of my bedroom wall or the vinyl seat back in Mom's
Buick station wagon or math equations scrawled on a blackboard.
Often I would find myself, some afternoons after school, twirling
across the manicured lawns of our neighbors, wildly waving my
phantom sword. At church, when everyone recited the Lord's
Prayer, I would often whisper admonitions at certain inhabitants
of Extinction Land, until Dad elbowed me to be quiet.

I did pray, sometimes, but the prayer was usually an out-
growth of one fantasy or another. When the phrase "Kingdom
Come" rumbled under my breath, I saw myself soaring up into
an iridescent vastness, my arms outstretched, my hands holding
the hands of Mom and Dad, who held the hands of Dave and

Grandpa Ken, who held the hands of everyone else in our family, whose hands clutched those of every guest and family friend we've ever had, so that the chain of us, a hundred or more people linked together, would glide gloriously toward Salvation. I would sit sometimes before bed under my desk lamp and try to picture each face in the Chain of Salvation. I would time myself. If I couldn't fix the most important faces solemnly in my mind—the details of each face, the lines, the noses, had to be etched in exact focus—within about a minute and a half, that meant we were all doomed or, at least, would all become drooling quadriplegics. The most important faces were, of course, those of immediate family and grandparents and cousins and aunts and uncles and my friend Jeff and the visitors who had stayed with us at one time or another.

We had a lot of visitors in our home—foreign exchange students, touring musicians, a Fresh Air kid, the occasional runaway—mostly folks from other parts who found some reason to pass through Middlebury, Vermont. Ours was a house of strays, Mom would say, whether it was people or animals that we'd opened the door to. At any given time over the years, the house was overrun by stray cats that had scratched at the door for milk and that Mom never had the heart to turn out.

Our mother thought of our house as a cultural sieve of sorts, through which she could run the lives of people from foreign places, holding onto the bits and pieces that enriched us. When she announced the advent of a new guest, we would usually consult *The World Book Encyclopedia* to learn about their part of the world, and she would read out loud the relevant information from sections like "People," "Land," "Government" and "History." She also routinely read to us the encyclopedia's chapter on the *Mayflower,* since, after all, she said, our family was directly descended from John Alden and Priscilla Mullens, who had been guests of the Indians.

On the evening of the arrival of a guest, we would all sit around our living room on chairs or the couch—no beanbags allowed on the night of a new guest—sipping hot chocolate or

iced tea or some generic soda Dad had bought at Ames, and
Mom would ask the guest questions and we'd all stare and I'd
expect exotic things. Sometimes I got them. Eric, the Fresh Air
kid, described knife fights on Flatbush Avenue and showed Dave
and me how to use his hair straightener, telling us that if we
smeared it on our arms, we'd grow thick, manly hair, like his.
Carlos, a foreign exchange student, mesmerized us with tales of
cannibals in Ecuador. Islam, a student from Cairo, said that in
Egypt a horse would bow its head for you before you mounted
it. Manrique, the *Up With People* performer, sang a few Costa
Rican tunes for us in Spanish. Ria, a student from Indonesia,
performed for us with her shadow puppets. Inga, a student from
Belgium, told us about having to learn four languages in school.

But after the initial thrill of a visitor, Dave and I would begin
to realize how dull and unworldly our lives were. Listening to
Eric talk about New York City and describe violence I knew only
from TV cast my stories—of spying on women in the college
dorms and of damming up the tributary behind our house and
thus flooding our neighbor's yard—in the stale light of irrele-
vance. Dave and I came to accept that our lives would be predictable, and that our brushes with danger and intrigue would be
vicarious and, in my case, occasionally invented.

Sometimes I imagined our home as some kind of underground railroad refuge for fugitives fleeing a hell-born, three-
headed dictator who could never tread on the sacred ground of
the Green Mountain foothills. If he ever dared enter the Champlain Valley, Dave, Dad and I would shuttle our charges to the
cellar and then hole up in the attic with Grandpa's shotguns. The
shotguns were black, heavy iron things, as tall as I was, and could
surely drop a grizzly or a three-headed dictator.

Mom knew that we were the real strays, we stationary ones,
and hoped that by plying our lives with the accents and stories
of people from alien places, she could rescue us from the cultural
torpor of Vermont. But her motives also grew from a place of
fallow ambition. She had always dreamed of being a missionary,
in the tradition of Albert Schweitzer and Tom Dooley. Albert

Schweitzer, most of all. She had written a class report on him in high school and had known then that her calling was to work among the deprived and diseased in distant places. But the farthest she got was a mountain village in Greece, where she volunteered for Heifer Project, cleaning up a playground and digging the foundation for a school; soon after that, she met Dad at the University of Vermont.

We heard countless times, though, of Schweitzer's indefatigable reverence for all living things, even insects. When Dave or I spotted a wasp on a windowsill and told Mom about it, she would pluck a cup out of the kitchen cabinet and snatch a sheet of printer paper or a newspaper insert. The cup was carefully placed over the wayward wasp, and the paper or newspaper insert was gently slipped under the down-turned cup. Mom would then carry the cup to an open window or screen door, where the wasp could be released into the clear summer air.

Mom did devote herself to a humanitarian career, opting for an unextraordinary but, arguably, no less altruistic alternative to working with leprous children in the jungle. She became a junior high special-education teacher focusing in speech therapy. It was a great frustration to her, I think, that she could eradicate the speech defects of her students but could not cure me, her elder son, of my frequent stuttering sprees. She would sit with me at the dining room table, her half-rimmed glasses perched low on her nose, as the fragments of my words spilled out recklessly like pieces of a puzzle scattered across the table. "Adam, you'll grow out of this," she would assure me. By the time I reached eighth grade, I did, for the most part, using a technique she had taught me, filling the jolting gaps in my sentences with "ahs" and "ums" and inhaling deeply before a consonant-crowded word.

Dad was a local family doctor and a good one—a lot of people told him that. He was obsessive, and not just about his patients. When he involved himself in certain activities, even hobbies—whether developing photos in his darkroom, assembling model train sets, repairing his collection of outboard motors or advocating his flagship political cause, nuclear disarmament—he would hone in with a ravenous attention to detail. When we were all watching the news one night and Dan Rather was talking about nuclear proliferation, Dad frowned, shaking his head, and said: "He doesn't know what the hell he's talking about. For Chrissake, he can't even pronounce the word right."

"Bill," Mom said. "Just listen."

"Jean." Dad was emphatic, twisting his wedding ring back and forth, pumping his knee like a piston. "All these guys—the newscasters, the politicians. They can't even pronounce the word right. They all say 'new-kya-lur.' The right way is 'new-clee-ur.'"

Since my ninth birthday, Mom had insisted that both Dave and I watch the nightly news. We couldn't talk, so we'd shoot rubber bands at each other or duel with action figures. One night, while we all sat wedged together on our new velvet sofa watching the news, Mom and Dad suddenly became quiet and concentrated. The pictures on the TV showed tiny, near-naked children clustered together in a dark, dirt-floored place, peering up with frightened eyes. The newscaster's serious voice layered over these pictures: *starvation . . . slaughter . . . atrocities . . .* When a commercial broke the newscast, Dad shut off the TV and clenched his jaw and said something about a holocaust, a regular goddamned holocaust, and told Dave and me it was time for bed.

Gee and Soeuth awoke with the cry of the work whistle, on a dim, cold morning. As the other boys groggily plodded down the steps of the hut to report for work, Gee and Soeuth lay on the plywood floor, curled up and breathing slowly. The group leader marched into the hut and, upon seeing them on the floor, demanded to know why they had not risen. Groaning, they told the leader they had bad headaches. This leader was not as bad as some. He was eighteen, with a soft, unserious face, and was not so strict. He looked at them suspiciously for a moment and finally said: today you may stay here and you may not leave the hut without permission.

After the group leader had gone, Gee and Soeuth remained there on the floor for a few minutes. Then Gee hopped up and ran to the door and peered out into the brightening morning and motioned to Soeuth that it was time to go. The boys delicately climbed down the steps and Gee led the way, walking quickly but quietly to the west, toward an expanse of empty, unworked rice fields. Their village was three or four miles to the north, but they couldn't walk directly north, Gee explained, because that was where everyone was working.

Gee glanced now and then back at Soeuth. He talked in rhythm with his walking: quick, quiet and breathless. Soeuth nodded, following Gee, and scanned the surrounding fields. He wondered what would happen if the guards caught them.

They walked along the edge of a rice field until they came to the clay levee that separated this field from another one. Without looking back, Gee hopped onto the levee and darted into the vastness of the rice fields. Soeuth followed. They crept quickly along the sun-hot levee, the surrounding rice grass hissing in fickle gusts of wind. In the distance, a line of palm trees rose up stiff and sharp, like claws in the sky. Soeuth felt small creeping between the rice fields under the palm trees, but also felt excited. He hoped to see his family very soon and eat sugarcane and drink coconut juice.

Gee's western detour had them switching back along a maze of levees that stretched on indefinitely, it seemed, and Soeuth was glad that Gee knew where they were going. He trusted Gee, because Gee had so far made sure they remained a good distance from the severe silhouettes of Angka guards in neighboring fields.

There were a few roads they had to cross; Gee would peek out and motion for Soeuth to follow and then sprint across the open road to the relative safety of the rice fields on the other side. Around noon, Gee guided Soeuth along a levee that followed a road.

"This road will come to another road which will take us to Asrolaub," Gee said, panting. "And then we'll be home."

It was midafternoon when Gee found the road to Asrolaub. He walked onto the sun-lit dirt of the road and beckoned Soeuth to follow. The road was quiet and empty, and the boys walked wordlessly side by side. The leaves of banana trees and smaller leaves of other trees sprang up in places, shading the road peacefully.

When they were within a hundred yards of Gee's family's hut, Gee announced: "I'm going to walk off the road and see my family, and you keep going down the road to your family, don't stop. Younger brother," Gee added, "we will be okay. Meet me here tomorrow, here in the road near my family's hut, at noon."

Soeuth nodded.

When they reached Gee's house, Gee walked past a thick stand of bushes and disappeared. Like Gee had advised, Soeuth did not stop. His family's hut was a half mile or so farther. He kept glancing behind him as he walked, because he had seen not a single person and there were no sounds coming from the huts set back from the road, and he was now afraid.

His family's hut was on the right. He recognized the path that arrowed off the road and recognized his father's banana and jackfruit trees, whose leaves shone bright in the sun, and a sudden anticipation swelled in him. He walked faster, his bare feet thudding on the clay of the road. But as his excitement grew, his fear grew also. What if his family's hut was empty or burned down or taken over by some other family?

When he walked past the bushes beside the path, he saw his grandmother in the yard, bent over, pulling weeds out of the dirt. He watched her until she looked up and her hands flew to her mouth. Soeuth stood where he was, smiling. His grandmother held her hands out to him; her hands were shaking.

Soeuth walked to his grandmother, and she crouched down next to him, looking him over, and clasped his hands. "I have prayed for you," she whispered. "And you have come home."

Someone came into the doorway of the hut. Soeuth looked up to see that it was his father. He was on crutches and his leg was swollen, but he was grinning; he hardly ever grinned. Soeuth looked away.

"A centipede bit him," his grandmother explained. "And he cannot work."

Three little faces floated in the darkness behind his father. They were his two younger sisters and baby brother. He smiled at them, and they stared back timidly. They were all still far too young to be of much use to Angka in the fields and had been allowed to stay with the family. In the evening, his mother returned from her work in the fields and wept upon seeing him and his grandmother wept, too, and Soeuth chewed on sugarcane and ate cassava. Because they were peasants, or "old people," in the eyes of Angka, Soeuth's family was still allowed to pick fruit from the trees in their yard and to cut sugarcane on their land. The "new" people, people from the city transplanted to their village, could not have their own fruit or sugarcane, his grand-mother explained.

They sat that night on the floor of the hut, his family once again complete, slurping rice gruel. After dinner, everyone shuf-fled into a circle around him, and his mother asked if he was okay. I'm okay, he replied with a shrug, and then he lied, saying he had permission to visit home but must return tomorrow. As his father lit a kerosene lamp, Soeuth gnawed into a fresh, stringy stick of sugarcane. His brother and sisters watched him eating, their walleyed faces painted soft and orange by the light of the lamp. His father smoked a hand-rolled cigarette and watched him, too, through the smoke.

He slept that night under a blanket, curled next to his grand-mother. He felt safe and warm sleeping by her, and his stomach, for the first time in months, was full. Listening to his family's breathing and to the sounds of the night outside, he slipped into sleep.

The next morning, early, he said good-bye to his mother, because she had to go to work in the fields. She was frail, with wrists as thin as a child's, and her face now almost always wore the same squinting, fearful expression. Soeuth waved to her, hop-ing Angka would not hurt her too much.

Just before noon, he left. His father and brother and sisters and grandmother stood outside the hut to say good-bye and good luck. His grandmother prayed: "May Lord Buddha watch over and protect you."

Gee was standing in the road where he had promised he'd be. They followed the same route back, clambering onto the levee in the rice fields. After about a hundred yards along the levee, Gee halted. His brow was wrinkled, and he chewed his lip.

"Let's stay another day," he said suddenly.

"Another day?" Soeuth asked.

"One more day." Gee looked both ways down the levee. "It's okay. We can hide under my parents' barn."

When they neared Gee's family's hut, Gee held his finger to his lips and then slipped quickly into a copse of banana-tree leaves. The two crept along, parting the broad, heavy leaves, until they reached an old plywood shed on stilts, three or so feet off the ground, its wood weathered and gray.

"My parents' barn," Gee whispered. He was bent over and his hands rested on his knees. "Use to store rice."

Soeuth nodded.

"We can hide under it."

They spent that afternoon in the shade beneath Gee's family's rice shed, chewing on sugarcane and waiting for night. It was safe, Gee had assured Soeuth several times, because it was far from the road, unused and surrounded by bushes and trees. When the clouds crouched low in the sky, Gee said it was time for dinner.

"Your family has chickens?" Gee was squatting, tracing circles in the dirt with a stick.

"Yes," Soeuth said. "We do."

Gee nodded. "We need to steal one."

Soeuth offered a noncommittal shrug.

"And come back here and cook it."

Soeuth examined the dirt at his feet.

"I have matches." Gee pulled a book of matches out of the pocket in his shorts. "And a knife." He produced the knife. "We just need the chicken."

"Okay," Soeuth finally said.

When it was dark, they crept back onto the road and walked the half mile to Soeuth's family's hut.

"You get the chicken," Gee said, "I'll wait here."

Soeuth felt guilty about stealing from his family, but he was hungry and he hadn't eaten meat in a long time. And he knew that, officially, the chickens didn't belong to his family anyway—they belonged to Angka.

He crawled carefully beneath his family's hut. The chickens, ten hens, were huddled together, asleep. He slipped his hand under one of the hens and broke her neck with a quick, twisting jerk. Cradling the limp hen under his arm, he went back to the road. When Gee saw him, he smiled approvingly.

Back under the rice shed, Gee built a fire with twigs, lighting
it with his matches. They did not pluck the hen's feathers; Gee
skinned it instead with his knife. With a stick Gee had sharpened,
Soeuth spitted the hen and they took turns holding it over the
flames. When it was cooked, they ate everything except the bones,
which they subsequently buried. Listening to the chirping of the
crickets, they picked their teeth, until they fell asleep on the
cool dirt.

They arrived at the slave camp the next evening just in time
for dinner at the canteen. When they returned to their sleeping
quarters, the group leader was there waiting for them.

The group leader accompanied them to the head leader's
quarters, a big building high off the ground. They filed up the
steps to see the head leader standing in the hallway. He had a
hard, lean face, unblinking eyes, and was feared by everyone. A
gunshot wound had left him with a limp, so that his weight rested
mostly on his good foot.

"Where did you go?" The head leader's voice was low, blunt.

Soeuth studied his own feet before mumbling, "I went
home."

The head leader glared at him for a few seconds, then said:
"You did not have permission." The words were uttered in quick,
staccato succession. "You lied. You said you were sick. And then
you were gone."

The head leader folded his hands behind his back and walked
around the boys until he stood behind them. No one moved. The
boys listened to the head leader's breathing and to their own
breathing, Soeuth wondering when they would be whipped.

Suddenly, then, the head leader gripped Soeuth by the ears—
the way one grips a two-handled jug—and hoisted him six or so
inches off the floor. Soeuth's hands flew up and grasped the head
leader's hands, but the head leader did not let go. Soeuth saw
his feet dangling beneath him. The pain was acute; it felt like his
ears would tear or the skin on his face would split. The head
leader held him up for a long time. Soeuth closed his eyes, and
then, finally, the head leader dropped him.

He sat on the floor, clutching his ears.

"Do not run away again," the head leader said and pivoted abruptly and strode down the hall.

Gee stood glancing guiltily at Soeuth. Soeuth knew why the head leader had hurt him and not Gee. Gee's father was a soldier for Angka—Gee had told him this—and the head leader knew Gee's father. Gee offered a hand to Soeuth. The group leader led them back to the sleeping shed, where Soeuth's ears stung all night.

Within a few days, Gee was sent to another camp. Soeuth never saw him again.

We moved into the farmhouse in the early fall of 1983, as I was starting sixth grade, because our baby-blue, single-level ranch house in town was too small, Dad said, and it wouldn't be long until it squeezed us out its doors. It was obediently fixed in a line of similar ranch houses, all neatly hugged by shrubs, all painted drowsy shades of yellow, brown or blue. Gorham Lane, Middlebury's postcard-perfect neighborhood abutting the campus, was pleasant and antiseptic. The lawns were so well groomed they looked vacuumed, the children played Wiffle ball—but not past eight o'clock—the yuppies had their barbecues and the retirees walked their Labrador retrievers. It was a friendly place, except if you accidentally wandered onto the lawn of some old man who came out waving a golf club at you and yelling that he didn't survive Korea for nothing. Some nights after dinner, I'd perch myself in the front-yard willow tree and observe our neighbors through their windows, basking in the glow of their televisions, eating, fighting, loosening their belts, scratching their asses. But Dave and I couldn't really explore that much outside, with so many well-kept lawns and finished fences.

There wasn't a farm anymore with the farmhouse, or cows or chickens or pigs, only two sober old barns and a few gray sheds. But it was a mansion compared to the house on Gorham Lane. It stood by itself in the wind-whipped Champlain Valley, rising up from the dark plain like a lonely monument, a fortress against the world. Its rooms—twelve in all—had high ceilings and tall windows. It had an attic, a fruit cellar and an in-ground swimming pool.

The day we moved in, Dave and I ran around like plunderers, the old floorboards barking beneath us, in a race to claim our new rooms. Dave found his first and, for lack of a flag, quickly sprawled on the floor and spread his arms and legs to signify his space. His room was large and crooked with blood-red wallpaper and willow branches scratching the windows. Mine was smaller and darker and had dull brown wallpaper with faded, lacy stripes. But I was satisfied; it was bigger than my old room on Gorham Lane and had a secret door to the attic.

Outside, it was a grand, open, empty place. The wind tore through in stout gusts, searing your face, dancing the trees, lapping up the leaves. The East Middlebury River, which ran a few acres south of the house, swelled up in the spring and narrowed to an icy trickle in the winter. Bumpy cow pastures spread south and southwest for miles, like the knuckled tops of giant hands, interrupted only by the river and an occasional tuft of trees. Bruise-colored loaves of mountain loomed on both the east and west horizons. Deer drifted in and out of the rim of trees that marked the swamp to our north, glancing at the aberration of civilization that was our house. The cornfield to our east muttered in the summer breeze, its dense green lushness inviting and mysterious. Life was big out here—we could roam and explore and not be watched by neighbors.

Down the road from our house, about a hundred yards, was the Anne Story monument. A small obelisk, six feet high, blemished with moss and age, it stood in the corner of a field near the road, erected on the site of the first house in town. On a walk one day to visit our new neighbor Charlie Bascom, who raised racehorses, we passed the monument, and Mom told us that when Anne Story lived on this very spot, she had made her house a refuge for the Green Mountain Boys when they were fighting the Iroquois Indians.

Grandpa Ken, Dad's father, had taught industrial arts on the

St. Regis Mohawk Reservation in upstate New York back in the '50s and had been inducted into the tribe as a blood brother. When we were visiting one afternoon, he sank back in his recliner and explained through hands tented before his mouth: "You see, boys . . . Indians are bad and good, smart and stupid, just like the rest of us. Rotten apples belong to every race, creed and color, you see." He had unfolded his hands and his mouth had frowned like a horseshoe. "When I joined the tribe, boys, I had to do a war dance. Never really got the hang of it, tripped on a root." A thick-throated laugh had rattled, gravel in a blender. "They called me Kayiendio, which means Good Wood. I figured, with their sense of humor, it could have also meant Block Head." He had looked at us levelly and something had twisted in his eyes and he had said: "Boys, I have the utmost respect for the Indians. They treat their women well, not like the White Man. They don't have crime. Not like we do anyway. And everybody does their share of the work. Everybody. And the Indian religion . . . well, in their religion, God is Nature, and if ya act against Nature, ya act against God." He had chuckled to himself and swept a gnarled hand over his near-bald head and added: "Not bad for a bunch of savages."

The people who had lived in our house during the old days, I surmised, had probably hung the scalps of murdered Indian women, soft flowing shocks of headless hair, on the wall of what was now our front room.

We had moved in when the trees guarding the house were still kingly with their leaves. As fall stripped the leaves away, the house was left standing alone. Dave and I helped Dad put in the storm windows in October. We held the ladder still as he climbed up it, shaking—he was afraid of heights. Then we'd run back into the house and hand him the new windows through the old frames.

I stood in Dave's room as Dad inched up the ladder, his face pallid, his knuckles white. Leaves twirled around him. As the wind picked up, I felt a stab of panic. If we didn't install these windows in time, I feared, the storm's tendrils would reach inside our house and snatch us away. It was a race, and with Dad's worsening acrophobia retarding our progress and the empty guest room still to go, the storm was winning. I couldn't stop myself before I yelled: "C'mon, ya old fart, we have to hurry!" He glanced up at me, grimacing, and managed to say above the wind, "Cut the crap up there." Dad was usually categorically composed, his face refusing to reflect the everyday tremors brought on by harried traffic, combative patients, mortgage anxieties, office politics. He was widely reputed to have one of the best bedside manners of any doctor on staff at Porter Hospital, but he would never tell you that. He had learned to maintain his calm by managing trauma at the local emergency room, the way a sword swallower learns to make his body go limp after years of sliding a blade down his throat. One night he had been called to examine the remains of a nursing-home groundskeeper who had fallen headfirst into a rototiller. His head, what was left of it, had disappeared into the rototiller's teeth and his body had slumped to the side, like he had passed out while dunking for an apple. When Dad had looked up from the ground-up groundskeeper, he had seen a bevy of bats flitting across the bright ivory circle of a full moon. When he told me that story, I developed a freshly minted idea of my dad: a superman doctor, unafraid of anything. Seeing him like this now, so visibly affected by being fifteen feet off the ground, made me muse on the randomness of God's endowment of strengths and weaknesses, how a towering man could be afraid of the dark, how a fearless soldier could stutter.

By the time Dad reached the top, the wind had temporarily abated, and we installed Dave's last window in no time. We finished the windows for the guest room just before the wind picked up again. As Dad leaned the ladder back against the garage wall, he said to us: "Well, boys, we should be ready for winter." I hoped so.

Midway through the dry season, Soeuth was sent to a new camp, Cave, about twice as far from his village as Wat Slar Gram. The work at Cave was more onerous, and as the next rainy season approached, the servings of rice gruel grew smaller and more infrequent. Hunger roared in his stomach, and a throbbing vacancy claimed his mind. Open sores sprouted on his arms and legs, more with the passing of each week, but he accepted them as an old man resigns himself to liver spots.

Unlike at Wat Slar Gram, though, there was a one-hour rest period at Cave at noontime. Some other boys from Soeuth's sleeping shed made slingshots during their rest period and asked Soeuth one afternoon if he wanted to make a slingshot, too, and he quickly nodded yes. One of the boys had a knife for which he had bartered his rice servings on Cave's black market. Another had traded his servings for a few strips of inner-tube tire rubber. With his knife, the boy cut a half-dozen forked branches off a tamarind tree and handed them around. Then all you had to do was tie a piece of inner-tube rubber around the two ends of the forked branch and you had your slingshot. The boys, four or five of them usually, would then scoop up handfuls of clay from the rice fields, round out their shots from the clay and let the ammunition dry in the sun.

They would meet the next day at rest period, gather the sun-hardened pellets and head out to the levees. Prowling the edges of the rice grass, they would look for snakes, lizards or field rats. Rats were especially good because they had a lot of meat. Sometimes the boys would scan the trees for birds.

One of the boys would build a fire out of brush and light it with his contraband cigarette lighter. They would all sit around the fire, holding their rats and lizards and snakes on sticks over the flames. If there wasn't time for cooking during the rest period, they might cook their catch after dinner. There was a curfew at dark, but if it was still light after dinner, the children were allowed to stay out until dark.

If Soeuth was unlucky with his slingshot, he would venture into the rice grass during his rest period to catch water bugs or spiders, which he would then lay out near the embers of a fire or just eat raw. A few children ate leaves from small trees and plants. Some leaves were poisonous, though, and many of the boys who ate them would soon vomit their daily meal on the floor of the sleeping shed. Soeuth would often mix leaves in with his rice gruel to increase the volume of his serving, even though such a mixture would result in vomiting or an insistent case of diarrhea.

Angka was building a lake, the children had been told, and so needed them to dig irrigation canals and build dams and levees. Soeuth had been assigned to dig canals. Working in a long line of other children, he would swing his hoe, throwing all his weight behind it, and break the earth and try to break apart the hunger, too. But in the afternoon he would grow tired, and the scrape and crunch of all the other hoes hitting dirt would somehow deepen his fatigue, and so he would merely let his hoe drop.

Boys with baskets would scurry in front of the boys with hoes and scoop the loosened dirt and mud and then deliver it to the boys constructing the dams. Sometimes the boys with hoes, who had grown tired, would accidentally strike the boys with baskets in the head and blood would spill into the mud and someone would get whipped.

One night as he stood in line at the canteen, Soeuth examined his hands. They had become callused and cracked. He ate his rice gruel and went to his sleeping shed and rubbed his hands together, wondering how long he had been away from home. It was deep into the dry season now, but he didn't know what month it was. He knew it had been a long time since Angka had taken him from his family, a year maybe, but he wasn't really sure. All he knew of time was the shift of the seasons, rainy to dry, dry to rainy, and that he was getting older—he was now eight years old, he guessed—and closer to being a man.

When the rainy season soaked the fields, the children were once again sent to plant rice seedlings. One sunny afternoon, one of the leaders ambled out to the rice fields carrying a pad of paper and a pencil. He was a new leader, short, chubby, mid-thirties. He walked along the rows and stopped at each child working to ask questions and record the answers on his pad. As Soeuth heard the squelch of the leader's sandals advancing down his row, he vigorously pushed his seedlings into the mud.

When the leader reached him, Soeuth continued to push seedlings into the mud—to show that he was a good worker—until the leader cleared his throat. Soeuth looked up.

"Can you tell me," the leader began in a nonchalant voice, "what your father did in prerevolutionary Kampuchea?"

"Rice farmer," Soeuth blurted, staring at the mud. His answer was truthful, for the most part. Soeuth's father had, for a short time, carried a gun as a reserve soldier for General Lon Nol, the former head of Kampuchea, who had been backed by the Americans and whom Angka had ousted. Soeuth had heard the rumors from boys in his sleeping shed: anyone who had been a doctor, teacher, student, landowner, city dweller—and, most especially, anyone who had had anything at all to do with General Lon Nol—was on Angka's elimination list.

The leader wrote down his answer.

"Can you tell me what your mother did in prerevolutionary Kampuchea?"

"Rice farmer," Soeuth said again. This answer was entirely truthful.

Things were getting worse, Soeuth knew that. Angka was becoming harsher and more paranoid. One night, after dinner, a fight broke out between two leaders. Soeuth and a few other boys slipped out of the sleeping shed to watch. The rice grass, which was painted silver by the moon, shivered in an evening breeze. One leader yelled at the other. Suddenly the leader who was yelling brandished a machete and chased the other leader into the rice grass. The leader with the machete returned some time later, alone, but told all the boys, who stood staring at him, not to worry, that he had not killed the other leader and to go to bed.

One of Soeuth's childhood friends, a boy who had been a neighbor in his old village, was assigned to the same sleeping shed at Cave. Their fathers had farmed together before the revolution. His name was Roeun. He was tall and muscular and had a high-pitched, cracking voice. Like Gee, he was a few years older than Soeuth and tried to look after him. The two would often shoot their slingshots together and sometimes, after dinner, share a contraband cigarette.

One such evening, while puffing anxiously on a cigarette, Roeun suggested to Soeuth that maybe it was time to visit their families. He passed Soeuth the cigarette, and Soeuth inhaled deeply, thinking about what had happened the last time he had run away, about the fact that Cave was at least a full day's journey from the village and about how Angka was more strict now. But as he tapped ashes to the ground, he also thought about his grandmother and eating sugarcane and cassava and a chicken, like last time, and so said, okay, let's go.

At sundown, Roeun told the group leader that he had to relieve himself and trotted out behind a stand of trees. Soeuth waited five minutes and then told the leader that he, too, had to go and met Roeun behind the shitting trees. The sky was a charcoal gray, not black yet, and so they scampered hurriedly along a levee between rice fields. Soon it started raining, but they continued on, gripping the slick levee with fast feet.

After the rain tapered, they climbed off the levee and walked along an irrigation canal that ran parallel to it. At one point, Roeun, who was leading the way, halted. He had heard something. The two boys stood as still as bamboo stilts. They squinted into the rainy distance and, eventually, were able to make out the forms of two adult figures ambling toward them along the irrigation canal. The adults were smoking and their cigarettes winked as they dragged on them. The only adults who would be walking freely in the open like that were guards or soldiers for Angka, and so Soeuth and Roeun dove into the rice grass. They crawled, hands and knees in the mud, through the tall, sharp grass for several meters and then lay flat in the shallow water, floating on their bellies, quiet and waiting. The footsteps of the adults grew louder. Finally, the two sauntered by, chattering, their sandals smacking against their heels. The boys waited motionless for several minutes before peeking up over the tips of the grass. The adults were gone, and so Soeuth and his friend went on into the night toward home.

They reached the village at sunrise and split, agreeing to find each other in a few days.

Soeuth was happy, once again, to be home, but his mother was not so happy to see him. She hooked his arm, roughly, and hauled him inside the hut.

"You should not have come home again," she said brusquely. "If Angka sees you this time, the whole family will be in danger."

His brother and sisters gawked at him. He gazed at the floor.

"Things are very bad now," his mother explained, her voice softening a little. "We cannot go outside without permission. We cannot pick our own fruit anymore. Or cut our own sugarcane."

This was particularly bad news. Soeuth had been looking forward to a fresh stick of sugarcane.

"We must all eat now in the canteen," she continued. "I cannot take food out of the canteen for you, son. I don't know how you will eat."

Soeuth sat down in one motion, as if this last comment had suddenly drained him of all his strength.

That evening his mother told him that a lot of people had been taken away and never seen again. They were mostly "new" people, people from the city or those who had had land or money before the revolution. A taxi driver from Battambang City who had been their neighbor before the revolution—he was gone. A man who had owned a house in Battambang City and had owned many acres of rice fields near Soeuth's father's fields—he was gone, too. Another neighbor had been taken away, she said, and yet another had been shot dead in front of his own hut.

We must be very careful, his mother cautioned, and you must not let anyone see you. Guilt stabbed him when she said this.

Soeuth's father was not around; he had been sent to another camp far away, but no one seemed to know why. His mother was allowed now to stay home to care for her young children, but his grandmother had been put to work in the fields. When she returned home after dark, she smiled upon seeing Soeuth but was too weak to smile for long. Soeuth slept that night curled up next to his grandmother.

For the next two days, Soeuth stayed inside the hut with his mother and little brother and sisters. His mother told them all to be quiet, and so they sat, hungry, on the floor all day. On the third day his mother stumbled in from outside, her eyes wide and blinking. She said to Soeuth, "They have come for you."

Two guards for Angka in black suits paced into the hut and stood next to his mother. They were both young and did not appear mean or dangerous. They were very polite.

"We do not mean to trouble you," one of the guards said to his mother. "But your son has come home without permission."

His mother regarded him sadly and then averted her eyes to the floor. Soeuth rose and shuffled outside with the guards. His mother and brother and sisters watched as he walked, flanked by the guards, down the road to Roeun's family's hut. The guards snatched Roeun, too.

"You are troublemakers," one of the guards said as they left the village; his voice was no longer polite. "When we get back, you will be in trouble."

They walked all day on the road in silence, reaching Cave in the evening. The guards escorted Soeuth and Roeun to a clearing in back of the sleeping sheds and stood with them wordlessly for a few minutes, until the head leader appeared with a few coils of rope. Darkness had fallen quickly, and the crickets were creaking now in a chorus. One leader guided Soeuth over to a tree and told him to stand with his back against the tree; Soeuth obeyed. Then the leader pulled Soeuth's hands behind him and around the trunk of the tree. He tied the rope around his wrists and then around the tree. The rope was thick and bristly and tied very tight. The other leader had tied Roeun to a tree five or so feet away. Then the leaders left.

Soeuth and Roeun glanced at each other, and Soeuth panicked, because he had heard that when someone was tied up like this, he would die. He remembered that at the base of these trees were large red ant nests. As if cued by his recollection, the ants emerged from little holes in the ground, solid lines of them, and crawled onto his feet. A few of them bit, and the bites stung, but he did not move, because he knew the more he squirmed, the more they would bite. Soeuth and Roeun stood tied against the trees all night, streams of red ants marching up their legs and into their pants. Soeuth kept his eyes closed tight, waiting for light.

At dawn, the boys were untied and, that afternoon, were sent under heavy escort to a camp very far away, deep in the jungle and against the mountains. The nights were dark and full of the sounds of gunshots and mortar blasts and, sometimes, the howling of wolves.

The rainy season at the new camp was soon engulfed by the dry season. Soeuth hacked the earth with his hoe and felt himself growing older and harder. He thought about his family every once in a while, wondering if they were okay, but he knew now that he did not need them like he used to.

★   ★   ★

After several more seasons had passed and the mortar blasts
in the jungle now thundered close to the camp, Angka marched
the children back to Cave. It was the rainy season at Cave, and
they resumed planting. During the afternoon rest period, there
were plenty of rats and lizards to shoot with their slingshots and
catfish in the rice fields to catch with their hands.

One of Soeuth's cousins was working at Cave now, too, but
he did not see her much. She was his father's niece and many
years older. Her name was Sao. One afternoon, as Soeuth was
planting, he noticed Sao working nearby, a few rows over. She
shot a few sharp-eyed glances at him, but he did not stop working. At some point she traipsed toward him, quickly, across the
rows and, when she reached him, whispered: "Your grandmother's dead."

Soeuth stood still. "No," he said.

"It's true. She's dead."

"It's not true."

"It is."

Sao left and continued planting.

The following morning, Soeuth asked the leader if he could
go to the bathroom and again sneaked out through the rice fields.
He knew that if Angka did not catch him, they would soon figure
out that he had left, and when he got back, they would hurt him
very badly this time, or kill him. But he loved his grandmother
more than anyone, and if she had truly died, he must see her
body before it was buried.

He arrived in the village just before dark. He walked down
the path to his family's hut, and as he crossed the front yard, his
mother hurtled out of the hut and down the steps. Her eyes were
focused and scared and she was breathing hard.

"What are you doing here?" She glared at him.

He said nothing.

"You cannot be here!" his mother whispered raspily. She bent
down close to him. "You have to go back. Now!"

"I want to see my grandmother," Soeuth said.

"You're too late." His mother stood up. "We buried her yesterday."

Soeuth rubbed his eyes; he felt suddenly alone. He knew his mother couldn't be seen talking to him, knew that it would put her and everyone else in danger—but he had traveled all this way and was determined to say some sort of farewell to his grandmother.

"I want to see her grave," Soeuth demanded.

His mother breathed heavily, clasped his hand and tugged him precipitously to an oblong mound of loose dirt behind the hut. There were no markers or flowers. Soeuth wept as quietly as he could.

"How?" he asked.

"Sickness," his mother snapped. "Bad sickness. Now, you must go."

She led him to the front yard. "You must go." His mother nudged him away from the hut. Soeuth left.

He returned to Cave the following evening and slunk to his sleeping shed. They were there waiting for him, two guards for Angka. One of them Soeuth knew. He was very young, only a few years older, and had been his neighbor before the revolution. His name, similar to Soeuth's, was Sut. Tall, with an elongated, pinched face, he had become arrogant and reckless with the power Angka had given him.

The guards approached Soeuth. The older-looking one, with a single motion, pulled his hands behind his back and tied his wrists together. Then they both pushed him onto his knees. Kneeling, staring at the dirt, Soeuth became angry. He had never done anything to these boys. In sudden unison, and with sudden laughter, they kicked him in the ribs and stomach. The blows were solid, and his body soon folded, collapsing to the dirt. Sut, whose face Soeuth vowed never to forget, kicked him as he lay on his side, the thud of his foot loud and hollow on the small of Soeuth's back. Occasionally Sut would interrupt the kicking so he could land a few lashes of his whip. The pain was total, and at some point Soeuth could no longer feel anything, and was not even really aware when the beating had ceased. He lay still, unable, even, to feel his own breathing. They untied him and told him to get up, but at first, he couldn't. Then, somehow, as if yanked up by marionette strings, he was on his feet. Go to bed, they ordered him, and he did.

It was one of those fall days when the sun shoots through tattered clouds like spokes of a wheel, when the bright yellow, brown and red leaves of maples undulate in the breeze, when the air seems edged with a cool electricity. Dave, my best friend, Jeff, and I were preparing to probe the wilderness behind our house, expansive fields and twisting swaths of old forest that reached back farther than you could walk in a week, according to Farmer Seeley. We sat on the steps of the porch oiling our BB guns. I was peering down the muzzle of my gun when Jeff started talking about bagging a deer. He had seen a deer that his uncle or a friend of his dad's had brought home in the bed of his pickup, he said, its mouth caked with blood, the bullet hole in its neck gaping like a poked-out eye, its antlers sticking up out of the truck like crooked bayonets.

"You can't kill a deer with a BB gun," Dave informed Jeff, his chin jutting defiantly.

"Well, that's why I got this," Jeff answered, brandishing his brand-new black pellet rifle. "This'd kill a bear."

I wondered if I could muster what it took to shoot a deer, to squeeze off a hunk of metal into its silky neck and watch it thrash incredulously to the ground, its eyes fluttering, asking: what did I do to you? I could gut and clean a fish without any moral problems, but anything with legs and fur and a tail—that was hard.

But Jeff was a man, as he'd say, who enjoyed the kill, who liked the smell of blood. He had bragged of exploding frogs by jamming lit fire crackers up their asses. He had been my neighbor at Gorham Lane, his house a few treated lawns and stained fences away from mine. He was a good friend who stood up to bullies for me and routinely allowed me into his baseball-card trading ring. Jeff was chubby—but in the right places—had a Raggedy Andy bowl haircut and freckles.

We laced up our shitkickers and set out. We scurried under the barbed-wire fence and stood panting, and Jeff remarked: "Damn! It's hotter'n a crotch out here!" It wasn't really hot, but Jeff was always saying things like that—tough, crass phrases he had presumably lifted from his uncle or dad.

Dave and I nodded our contrived agreement, and I wiped my brow as if I were sweating.

Jeff looked all around, drawing in the landscape, and then exclaimed: "Okay boys—cock your rifles!"

We obeyed, in unison.

Just past the fence was a tepid, slug-shaped body of water bordered by rambling wild grapevines. Here the effluent from our sewer tank spilled out, and on a day like this, the stench was pungent.

We skirted the pond, batting our hands at the envelope of odor, until we reached the edge of the open cow pasture. The terrain to our south was littered with the prostrate hulks of willow trees felled by the Hurricane of '54. Farmer Seeley had told us of a series of legendary natural disasters that had befallen our new neighborhood over the years, including the Hurricane of '54 and the even more ominous-sounding Storm of '27, which had flooded everything in sight, including the basement and a few feet of the first floor of our house. The willows had been knocked over by the hurricane but had survived and continued to grow downward and outward, so that their branches now pushed against the ground, trying, it seemed, to right their torsos. Something struck me as sad but noble about a tree that had been felled but refused to surrender its life, like some prehistoric creature that had, for some reason, evolved backward.

The pasture stretched ahead infinitely, its tall grass sharp and bright in the sun and full of thistles. We eventually found a spot in the river where we could cross. We removed our shoes, rolled up our pant legs and padded through the icy water, wincing at the riverbed stones under our feet.

After we got across, we followed the bank until it became too steep and crowded with trees. When we located a clearing, Jeff said: "It's time to start a fire, boys."

We gathered some sticks, made a tepee with them, and Jeff lit it with his matches. The fire crackled, fighting the wind. Jeff brandished his Barlow jackknife and said: "Now for the ceremony."

"Ceremony?" I asked.

"Yes," he said seriously. "To go on this adventure, we have to be brothers."

"But we are brothers, Adam and me," Dave protested, pouting.

"No, dummy," Jeff said, grinning. "This is a special kind of brothers—blood brothers."

He sharpened his knife on a rock, a glint of sun shimmying on the blade. Then he regarded me and ordered nonchalantly: "Gimme your hand."

I knew it would hurt, but I had to do it. I knelt down beside him and gave him my hand. He grabbed my wrist and pressed the blade down into my palm until blood welled and my hand burned. I wanted to scream but held it in. He then cut his own hand, his face tight and concentrated. Then it was Dave's turn; he was crying. "C'mon, man," Jeff said, cringing. "It ain't that bad." So Dave let Jeff cut him.

Jeff tied my bloody hand to his with a rag. The rag reddened. Then he untied our hands, cut himself again and tied his hand to Dave's. Blood dripped onto the ground.

He told us to hold our hands over the fire. We sat there cringing, our bloody hands over the flames, and Jeff announced: "Now we're brothers."

A few weeks before the dry season, Soeuth was transferred to a work camp only a few miles from Battambang City. Everyone slept on floors of open-air sheds, no hammocks, and listened to the war thundering inside the city and watched it blooming in sudden bright circles against the night horizon. While most boys slept, a few would remain awake, whispering about rumors that the Vietnamese were now invading Kampuchea. Soeuth lay on his side on the cool wood floor, listening, wondering what would happen if the Vietnamese won—whether he would be able to find his family. If not, he could probably survive, he figured, by wandering around and stealing coconuts and sugarcane.

On one morning he did not wake to the cry of the work whistle. It was the first morning since Angka had separated him from his family, the first morning in several years, that he had roused naturally. He knew by the sky's brightness and the heat that it was late. But several other children were still asleep. He lay awake until the group leader finally stomped in and told them all to get up and go to work.

For the next several days, there was no whistle, and the group leader, who was only fifteen or sixteen and very nervous, woke them. When they filed out to the fields, Soeuth saw only two or three other leaders. They were all young and none had any seniority. All the head leaders and middle leaders were nowhere to be seen.

As the dry season wrung the sky of its moisture, the number of leaders continued to decrease. Those who remained grew progressively more anxious and distracted. Every day there were fewer children out working, too, and Soeuth guessed that it would be easy now to leave the camp.

Soeuth and Roeun awoke very late one morning and stumbled out to the fields to report for work. Some other children were working, but there were no leaders supervising them, not a single one. So Soeuth and his friend wandered cautiously around the camp grounds, wary of the vast, brooding silence, half expecting a machete-wielding guard to leap out of the shadows at them. But except for the handful of children working, no one was around.

Soeuth slipped into the canteen to discover that even the cooks were gone. Behind a leaf-thatched partition, where their meals had been prepared, he and Roeun found a long wooden table upon which a dozen or so pots and pans were neatly laid out. They stole a few pots and scurried to the rice house. Then Roeun made a fire outside their sleeping shed, and they boiled the rice in water from the paddies.

"Maybe we should leave," Roeun said, squatting, stoking the fire. "Almost everyone else is gone. The leaders, too."

Soeuth watched the water boil and his stomach lurched with hunger. He nodded distractedly at Roeun's suggestion.

"But we have to be careful," Roeun intoned somewhat paternalistically. "Because of last time."

Soeuth nodded.

"Angka could be playing a trick."

With great weariness, Soeuth lifted his head to regard Roeun.

"We have to be careful," Roeun said.

After a few days of eating their fill of rice, Roeun said it should be safe now to return to the village. On the morning they left the camp, there were still a few young children out in the fields, obediently cutting and bundling stems, waiting for their captors to return.

It was early afternoon when they arrived in the village. The road was quiet, and the thatched roofs of huts were bright in the sun. They reached Roeun's family's hut first, but it was empty, and so they went to Soeuth's family's hut. It was empty, too, its dark doorway gaping mournfully. They stood outside on the packed dirt and Soeuth suddenly felt spent.

Roeun fished a cigarette from a pocket, and as they smoked it, a man's voice yelled Soeuth's name. He swung around, and through spaces in the wall of banana-tree leaves, he could see that it was his family's next-door neighbor. The man was standing alone in his yard, next to a pile of things he had packed for a journey.

The man said, "I know where your family went."

Soeuth stood still; his heart quickened.

"They went to Cave," the man said. He put his hand up to shield his eyes from the sun, and added, "Maybe you can find them there." Then he returned to his packing.

Soeuth and Roeun reached Cave, their old slave camp, just before dark. It was crowded and clamorous. The sounds of babies crying, livestock squawking, pots and pans clinking, and people chattering all melded into an undulant, echoing din. Families huddled around fires or cowered under lean-tos. Soeuth and Roeun meandered carefully, quietly, among them, peering into shadows to see faces.

A man barked out Roeun's name from a few yards away. He beckoned the boys to follow him. He led them through a snarl of encamped families, and there in the midst of the clamor was Roeun's family, busy building a lean-to out of sticks, leaves and brush. When they saw Soeuth and Roeun staring at them, they flinched—as if the boys had materialized suddenly like apparitions. Roeun's mother and grandmother reached out to Roeun, crying, and bent down to whisper soft, sweet things to him. Roeun's father was not there, but most of his family was, and Roeun was smiling widely. Soeuth stood quietly, observing his friend with his family.

There was only enough space under the lean-to for Roeun and his family, so Soeuth slept in the open. He curled himself into a ball and listened to the gunfire and mortar blasts and drifted into fickle sleep.

The morning erupted with the same cacophony of sounds. Soeuth was sitting with Roeun, sharing a cigarette, when a skinny, smiling man ambled over, calling Soeuth's name. He stopped close to the boys.

"Soeuth, are you okay?" the man asked in a gentle voice.

Soeuth dimly recognized this man as an acquaintance of his father's. He squinted at the man. "Yes," he replied.

"My name is Snuy," the man said. "I was your neighbor before." His smile engraved his face with deep and sincere parentheses.

Soeuth nodded; he remembered him better now, could picture his hut a few huts away from his family's.

"Why don't you come by?" Snuy said.

Soeuth went with Snuy and said hello to his wife and ate rice with them that afternoon. They did not have any children and told him he could stay with them until he had found his family. They were better off than many families at Cave, because they had an ox cart and two oxen and a few sheets of tin with which they could quickly assemble a rainproof shelter.

Each day Soeuth snaked through the vast tangle of people at Cave, hoping to find his mother or father or brother or sisters. But there were a lot of people, over a thousand probably, and they weren't always in the same places, and so he told himself that Roeun was just lucky.

In the afternoons, most everyone ventured to the rice fields to cut stems which were now heavy with kernels. There were many Angka soldiers at Cave, but they didn't seem to mind if the people collected rice from the fields; they were too worried about the Vietnamese. AK-47s slung over their backs, they strode through the camp, holding up megaphones and announcing that Angka would protect the people from the Vietnamese aggressors. Sometimes Angka soldiers would shoot in the direction of the advancing Vietnamese, even though they were nowhere in sight.

Indolent cows wandered here and there around Cave. They had become the property of Angka after the revolution, but now the civilians were taking them back. When a cow was claimed, its new owner would often immediately strike it in the head with an axe, carve it up and cook it. If there were any leftover parts—hocks and viscera, usually—they were tossed toward groping hands.

Snuy had given Soeuth a coil of rope one afternoon so he could catch a cow. The cow he found was old, slow and bone-thin with a rough, grayish coat. It hadn't put up any resistance when Soeuth looped the rope around its neck and tugged it back to Snuy's camp. That night, after tying his cow to a stake Snuy had hammered into the ground, Soeuth fashioned a pair of saddlebags out of a piece of rope and two rice sacks.

After a week at Cave, Angka said through its megaphones that the Vietnamese—the *k'mung*—were coming and it was time to pack up. Everyone tied together his belongings and followed the megaphoned voices out of Cave and along a narrow road that sliced the rice fields. Soeuth rode his cow like a horse alongside Snuy's oxcart. Maybe your family will be in the next group of people at the next camp, Snuy offered as they rode side by side. Maybe, Soeuth agreed.

They settled soon at the same faraway camp in which Soeuth had worked for several seasons, the camp deep in the jungle and against the mountains. His family was not there.

It was only another week or so before Angka said it was again time to relocate. They climbed now into the mountains, and the air was sharp with the stench of sun-baked corpses heaped alongside the road.

Sometimes a group of people would split from the caravan, directed by Angka in another direction, and sometimes a new group would join it. The caravan strained up the road as the sounds of its squeaky wheels, hacking coughs and crying babies mingled with the twittering of birds. The food was running out now, and Snuy and his wife carefully rationed what rice they still had.

Snuy told Soeuth that maybe he shouldn't ride his cow so much, because it would tire and die, so Soeuth rode in the oxcart with Snuy and his wife.

"I heard Angka is planning to use us as shields against the Vietnamese," Snuy said to his wife one afternoon as they all rode in the oxcart.

His wife looked at him; she was small, quiet and pretty.

"Because the Vietnamese don't know who are civilians or not," Snuy went on. "We're just Khmers in their eyes—that's why Angka has gone up ahead and left us in between them and the Vietnamese." He paused and frowned, adding: "These men— they are cowards."

Snuy's wife smiled at Soeuth, as if to say, don't worry, this doesn't affect you. Soeuth smiled back.

The roar of a Vietnamese jet would sometimes rupture the afternoon; the sounds of mortar blasts boomed behind them like a continually approaching storm. After camp had been set one afternoon, Soeuth returned from a slingshot excursion to find that his cow was gone. He stood by the tree where it had been tied, quietly fuming, though he knew there was nothing he could do; it was probably already being cooked by now.

Two nights later, camp was set in a damp clearing beside a pond. The pond's surface was placid and shone with stars. After everyone had set down his bundle, many scurried to the edge of the pond, sank to their knees on its muddy shore and slurped up water with their hands. There hadn't been a water source for many days, and everyone was thirsty. Soeuth, Snuy and his wife staggered to the pond and drank up water until they were full with it.

In the morning, several boys were out hunting with their sling-shots for rats among the pond reeds when one of them screamed shrilly, pointing into the water. The other boys stared into the pond and immediately buckled over and vomited. Soeuth padded over to the pond's edge to see what had caused all the commotion. Submerged a foot and a half beneath the surface, and only a couple of feet from where he had knelt to drink the night before, were a half-dozen corpses. Some were facedown, some supine, some contorted in uncomfortable-looking positions. Although just bones now, they still wore their clothes. Soeuth could see the closest one clearly. The skull had separated from the body, and although the flesh was gone, its black hair floated up and fanned out at the surface. The hair was long, probably a girl's hair, Soeuth thought.

A lot of people were vomiting now. Soeuth went back to where Snuy and his wife were camped and sat down, vowing to himself from now on not to drink from ponds or lakes or rivers at night, even if he was very thirsty.

Soeuth sat with Snuy that afternoon, wishing he had a cigarette, and listened to some angry adults in a nearby lean-to saying that Angka's men were monsters and demons and murderers of their own people. He listened to the hushed, harsh voices, hoping his family had not been dumped in a pond or roadside ditch.

Later that afternoon, a boy found the body of an Angka soldier, sprawled on the ground in the shade of a wild apple tree and missing his head. Word had radiated fast and a gaggle of people had gathered to inspect the headless body. Soeuth wandered over toward the congregation, but did not go close in case the body's ghost was still nearby. He saw the body, though, the maroon stump of a neck, the blood dried and dark in the dirt. No one seemed to know who had killed him, but the rumor was that his death was an act of revenge.

After seeing the dead Angka soldier, Soeuth realized that he had not seen any live Angka soldiers at all today or the day before. He returned to Snuy's camp. Snuy and his wife were packing their things, and when Snuy saw Soeuth, he said in short, quick breaths: "It's time now. To leave. Before Angka . . . comes back."

The next night at sundown, Snuy had loaded his oxcart, and he and his wife and Soeuth were standing next to it, waiting for the word. The moon had flown up as soon as the sun had gone down, it seemed, and the reeds and bushes hummed with the chirping of the crickets, and everybody stood still as if transfixed, listening.

Then the word arrived, whispered all around, and they were driving in one great surge, hundreds of people, across the dry, dusty fields toward the national highway and the Vietnamese. Soeuth felt that familiar, tingling thrill of escape. He was riding with Snuy and his wife in the oxcart, which trundled roughly on a path between the fields. Some other families were in oxcarts; most, though, were on foot, lurching across the fields, tugging their children and possessions behind them, straining in the soft moonlight.

Snuy's oxcart was rickety and swayed from side to side, and its wooden wheels wobbled and creaked on the hard clay. Another oxcart lumbered beside them, and Soeuth could hear the driver speaking to his wife. "We have to hurry," said the man, urging the oxen. "If the *K'mao* catch up, they will kill us." Soeuth knew *K'mao*, the Khmer word for "black." Angka's men all wore black clothes and their hearts were black, too. They were sometimes called the *Khmer Gra-Horm*, the red Khmers—because they were Communists—but *K'mao* was easier to say.

They traveled all night and on into morning. The dust hung in the air like fog. At sometime past noon, people all around were yelling that the highway was near and that up on the highway were the Vietnamese.

"Once we get to the Vietnamese," Snuy announced, coughing, "we will be safe."

Soeuth peered ahead through the dust and could dimly make out the highway raised above the fields. He felt a strong jolt of hope.

Then gunshots reported from somewhere behind them. Soeuth swiveled around to see four of Angka's men on horses racing toward them, rifles raised, furious and firing. They were about a quarter mile away, but moving fast. People began sprinting for the highway and screaming. Snuy was whipping the reins of the oxcart and exhorting the oxen to move faster. The highway was close now, maybe a hundred yards away, lined with a large regiment of Vietnamese soldiers.

As Snuy's oxcart rumbled toward the highway, Soeuth sank down among the pots and pans and sheets of tin. The dust swept over him, and he peeked back at Angka's men on their horses shooting at the people in the fields, shooting at him. He was too angry to be afraid. He hoped Angka's men would ride in closer, close enough for the Vietnamese to gun them down.

Then, suddenly, they were on the highway, and the Angka soldiers, who must have known they were outnumbered by the Vietnamese, turned and galloped away. People stumbled onto the highway, breathing raspily, glancing back in awe as their captors and the murderers of their families retreated. Soeuth jumped down from the oxcart with Snuy and his wife. There were twenty or so Vietnamese foot soldiers in olive-green suits, cradling their rifles and marching toward them. *Do not worry,* the soldiers yelled out in Khmer, *it is safe now, do not worry.* Behind the soldiers were a few tanks and equipment trucks, growling slowly down the highway. The soldiers asked the people where the red Khmers had gone, and everyone pointed eagerly toward the cloud of dust that had enveloped the retreating Angka soldiers.

It was hot, and Soeuth was soaked in sweat and powdered with dust, and all the people around him were weeping because they were free.

The highway was National Route 5 and would lead them north to Battambang City, Snuy said. They walked, because Snuy wanted the oxen to rest. They reached the outskirts of Battambang City in just under a week.

It was not yet safe to return to the villages, a group of Vietnamese soldiers informed them, because there were still land mines that had been sown into the fields and roads. So they set up camp with a few other families on a dusty swath of dirt along the highway on the city's eastern rim.

Thirty yards up the road was a worn cement bridge that crossed the Sangker River, in which Soeuth used to bathe with his brother and sisters. He walked to the bridge that afternoon to see how high the river was. But the dry season was severe this year, and the Sangker River, which had always run deep and wide, as Soeuth remembered, had now mostly run dry. A trickle of water dribbled down the river's naked bed, which now reminded Soeuth of a massive, empty irrigation canal.

Within a few days, Snuy and his wife left. They were going north, they said, to look for relatives. Good-bye, Soeuth, they said, we will pray for you—and then their oxcart trundled onto the road and disappeared in its own dust. Fortunately, within another few days, an old neighbor approached Soeuth. The man, who had a wife and son, was muscular and serious. He offered to take Soeuth in and feed him, on the condition that Soeuth look after his two oxen. The family lived in a small, stilted bamboo shack the man had built there in the dusty area along the road by the bridge. Soeuth slept on the floor of that shack for the next two months.

When word was released from the Vietnamese Army, dispersed mouth to mouth, that the land mines had been cleared, everyone wearily dismantled his shack and once again packed his things. Soeuth journeyed with the serious, muscular man and his wife back to Asrolaub, his old village.

Many people were returning to the village now to reclaim their homes. But the land was stripped of its crops and many of the huts were burned down or wrecked. The serious, muscular man's hut had been ruined and he cursed over it, because now he would have to build a new one. Roeun's family's hut had been wrecked, too. Where Soeuth's family's hut had stood was now just a smooth patch of dirt. He lingered on the path and stared at the bare dirt and thought that his family must surely be dead.

He walked across the river's bare bed to see if his aunts, Him and Pai, had returned to the village. They were there, but had no food for him and had not seen his parents and didn't know what he should do. They were both pale and gaunt, their skin clinging urgently to their bones. Smiling wanly at him as they sat on their bamboo beds in the shade beneath their huts, they seemed as indifferent as corpses—and so he left.

He stayed with the serious, muscular man and his family, watching his oxen and sometimes sneaking into other people's fields to sling stones at rats and steal corn and sugarcane. The man's wife was kind and gave Soeuth rice and a *khrama,* too. Within a month, the rainy season swelled the Sangker River, and Soeuth swam in it on many afternoons.

One day, several months into the rainy season, after a sling-shot excursion, Soeuth plodded home to discover that the serious, muscular man's oxen had broken loose and eaten all of the family's mung beans. Realizing that he had somehow forgotten to secure the gate, Soeuth crept into the man's citrus grove, stole two grapefruits and ran.

Blisters broke on the soles of his feet, but Soeuth did not stop walking until he reached Battambang City. The city was dusty and full of ragged, barefoot people. Its rubble-strewn streets were lined with lean-tos, makeshift tin-and-plywood shacks and road-side stands where you could barter rice for candies, soup or ciga-rettes. Soeuth had only his grapefruits and figured they wouldn't earn him much—maybe a few cigarettes—and so held onto them. The sun was hard and bright against the bombed-out buildings and there were cooking fires all around and funnels of smoke twisting toward the sky.

The city was sad and smoky, and so he left, traveling north on National Route 5. He walked for days, sweating and shivering with the heat and hunger. It rained only a little at night. He met up, one afternoon, with a large group of people camped on the side of the highway, thirty or so families with children and babies. He traveled with them for several days and camped with them at night. A few of the adults were saying, around the fire one night, that it was time to venture off the road. The next day they all crept down a steep bank and waded across a chest-deep, fast-moving river. On the opposite side, looming over the lip of the bank, was the jungle.

There was a rough path, hacked by others who had come

this way, that wormed through the close-woven undergrowth and beneath the low-hanging vine webs. Sharp leaves jutted like bayonets from thickets encroaching on the path. Some of the adults had told Soeuth to be quiet and to go slow, but there were others who were not so quiet and there were many crying babies. They trudged in tandem along the path, and Soeuth was glad that he was in the middle of the pack; if there were any land mines, the people up front would set them off.

It rained continuously for several days, and the jungle was heavy with the moist reek of corpses strewn alongside the path. No one had time to build lean-tos and so slept in the mud under blankets and *khramas*. Some families had oxcarts under which they could sleep. Soeuth slept in more than three inches of water, nestling at the base of a tall tree.

One afternoon, after more than a week in the jungle, the chattering of distant voices reverberated through the walls of leaves. Everyone staggered toward the voices, dozens of feet pattering like rainfall, until the path deposited the group in a vast clay clearing. In it was a muddy stew of skeletal people like them who had come the same way.

This was the border camp, Soeuth soon learned. This was where you waited for a new life. Every morning ten large flatbed trucks would nose out of the jungle, and people would climb on board, and the trucks would ferry them to Thailand. Soeuth overheard some people whispering by their fire one night that those who boarded the trucks were driven to a cliff and pushed off the edge. But after several weeks of stealing fruit and cigarettes and sleeping in the rain, he knew that if he did not leave this place, he would starve. One morning he joined thirty or so others, hopping onto the bed of the nearest truck. Its engine growled and sputtered, and then they were racing under the leaves toward Thailand.

The new house was too big for just the four of us. Mom had been saying that ever since we moved in. One night in November, when my thoughts were marshaled toward Christmas and new action figures and Atari games and Lego sets, she called a family meeting. She sat in the north corner of the living room, her legs crossed at a businesslike angle, her hands folded in her lap. Her oval face always had a ready arsenal of distinct and strategic expressions; today, with her metallic-blue eyes bright and hopeful, and her lips pushed up into a half smile, it was her "proposition" expression.

Dave and I slumped side by side on the couch. Dad was always the last to join us. We heard him in the kitchen crinkling up a Lay's bag and stuffing it into the bread box. He came in wiping potato-chip crumbs off his hands, hiking up his trousers. He sat in the engulfing armchair, his bony knees jutting up, a bright white skin gap suddenly appearing where his socks and pant legs failed to meet. He winked at us and wriggled his nose. He didn't like the meetings any more than we did.

"Boys." The tone of Mom's voice was cheery, insistent. "Your father and I have been thinking."

Your father and I have been thinking—that was never good. I began to rap my fingers on the coffee table as Dad would often do. I caught Mom examining me for a reaction, and my eyes shot down to the safety of the beige carpet. Dad sat in the opposite corner, his eyebrows innocently inclined.

"We've been thinking about adding another member to our family," Mom finally said. "But we wanted to talk to the two of you about it to see how you feel."

I looked over at Dave; his face was frozen, his eyes anchored to the coffee table. I nudged him.

"Stop it, you idiot!" He was glad for the diversion.

Mom sighed. Was she having another baby? I looked at Dad; his brow went up even farther and he began to nod, as if answering my unspoken question. I looked back at Dave, who was now kneading the couch pillow like it was bread dough.

"Boys?"

I resolved to speak. "Mom, are you . . . having a . . . you know?"

Dave's head snapped up, as if I had been part of the stork conspiracy committee.

"No," Mom answered quickly enough.

Relief. Dave sat back and dropped his pillow. Mom's eyes narrowed thoughtfully, and she leaned forward, placing her hands on her knee, forcing our eyes to meet hers. Then she said, "There's a boy."

She might as well have said, there's an alien. Dave and I looked at each other and studied each other's faces for a clue to what or whom she might be talking about. I looked at Dad, but he was looking at Mom.

"There's a boy from a place called Kampuchea," she said. "A place on the other side of the world."

Kampuchea. The word filled the room like mist. It made a picture in my mind of a jagged, mysterious landscape of shark-fin peaks and foggy, dark forests, full of the sounds of spirits and goblins and whispered riddles. The way Mom said it, the way her lips rolled it out like it was some ancient, powerful secret, sent a cool shiver down the back of my neck.

"His name is *Suit*."

Suit. I guessed at what his last name might be. Jacket or Pants, maybe. Mom's eyes angled at me.

"And he needs a home."

I wondered if he knew magic, like the characters in Narnia; if he could show us how to use our closets to get to his and other worlds.

"He's a very nice boy," Mom assured us casually, as though she were talking about a new dog. "And he might become your foster brother. What do you think about that?"

The truck rolled shakily along a pocked, winding road. Soeuth could see wedges of sky and sometimes leaves when he looked straight up, but he couldn't see the landscape all around; there were too many tall adults packed tight against him. After three or four hours, the truck turned off the road and grumbled down another road for a while and then turned off somewhere else. Loud voices and footsteps and children's shrieks now surrounded the truck, and soon it reversed, stopped. The people on the truck shuffled and jostled each other until most of them had jumped or been pushed off. Soeuth could now see out. Beyond the gate of the truck lay an area more vast and crowded than any place he had ever seen. The size of it stunned him for a second. It was like a giant ant farm: a few clusters of people scampered here and there through a maze of tiny narrow roads and regimented rows of bamboo huts. The roads were striped with shadows into which the people occasionally disappeared and reemerged again, sun-lit.

This was Khao-I-Dang, a United Nations-run refugee holding center, and would become Soeuth's home for the next six months. He liked Khao-I-Dang. He was fed a full bowl of rice or stir-fried long beans every morning, afternoon and evening. Sometimes he was given fruit. He was issued a set of clothes, pants and a shirt, and a pair of sandals. During the day he went to school. At night he slept with a blanket on the floor of a building with a tightly thatched roof that admitted no rain. There were twenty other boys in his sleeping house. These boys hadn't been able to find their families either, and Soeuth felt better knowing that he was not alone anymore and that there were other children like him without families.

It was the rainy season again when he was sent to a new camp, where he would remain for many more seasons until he lost track of how many seasons had gone by. He made friends there and entered adolescence and learned how to write in Khmer and to count in English. He played soccer and volleyball and other games. When there was a gunshot—and there were many— he ran, with the other boys, to the tall chain-link fence that enclosed the camp to look out at who had tried to escape and been shot by the Thai soldiers. He learned auto mechanics. He went to temple. On many occasions he witnessed the Thai soldiers kicking and beating someone into unconsciousness for one reason or another. He saw a Cambodian man electrocuted as he tried to crawl underneath a high-voltage fence that surrounded a wood-storage shed. He got into a few fights, one involving a dispute over how many days there were in the calendar, in which he punched his adversary in the jaw and near dug out the boy's eyes with his thumbs before other kids pried him off. He learned how to play cards.

During the rainy season he was called to the office for an interview. The office had been built with good, solid wood and had a tin roof and was bordered by rows of brightly colored flowers. The interview was held inside a small room with a table and two chairs. The interviewer was a white man, who spoke in a soft voice. Through an interpreter, he asked Soeuth questions about his family. Soeuth answered that he had no family, hadn't had one in a long time. The interviewer asked him many other questions. Finally, Soeuth was instructed to stand against the wall and handed a placard to hold. Then someone snapped his photograph.

After the first interview, he was called for several more interviews and the interviewer was a different person each time but always nice. Other boys told him to look for his name on a list that was posted each day on a bulletin board outside the office. The bulletin board was shielded from the rain by a small plywood roof. The names on the list tacked to the bulletin board were those of children for whom new families had been found in new countries.

He checked the list once a week for several weeks but did not see his name. A few other boys in his sleeping house had found their names on the list and had gone to the office and been given a new shirt and pair of pants and shoes and then had been sent on a bus to Bangkok. After half the boys in his sleeping house had found their names on the list, Soeuth started checking the list every day.

On an afternoon in the fall of 1982, he went to the bulletin board and started to read down the list. He began to give up hope again when he got halfway down the list and had not seen his name, but read a few more names and then there it was, his name, typed in veritable black ink.

I put on my corduroy vest, donned my smartest, steel-rimmed bifocals, folded my hands behind my back and went to pacing to and fro across my room. This was how you jarred loose stuck ideas, Dad had said. The first thing I thought was: I already have a brother who dismembers my action figures, gets food in his hair and sometimes in mine, blows up his cheeks like Dizzy Gillespie on the trumpet and makes farting noises during dinner, belches, bites, badgers, smears ice cream and frosting on his face and has a penchant for collecting dirty, smelly and, sometimes, dead things. On my ninth birthday, Dave's gift for me was a dead mouse he had found under the porch; he had plopped it in a plastic margarine container and then had handed it to me, exclaiming: "Happy Birfday!" Little Dave, whom Dad called "Davy Crockett" or just "Crockett," was enough brother for me.

What if our new brother turned out to be some primitive living in our midst, building fires in our living room, sacrificing our cats? What if he walked around naked and ate with his hands and made grunting, guttural noises? What if he pierced his cheeks with one of our shish kebab skewers? It occurred to me that he might have tapeworms or fleas and Mom would have to give him Frisbee's worm medicine and get him a Hartz Flea & Tick collar. I assumed he would be dirty, any way you sliced it.

The phrase kept pulsing in my head like some emergency warning signal. *Foster brother*. How can you just become someone's brother? I understood the granite reality of it: once he did become our brother, there was no going back.

One day over a few bowls of Life cereal, Dave and I conferred about the new-brother question and, after an exhaustive and circuitous conversation, decided it might have its advantages. Dave said that with someone from the other side of the world around— since he had probably seen some R-rated things in real life— maybe our parents would forget about their TV rule and finally let us watch the only two shows we were prohibited from watching, *Kojak* and *Starsky & Hutch*. It was a good point. I added that he could accompany us on our adventures in the woods out by the river, since he might know how to live off the land, trap animals and build forts from sticks and leaves. I also wagered that he could climb any tree, even the monster willows in the front yard whose branches wandered like tentacles. Dave wondered if he could communicate with animals and possibly teach us how to talk to Smokey, an ill-tempered old swayback who usually acknowledged most people by trying to bite or kick them. Our new brother might know how to make slingshots out of twigs in Dad's brush pile, I offered, with which we could brain beavers and muskrats and coyotes.

We watched *ET* again, because this boy came from a faraway place. Dave suggested that we try offering him Reese's pieces, like they did in the movie, or, if we didn't have Reese's pieces, fruit roll-ups. The other side of the world, where he came from, might not be that different from ET's world, we figured. It occurred to me that he might have telepathic and telekinetic powers, that he could riffle through my thoughts like Mom going through the mail. I began to picture him with a long neck, huge head and peering eyes, except in a suit.

His name was actually pronounced *Soot*, Mom told us, like the silty remains of a fire in our chimney. She wrote it down for us and made us repeat it so we'd get it right when he came.

One night, as Dave and I played Pac Man, Mom carefully lowered herself into the unoccupied beanbag. She lolled awkwardly, legs crossed, hands tented. Her face was half smiling, half frowning. As I turned off the Atari, she told us about our new brother. He had been through some really bad things, she said. Like losing his entire family and being a slave and living by himself in the jungle, eating rats and water bugs. His country had had a war and children like him were left with no parents or homes and had to live in crowded camps with other lost, starving children. She said the bad guys were called some fancy French name that sounded like a gourmet dessert.

The fancy French guys had killed a lot of people, Mom said. *Two million* people. They had taken children away from their parents and made them dig ditches and harvest rice. They had killed doctors, like Dad, and also schoolteachers, monks and lawyers, and had outlawed money and religion and broken apart families. They were Communists, she said, and as bad as bad guys get. As bad as the Nazis whom Grandpa Al had fought in World War II. Their Hitler was some guy whose first name was Paul, a pretty bland name for a mass murderer, I thought. She said that our government should have gone over there and stopped Paul and the fancy French guys but didn't.

After she told me all this, I sat down in Dad's study, under his green banker's lamp, and tried to work out how many people two million was. Dad had said that it was four times the number of people in Vermont. I imagined everyone in Vermont being dead, pictured the aisles of Ames brimming with corpses, envisioned skeletons heaped up on the town green and laid out neatly along the yard lines of the high school football field. I had seen a few cow carcasses out back by the river, crawling with flies and maggots and giving off a swollen, vinegary odor. But I had never run across any dead people.

At the next Fifield family meeting, Dave and Dad voiced their reservations about the boy from Cambodia. Dad folded his hands under his chin, furrowed up his brow, pistoned his knee and said that this boy might change the dynamics of our family and that we would have to do a lot of adjusting. When he said "adjusting," I couldn't help but think of our family as a fluttery old engine powered by the spastic pumping of Dad's knee, an engine that would have to be taken in for frequent tune-ups if any new parts were added to it. When Dad had finished with his comments, Mom nodded and answered that life was full of adjustments, that that's what it was all about; a thoughtful frown bobbed on Dad's face then, and I could see that he was reconsidering. Mom inhaled deeply and slung her gaze over at Dave, who sat ponderously working his thumbs. Dad's probably right, Dave said, we won't know how he'll work out, we just don't know at all. As Dave spoke, I let my eyes warm themselves in the lamp on Mom's antique table, and suddenly felt a surge of excitement. When Mom turned toward me, I decided I would take a stand, and as the others inhaled or rapped their fingers on the table or spun around their thumbs—the engine's components at work—I cleared my throat and declared: I'm down—let's do it. Dave looked over at me like I had sold us both out, and I shrugged and pushed my glasses up on my nose. Dave's thumbs stopped suddenly, and he looked all around the room, and finally said, wait, wait, okay, I'm down, too—I mean, he is from the other side of the world and that could be pretty cool. Then we were all tossing glances at Dad, who sniffled and nodded and finally said, yes, okay, Jean, yes, you're right, we should help this boy. We had a vote and it was 4 to 0, all for it.

We waited for our new brother. The snow banked halfway up our windows as the wind eddied around our house. The gunmetal-gray sky dimmed the sun, and time hibernated with the animals. I imagined that he was hibernating, too, curled up in the nook of some giant oak, waiting for the warm weather to unshackle him from sleep.

In November of 1982, after nearly a full day and night on the plane, Soeuth set his feet onto the vast asphalt floor of his new world. He was fourteen. Gripping the straps of a small tote bag that had in it everything that proved he existed, he wondered who, if anyone, would welcome him to this gray and windy place. When the big glass doors pushed open into the fluorescent warmth of Burlington International Airport, he spied Wiltrud and Walter Miller, his new American parents, waving to him from behind the felt ropes of the waiting area.

The Millers had arranged for Soeuth to emigrate to America and were his first foster family. They were always polite, and when I first met them, I remember thinking how my family seemed like a tribe of heathens in comparison. They had a circumspect manner of speaking, as if plucking their words from some invisible, ever-present TelePrompTer. Wiltrud Miller was a short, austere woman with an incongruously charming smile. Walter, a tall, natty man, was a local accountant (my parents' accountant, in fact), and everything about him—his thick-rimmed glasses, his close-cropped Mister Rogers haircut, his carefully calculated gestures—suggested the fastidiousness of someone who spent his days bent over an adding machine.

The Millers had taken two other refugee children before Soeuth. The first was Kim, a Korean girl, who had been living in an orphanage in Seoul; the second was Jessica, from the Philippines, whose father had dropped her off at a friend's house one afternoon and simply never came back to pick her up. When Soeuth was added to the mix, the Miller household swelled to eight people, including their three biological children, Johnny, Kenny and Sonia.

Walter and Wiltrud weren't ungenerous—they had engaged in a "two-year siege," as Walter puts it, to get Jessica out of the Philippines—but they presided over their motley gaggle of children with an unbending stringency. When a new child joined the family, Wiltrud laid down a regimen of house rules, including: no rock 'n' roll music (she often flooded the house with Beethoven and Brahms, as a healthy alternative), no soda, no junk food, sit up straight during dinner, finish what's on your plate, speak slowly and clearly, no more than one hour of TV a day (unless, of course, there was a double episode of *Star Trek* on) and do your homework the very minute you get home from school.

When Soeuth once flicked on Johnny's radio after school and Tina Turner's "What's Love Got To Do With It?" perforated the clockwork calm of the Miller household, Wiltrud hurtled suddenly into the room and quickly instructed him to shut off the radio. "Rock 'n' roll is junk," he remembers her saying. "People in the street listen to that—we don't listen to rock 'n' roll in my house."

Soeuth received a monthly allowance of $2 and change and was told he could earn extra money by doing chores here and there. Walter opened a bank account for him—like he had for all the children—to teach him fiscal responsibility. In his year with the Millers, Soeuth accumulated $150 in that account—mostly from mowing the lawn—not a cent of which he spent. (He was stunned, after coming to live with us, when his allowance rose nearly one thousand percent to $5 a week.)

One afternoon, when all eight members of the family were packed into the station wagon en route back from Wiltrud's parents' house, Soeuth muttered that he wanted to throw out half of a sandwich. Walter, who was driving, pulled the car onto the shoulder.

"Throw up? Soeuth? Did you say you need to throw up?"

Soeuth did not look up. "No." He held out his sandwich. "Throw out."

Walter glared back at Soeuth. "Soeuth," he said sternly, "you should know how to speak English by now."

It was on an afternoon in late December of 1983 when Soeuth knew, once again, that it was time to escape. Soeuth and Kim had walked to the Ilsley Public Library after school, where Wiltrud had said she'd pick them up. The library was a block and a half away from the Sheldons' house, where Sokkhan, a new Cambodian boy, had recently settled in. Soeuth told Kim, whose grasp of English was much better than his, that he was stopping by to see Sokkhan for five minutes, and that if Wiltrud arrived in that time, he would be right back. He spent enough time at the Sheldons to say hello and eat an orange. But when he trotted back to the library parking lot, Kim was gone.

He zipped his coat to his chin and made his hands into fists inside his pockets and decided he could never trust the Millers again. He did not panic, because at least his life was not at stake. No guns were aimed at him from behind the trees. There would at least be food for him tomorrow at school, and, if needed, he could hide in the school bathroom and sleep beside the radiator. He had made a map of Middlebury in his head and remembered that the Chittenden Bank was at the other end of town, up the hill and past the traffic circle. He plodded in the direction of the bank, because the bank president, Louise Sandburg, was the foster mother of Phun—the only other Cambodian kid in town besides Sokkhan, and Soeuth's best friend—and she could maybe help him.

After Louise dropped Soeuth off at the Millers that evening, Wiltrud grounded him for two weeks, forbidding him to go outside after school or to see his friends (his only two friends were Phun and Sokkhan).

The next morning, he stowed a few clothes in his backpack. At school, he told Phun he wasn't going home because his American mom had left him at the library and had yelled at him and had said he couldn't go outside or visit Phun's house. Phun said, why don't you come to my house right now and live with my family, they're pretty nice.

Phun's foster parents, the Sandburgs, were an amiable couple who smiled contagiously, talked about feelings a lot and were careful not to do or say anything that could be remotely insensitive to their new Cambodian foster son. When Soeuth went to the Sandburgs that afternoon, he told Gary he would never return to the Millers—even though he feared the consequences of that decision might land him back in the Thai refugee camps. He stayed with the Sandburgs for a week or two, until Mr. Silverstein paid a visit and told him he had found a new family who had only two kids, both boys about his age, and weren't so hung up on rules.

PART THREE

After we returned home from Grandpa Ken's, and Mom, Dad and Dave had gone inside, Soeuth stood in the garage in the corner by Dad's outboard motor rack, puking into his baseball cap. He puked quietly and deliberately. His back was hunched up and his head hung low enough so that I could see the string of vertebrae on his neck. He turned toward me, the soles of his sneakers scraping on the pavement, and glanced up from his hat to see me and swiveled away to lean on one of the outboard motors—as if that would erase what I had just seen. This had happened a few times before, and I should have known to leave him alone.

He became carsick only after long rides, rides over an hour. After he was done puking, he would dump out the contents of his hat somewhere behind the barn and then sit on the cement steps outside the garage and vigorously rub a quarter or a nickel up and down his arm. The coin rubbing broke blood vessels and made an auburn streak on his skin, like a dull dash of war paint. He did this, Mr. Silverstein said, because Cambodians believe you can release sickness or fever by traumatizing the skin with a coin, spoon or any thin metal thing with an edge that wasn't too sharp. When I had a cold, I tried it once, with a nickel, not a quarter—a nickel's edge was smoother. I rubbed it hard on my left arm just above the elbow for about five seconds. When I felt an acute burning sensation, not unlike frostbite, I stopped. In the next few days my cold only intensified, and so I figured that non-Cambodian people should just stick to Dimetapp and Tylenol.

Soeuth would grate a coin on his arm for headaches, too, which would last sometimes for several hours and often hold him prisoner in his room. As I was about to knock on his door one morning to offer him my coin collection—I figured the silver dollars and maybe the imitation doubloons would cure head-aches—Mom stopped me and closed my coin box. "Leave him alone, Adam," she said.

But Soeuth never complained about the headaches or reacted, in any visible way, to physical pain. Sometimes he would roast trout he had caught in the river on willow-tree twigs in the wood-stove or lay them out on a sheet of tinfoil close to the flames. When he reached inside the woodstove to retrieve the fish, his hand would hover inches from the flames and he would break a sweat, but his face would not change at all: not a wince, nothing. Then he would bite the head off the charred, smoking fish with-out waiting for it to cool off, and Dave and I would try not to stare at him.

When Mom brought Soeuth to the dentist, the dentist discov-ered that one of his teeth was badly infected and that his whole upper jaw was beginning to rot. Soeuth had never said anything about a toothache. The night before Mom drove him to Burl-ington for a bone graft, he asked her, "Where they get the new bone?"

She smiled brightly and tilted her head. "From someone who doesn't need it anymore."

Soeuth nodded slowly. He put his fingers in his mouth and pushed his gums. "From dead people," he said through his fingers.

For a few days after the bone graft, he walked around the house dazed, his eyes wooden, his skin bagged, pale and loose beneath his eyes. Whenever Mom asked him if he was okay, he kept his eyes locked on some space between his feet and nodded quickly, as if she had posed an embarrassing question. One night when he and Dave were watching a PBS nature show before dinner, Mom and Dad were talking about Soeuth's tooth while they diced up carrots for the salad.

"I never know if he's in pain or not," Mom said.

"He is stoic," Dad agreed.

"I wish he would tell us if his mouth hurt." She scraped the carrots off the cutting board and into the salad. "When he went for the surgery, Bill, he didn't act scared or nervous at all. Our two guys would have been basket cases."

Mom turned to shout an aside toward the dining room table, where I sat pretending to read a *Spider-Man* comic: "Don't take that personally, Addie."

Dad carefully rinsed off the dicing knife. "It is difficult to know what he's thinking." He dried the knife and added: "He's one tough kid."

Soeuth had tested positive for tuberculosis, but Dad said that as long as he took his medicine each week, it shouldn't bother him. I knew that tuberculosis was one of those serious diseases, the kind that causes doctors to tent their hands and furrow their brows sympathetically. I heard Dad say to Mom one morning while they were getting dressed: "You know, Jean, his toothbrush is right next to mine in the bathroom."

"Bill," Mom said. "That's foolish."

"I'm just kidding." Dad yawned and buckled his belt. "It's a very hard disease to contract."

Because I sensed from the tone of Dad's voice that he was only half kidding, I darted into the bathroom and plucked my toothbrush from the communal toothbrush holder and sneaked into my room and tucked my toothbrush behind a stack of comics in my bookcase.

After a fruitful crayfishing expedition one afternoon a week or so later, Dave and I showed Soeuth the Seeleys' rope swing. Tied to the top of a giant willow tree that arched over a bend in the river where the bank slid precipitously into the water and the water was slack and murky and deep, the rope swing had always intrigued me and scared me a little, too. After you had snagged it with a stick, you were supposed to grip the rope in both hands just above a large, lumpy knot. Then you would stride along the bank and launch yourself over the river, ascending toward the pendent willow branches, and when you had reached a height of, say, fifteen feet, let go. Timing was important, because if you held on for too long, you could come rounding back toward the bank and crash into the willow's gnarled, muscular trunk.

I swung first on that afternoon and Dave went after me, and we both let go too early, and we were both disheartened that we hadn't adequately displayed the rope swing for Soeuth. When it was Soeuth's turn, he clutched the rope tentatively and studied, with quiet eyes, the distance between himself and the water. With a sudden start, he sprinted along the muddy, root-covered bank and then pulled himself up so that he sat squarely on top of the knot at the end of the rope and then flew out farther and higher than I had ever seen anyone swing. When he hooked back around, he didn't let go until he swept perilously close to the willow-tree trunk and then executed a flip in the air and dove in the water just a couple of feet from the edge of the bank.

He clambered up the steep bank, using the scraggly roots for rungs, and then stood shivering, lit in a shrill spot of sun. He had forgotten his towel. I still felt guilty about the toothbrush incident—even though he didn't know about it—and wanted to prove to myself that I wasn't afraid of catching any diseases from him, and so told him to use my towel. He wrapped himself in it snugly, the frayed edge of the yellow towel hanging just above his knees. Just below his knees, offset by the towel's yellow, were a dozen or more deep brown, dime-sized circles, mottling his calves. At first I thought they were leeches and panicked and inspected my own legs, but saw nothing and so reexamined the marks on his legs and realized that they were scars. Machine-gun wounds, I surmised and wondered if the bullets were still embedded beneath the skin. He was also shy a toenail on his second toe. I had only two scars worth a mention: a faint nick on the web between thumb and forefinger from a nail in Dad's wood chute, and another such nick on my wrist, sustained during a snowball fight at my friend Tim's when my arm brushed a piece of sheet metal nailed to the barn. I thought about showing them to Soeuth in the hope that he would reciprocate and tell me the story of those dark, dime-sized circles. But then it occurred to me how my scar stories would probably just make him squint and shrug and walk off, and so I left it alone.

One bright afternoon in early September, when the air was crisp with the chilly promise of autumn, the three of us went exploring in the swamp that lay behind the murky line of trees north of our house. Farmer Seeley had warned us not to venture into the swamp because there were hidden patches of quicksand. A lot of hunters had gone there looking for deer and had never come out, he said. A farmhand of his who was driving his tractor along the swamp's fringe had heard a giant sucking sound, and his tractor, all of a sudden, had started to sink. He had jumped off the tractor to watch the swamp swallow it, giant tires and all. "That swamp's a man-eater, boys," Farmer Seeley intoned while sitting at our kitchen table in his overalls, slurping coffee and filling our house with the smell of the barn.

For me, the swamp was vast and mysterious, and the threat of quicksand, whether real or imagined, was only another reason to explore it. We put on our parkas and laced up our shitkickers on the back porch. Soeuth's boots were hand-me-downs—Mom said she would buy him new ones—and he looked like a duck with the huge pumpkin-colored footgear. Dave and Soeuth had the two BB rifles, and I had my new pellet pistol, which, according to the red letters on the box, had as much firing power as a .22 and could shoot up to a mile.

We had shown Soeuth how to shoot the BB guns the week before, and he was already a better shot than both of us. Our targets consisted of Campbell's soup cans, plastic soda bottles, cardboard boxes, old Sears catalogues and the pole to which Mom's laundry line was affixed. We'd stand on the steps outside the garage and squeeze off BBs at the laundry pole and one of us would keep score. The narrow pole was warped and wavy

near the top, and that part was the hardest to hit. I had once hit
the top part of the pole three times in a row, but that was lucky;
usually, after I'd squared the rifle against my shoulder, my hands
would wobble, as if the ground beneath me were suddenly shud-
dering with rogue tremors. When Soeuth fired the BB gun, he
steadied the barrel on his left forearm, which he held out straight
as a two-by-four. He closed one eye, like I'd taught him to, and
narrowed his other eye to a mean slit and pulled the trigger
slowly. He smashed my record one day, sinking ten consecutive
BBs into the soft pulpy wood at the top of the laundry pole.
Sometimes Dave and I would pick out easier targets like the side
of the barn or the shiny tin roof on the Seeleys' farm-equipment
storage shed. Dave once shot out all the windows in the chicken
coop. I once shot up some red peppers Soeuth had bought at
the local health food co-op with his allowance money and hung
up to dry with clothespins on Mom's laundry line. When Soeuth
found out about it, he didn't seem mad, just shrugged and walked
off distractedly, mumbling, "Prob'ly pepper no good anyway."

We set out for the swamp across the cornfield. Dave and I
both tripped on old cornstocks; Soeuth, despite his ill-fitting
boots, never once tripped. The dark recesses of the swamp beckoned to us beyond the skeletal wall of pale birch trees.

"Now, listen up," I said, holding my pellet pistol straight up,
so that its muddy shadow was longer than the shadow of my
arm. "If one of us goes down, the other two gotta find something
close by to grab onto, so's we can reach down and pull the other
one out." I liked to say "so's" on occasions like this, rather than
"so"—it sounded more authoritative.

Dave nodded seriously. Soeuth eyed me sidelong, like I was
telling a dubiously embellished hunting story. We stood quietly
for a moment, our three shadows stretching toward the swamp.

Soeuth was the first to move. He tossed up his rifle and caught
it by the barrel in his left hand, swung it back over his shoulder
and plodded toward the swamp. Dave followed him, and I followed
Dave, and we proceeded like that for a few minutes, September
twigs snapping loudly underfoot, until we stood on a leaf-carpeted

slope that disappeared before us into a still expanse of cool, dark water. The water held the swamp's reflection with mirrorlike perfection, broken only by the occasional jutting log or the loop of a protruding root. Soeuth scanned the water with an expert's steady gaze. Dave began to pour BBs into the slot of his gun, spilling most of them into the leaves. I cleared my throat and loaded my pellet gun.

A bird cried out from somewhere further inside the swamp. Soeuth, in a blur, had aimed his gun in the direction of the sound.

"Won't shoot far enough," Dave advised. "Unless the bird's close up."

"Okay," Soeuth said.

We pressed on, skirting the water's edge, stepping carefully over rotten logs and lumpy, leg-sized roots, until we had neared the heart of the swamp. The sun was blocked out suddenly by a cloud, and the gnarled trees stood in the dimness of interlocking shadows. The swamp's quiet water went black then, and the mint-green moss that sheathed the logs and roots seemed to glow. As the cloud retreated, the shadows of the trees rotated around us like the arms of crooked clocks.

A gunshot reported somewhere from the southwest, I think, but not too far away. Dave and I stood still as the echo lingered.

"We should be wearing something bright," I said.

Dave said, "Oops."

"We should head back." I was thinking about all those stories Dad had told us about people who had caught stray bullets from hunters' guns.

"Yup," said Dave.

We turned to leave, but didn't see Soeuth anywhere.

"Oh, shit," I said.

Dave's face had suddenly blanched. "Do you think the quicksand got him?"

"Oh, shit."

A whoosh in the leaves rustled behind us. We jerked around to see Soeuth crouched behind a birch tree, his boots in a good foot or more of water. His eyes were set deep in his face, and his rifle was bolted in two tightly clenched fists. When he saw us staring at him, he stood up, and immediately started back to the house.

We followed him wordlessly, five or so paces behind, the sound of our feet on the leaves and twigs as loud as a family of bears tromping through the woods. The sun speckled his back and the wind kicked a cowlick in his hair, and as another cloud slid overhead and darkened our path, I wondered at how his eyes sometimes went dark like that, too. Except for his stories of eating rats and water bugs and catching fish by hand in the rice fields, he hadn't told us anything about Cambodia.

When Mom said she was going to take us all to Burlington to see *The Killing Fields,* a movie about Cambodia, I had hoped it might jar loose a story or two. She said it was an R-rated movie about an American journalist, Sydney Schanberg, and his Cambodian assistant, Dith Pran, and that it had a lot of adult content. Dave and I had never seen an R-rated movie before— we still weren't allowed to watch *Starsky & Hutch*—and I wondered if I would feel like a different person when I walked out of the theater. My friend Jeff, who had seen a lot of R-rated movies because he had HBO, said that watching one was a life-changing experience, like hitting your first baseball, and that most R-rated movies showed naked women and explosions and had really good car chases. And he said that by the sound of the title of this movie, we would probably get to see a lot of people being killed or a lot of dead bodies or both. I was thrilled.

We drove up for a Sunday matinee, and Soeuth's friend Phun came with us. Phun, who had started coming over to our house a lot after school, was shorter than Soeuth and his hair was curly for a Cambodian, a close crop of loops through which he was always running his hands. He was garrulous and inquisitive and prone to pranks—a Tom Sawyer to Soeuth's Huck Finn. He had taught his younger American foster brother, Tyler, some Cambodian expletives, like *Choi mai*—"fuck your mother." He would often walk close in front of Dave or me, stop suddenly and fart. When he first met us, he did his Michael Jackson impersonation, which consisted of perching himself up on his toes, gripping his crotch and emitting a high-pitched wail. It would be fun to watch an R-rated movie with Phun, I thought.

The theater was mostly empty. We sat near the front, in the middle section, so that we had to tilt our heads back to see the screen. Dave and I sat between Dad and Mom, and Soeuth and Phun sat on the other side of Mom. Dave and I shared one large bucket of popcorn, but Soeuth and Phun had their own popcorn buckets.

No one talked during the movie, but Mom cried a lot, and Dave and I cried, too. Dad didn't cry, but I could tell that he was upset; he kept patting Dave and me on the back. Neither Soeuth nor Phun cried or appeared upset at all. They munched steadily on popcorn, and during a scene when a prisoner was executed—shot in the face—Phun yawned.

I felt embarrassed crying, because Soeuth wasn't crying—but I couldn't help it. When the main character, Dith Pran, was forced to leave the French Embassy and walk into the hands of the Khmer Rouge, and Sydney Schanberg was standing in the rain watching him go and the music was building, tears spilled down my face and I hid my face in my arms. At the end of the movie, when Pran and Sydney were reunited at the Red Cross camp in Thailand and John Lennon's "Imagine" swelled, Dave, Mom and I were all wiping our eyes and sniffling. Soeuth looked at me blank-faced, and Phun belched.

After the movie, we went to Friendly's. Mom's eyes were red from crying, and she kept smiling to show that she was okay. We all ordered large chocolate sundaes. As we ate and our spoons clinked against the sundae bowls, Dad asked Soeuth and Phun if they were okay. They nodded, eating their ice cream.

"What did you boys think of the movie?" Mom asked, sipping a glass of water.

Soeuth had finished his sundae. He shrugged and said, "Pretty good."

"Phun," Mom said and tilted her head, gazing sympathetically at Phun. "What did you think about the movie?"

Phun lapped his sundae spoon. "Movie okay," he mumbled. Then his face became honed and thoughtful and he said, "Movie okay, but movie no show smell." He pinched his nose for effect. "Dead people is really smell," he explained. He slurped the last of his Coke through his straw and then looked at Mom and added matter-of-factly: "Movie no show maggot."

Mom nodded and glanced at Soeuth, who nodded back, agreeing with Phun.

Sometimes when Phun and Bi, another friend of Soeuth's, came over after school, they would huddle together on the pool patio or hole up in Soeuth's room and talk about the other things the movie didn't show, or things that had happened in Bi's country, Vietnam. Bi was Amerasian, Mom said, half Vietnamese and half Caucasian. His dad was American and had gone to Vietnam during the war over there, she explained, and had fallen in love with a Vietnamese woman.

Soeuth and Phun had met Bi in their English as a Second Language class in school. His sister Lan and brother Louis were also enrolled in ESL, and for the first few weeks, the class resembled two groups of diplomats from hostile countries thrown together without a translator: Phun and Soeuth spoke only to each other in Khmer, and Bi, his brother and sister spoke in Vietnamese.

One afternoon after school, while he ate rice with Soeuth in his kitchen, Phun scowled and remarked to his foster mother: "Vietnamese no good, Vietnamese eat dog." Soeuth, who had once eaten dog himself, stared into his rice bowl and kept silent.

Soeuth didn't distrust Bi because he was Vietnamese, although many Cambodian kids, including Phun, had learned to loathe their neighbors to the east, after centuries of warfare between the two countries. He was wary of him, just as he was of anybody he didn't know. But Bi was gregarious and given to dramatic gesticulations and eventually won them both over. He was big for an Asian kid, Mom said, taller than Dad and as broad as Farmer Seeley. When he sat or stood next to Soeuth and Phun, they looked like little Davids who had befriended a Goliath. He smiled with one side of his mouth, which stretched out a crooked set of parentheses on his face. Since his grasp of English was much better than either of theirs, and since he was given to moments of animated yarn spinning, he became the trio's spokesperson and ostensible leader.

In ESL class one afternoon, Bi stood up and told his classmates that he had discovered the wonderfully explosive capacities of the American microwave. He had put a goldfish in the microwave, he said, after seeing it done in a cartoon on TV. Setting the timer for two minutes, he had watched the fish flop around until it had blown up and splattered the microwave's glass door with a film of guts and fins and scales.

Mr. Johnson, the ESL instructor, a soft-spoken, bearded man who wore Birkenstocks and had studied Buddhism in Nepal, nodded thoughtfully at Bi's story and then asked him: "Did you think about karma, Bi, when you blew up the goldfish?"

Bi stood still for a few seconds, dumbfounded, until, with an abrupt resolve, he whacked himself on the forehead with the heel of his palm and exclaimed with an enthusiastic contrition: "Oh, Mr. Johnson—I forgot about karma!"

When I plodded down the stairs one afternoon after school, swimsuit in hand, on my way to the pool before Dad closed it for the fall, I spied Bi, Soeuth and Phun clustered around our kitchen table. Bowls full of rice were set out before them, and the white sunlight slanting through the bay window ricocheted blindingly off the table. Soeuth sat in front of the picture window, a hunkered shadow in the sunlight, and Bi and Phun sat on either side of him. Their voices were low and serious. I positioned myself in the doorway between the dining room and the vestibule, leaning against the doorframe, so I could see their heads and shoulders refracted through the wine and champagne flutes in Mom's new glass cabinet.

"When we live in Saigon, we borrow bikes, go ride in the city," Bi said, his voice edged with intrigue. "I sit on back, my friend up front. One day, two boys riding a bike in front of us. Then a bus come by. The bus pull into bus stop. The bike up front, his bike wheel hit the curb, because he don't want to hit the bus. His brother flew off and hit the bus and hit the pavement, and then his head between the bus tires. Then the bus ran over his head!" Bi paused, leaned in so his chin was almost touching the table, then continued with a punctuated deliberateness. "There no sound," he said, "like a human skull being popped. Brains come shooting out. Those kids were alive, and all of sudden, one of them just die."

Phun and Soeuth were nodding. "In Cambodia, I hear the Khmer Rouge throw the baby in the air and it come down on knife," Phun said.

Soeuth picked up his rice bowl and put it down like a gavel. "In the camp," he said, "I hear a story that the Khmer Rouge take a bamboo stick . . . you know, a long stick like this . . ." He held his arms far apart. "Then they take the end, the sharp end, and they take a woman, and they put the bamboo stick up her . . ." He made his hands into a V to suggest a pair of legs. "You know, up in her place."

"That's bad," Bi said, his face bobbing methodically. "The way I hear it is they rape the woman first, then they play games."

Soeuth shrugged. "Prob'ly do."

He was about to say something else, but glanced over to see me and swung his eyes suddenly into his rice bowl. Bi and Phun hadn't noticed me.

"One time," Bi mumbled, shoveling rice, "my older sister, during labor, went to county hospital. During break, we'd go down to cafeteria. And next to cafeteria was indoor pigpen. We go down late at night. The way the pigs crying, at first I thought babies crying. We're like, why hospital have some pigs? Then a woman say they feed the pigs the afterbirth or the abortions or the dead bodies. I get all goose bump. That's why those pigs sound like babies."

Phun was nodding. "I guess dead baby good food for pig," he said.

"It's very bad," Soeuth finally said. "Very bad."

"Yes," they both agreed. "Very, very bad."

When he was watching TV or movies, Soeuth would laugh at the oddest moments. He hadn't laughed during *The Killing Fields*, of course—hadn't cried either—or during other movies that we thought were really sad, like *ET*. But violence, in general, seemed to tickle him. Car crashes, shootings, impalings, explosions—especially when someone got blown out of a window—or any scene in which blood was spilled caused him to smirk or downright giggle. PBS nature shows featuring encounters between predator and prey could have been episodes of *Benny Hill* as far as Soeuth was concerned. One night we watched a special about lions. When one of the head males in the pride downed a gazelle and began, with help from other lions, to rip open its stomach and eat the wet innards, Soeuth, who was lolling in a beanbag, smiled. "That deer stupid," he said, chuckling.

Dave and I sat on the couch watching him as he watched the lions.

"Yup," Dave finally agreed. "That deer was an idiot."

Most often, though, Dave and I would sit quietly while he laughed at these things and exchange fugitive looks. Soon, however, we laughed along with him, amused by death and accidents and mayhem and other things that we had always assumed to be matters of the utmost seriousness.

One afternoon Dave cut his finger while trying to extract Luke Skywalker from the rusty grille at the bottom of the refrigerator.

As he screamed at the bright blood spreading through his fingers, Soeuth started tittering; when Dave saw this, he screamed even louder. "Maauh!" he retched, not quite forming a word. When Mom raced into the kitchen and saw Dave bleeding and Soeuth laughing, her face grimaced like she had just drunk curdled milk. She blinked a few times.

Finally she screamed: "Bill!"

Dad's feet thudded down the stairs. He cast a calm over the room when he entered. Dave stopped screeching, Soeuth stopped laughing. All eyes were trained on Dad.

"David, I told you to be careful around those things." He smiled. "They get old, they get rusty."

Mom seemed even more shocked by Dad's nonchalance than she was by the scene itself.

"C'mon, Crockett." Dad put his hands lightly on Dave's shoulders. "Let's get you a Band-Aid."

"But, Bill. . . ." Mom's voice quavered.

"What?"

"Don't you think he'll need stitches?"

Dad knelt down and lifted Dave's hand close to his face. "No, Jean. It's not a deep cut. But I'll give him a tetanus shot just in case." He escorted Dave through the hallway and into the bathroom.

Soeuth had faced the wall and was silent, imposing his own punishment.

The rusty-grille incident was not discussed, and for a few days, Soeuth refrained from laughing at anything, even jokes Dad or I told or Dave's farting noises. He would squint and cock his head when everybody else laughed, wondering, perhaps, why a belch or an imitative flatulence sound was funny and Dave bleeding all over himself was not. Which is why, I suppose, he was so perplexed one afternoon when he saw Dad humming to himself while he whipped up a few batches of fake blood in the kitchen, mixing chocolate syrup and red food coloring in Mom's cooking pots.

Soeuth was standing in the doorway eyeing Dad when Dave

came in, saw the fake blood and shrieked with joy. Dad smiled at Dave and stirred the concoction—which looked as bright red and real as the blood that had oozed through Dave's fingers only a week earlier—and Soeuth squinted at me for an explanation. I shrugged dismissively, and so Soeuth's gaze floated errantly toward the bread box and seemed to hover over the napkins. Then he left. We stayed in the kitchen after he had left and smeared each other with the fake blood and laughed. I assured myself that Soeuth would soon understand the difference between real blood and fake blood—he would have to.

Outside, the color of the world had deepened from brown and green into russet and gray, and the air was leavened with the smell of dying leaves. As September shed its final days and the temperature burrowed below fifty degrees, it seemed that there wasn't much time, no time at all.

Maggie Seeley, who oversaw milking operations at the farm, had dropped off a pickup load of pumpkins out by the barn, and there was an army of people cleaning out the pulpy insides, dumping the seeds into buckets. A couple of half-done scarecrows, made of cornstalks and old grain sacks, were propped against the barn. A half-dozen plastic skulls were lined neatly on the floor of the back porch. In the living room one afternoon, I found Dad sitting on the couch listening to Bach's Toccata and Fugue in D minor, his face reflecting flashes of macabre inspiration from the ominous organ chords, his fingers tapping a strobe light in his lap. In the bathroom, I examined my werewolf costume in the mirror, and I could hear Dave grumbling in his room, searching for the most menacing timbre his preadolescent vocal range would allow. Outside, Farmer Seeley's son, John, was revving up his chain saw; he had taken off the chain, but you wouldn't know that in the dark. Everyone was getting ready.

That night we held the first meeting on our pool patio. Forty people, some in suits and ties, some in overalls spattered with cow manure, pressed themselves into tight plastic lawn chairs and huddled around Dad, who was feverishly drawing up the floor plans. We could see his arm hinging up and down as he scratched out room 8, room 9, room 10. The tendrils of his mad doctor's wig waved in a slight breeze.

"What he doing?" Soeuth and I were sitting at the back, behind the hulking flannel forms of Farmer Seeley and Charlie Bascom. Dave was up front, slurping cider.

"He's doing the floor plans," I whispered. "Shhh. You'll see."

The sound of his magic marker screeched urgently, people shuffled and the cheap chairs squeaked. Finally, like a circus master, Dad whirled around, his scarlet-stained lab coat billowing out like a cape. His face exploded into a crazed smile, his mad doctor's wig jostled. "All right, folks," he announced. "The floor plans are done. The Fifield and Seeley Haunted House is back!"

Some people clapped. Most just grunted.

"It's gonna be the biggest yet," he promised proudly. "Fourteen rooms this year, including Maggie's new and improved witches' kitchen and the guillotine scene!"

Every fall, one of our old barns out back became Dad's laboratory of horrors. He had built a maze into the front of the barn and installed strobe lights to disorient people. The corpses that he and I had created with plaster of paris and plastic skulls were positioned all over the place: some impaled on stakes, some slumped in rocking chairs, some infested with rubber snakes, some propped in coffins he and Dave had built. In the notorious mad doctor's scene, where Dad donned his wig and ketchup-and-Kool-Aid-stained lab coat, he used real cow entrails from a local butcher shop. In the witches' kitchen, Maggie Seeley, the head witch, set out a real, hollowed-out pig's head on a card table; she had poked out the eyes and put a candle in its cranial cavity, so it looked like some devil hog, eyes flickering wildly. She had also strung up fresh road kill from the ceiling, usually muskrats, and had affixed to the wall a witches' kitchen menu which offered the following entree choices:

Muskrat Sushi: Four Rats
Oxtail Creole: Five Newts

Mouse Guts Gispach: Six Ant Intestines
Special Fresh Bovine Livers: Eight Spider Abdomens

In the finale scene, a zombie—usually one of our neighbors who'd been lacquered white, so as to appear undead—emerged from a three-foot-deep grave Dad had dug outside the barn. At the head of the grave, he and Farmer Seeley had erected a real marble tombstone that Farmer Seeley had found in his basement. The following was engraved on the tombstone:

ELIZABETH

DAUGHTER OF

JAMES AND RHODA SEELEY

DIED AUG 28, 1849

AE 14 YRS & 10 MO

& 26 DAYS

"Well, Bill, the old girl is prob'ly lyin' around somewhere in my basement," Farmer Seeley half joked to Dad as they steadied the tombstone. "What's left of her anyway."

Our haunted house was locally famous—but no one could say it wasn't authentic. More than anything else, we all knew it was an escape for Dad from the nerve-stiffening responsibility of the hospital, the rounds, the fourteen-hour days, the concussions and seizures, the old women who thought he was their psychotherapist as well as their doctor. The rehearsals, the weeks before the big show—it was the only time of year when he could leave his bedside manner at the office and be the mad doctor instead of the reliable doctor. Each night, after all the guests had left and before we had cleaned up the garbage on our lawn, Dad would sit around the kitchen table with Farmer Seeley, Maggie and the other hard-core haunted hacks and rate the night's success. The measure of a good night was the number of teenage girls who had puked and the number of kids who had wet their pants. One notorious incident occurred when a little boy who had wrapped himself around his father's torso suddenly wet his pants at the sight of a vampire and wet all down the front of his father's shirt as well. There was also the smart-ass jock kid who, when wandering through Maggie's witches' kitchen, had proclaimed to his friends, "I bet that chicken's not real," and bit into its neck to prove it; he was wrong and lost his dinner as a consequence.

It had always perplexed me how Mom and Dad had been so careful about our exposure to R-rated movies but had never been worried about the haunted house. This year, however, they *were* worried. I heard them talking in their room one morning while I waited in the hall for Dave to finish brushing his teeth in the bathroom.

"Bill," Mom whispered. "You have all these plaster of paris corpses out there. How does someone who's seen plenty of real corpses process that?"

"Yes, Jean, I know." I could hear Dad rummaging through his drawer. "But I think we ought to talk to him about it, let him decide."

"He's just a kid." Mom's voice tightened. "I mean, if you'd seen what he's seen, Bill. If your whole country was a graveyard."

"Yes, Jean." Dad shut his drawer. "I'll talk to him."

So Dad talked to him. They sat in the living room, Dad saying very serious words, Soeuth nodding.

An hour or so before the opening on the first night, Dad, Dave and I were in the kitchen waiting for the show. My snarling wolf mask was strapped on, and clumps of hair that our horse, Smokey, had donated were glued to my shirtsleeves. Dave had donned his gargoyle mask and gorilla suit, a kind of hybrid monster. Dad was adjusting his mad doctor's lab coat.

"What's Soeuth gonna do?" we asked Dad.

"You'll see."

We heard tentative feet on the stairs. Then Soeuth, transformed, walked into the kitchen.

"Holy shit!" we both shrieked.

Fake blood was smeared all over his grinning face and encrusted in his hair. A fake knife protruded from his chest. A tattered overcoat hung from his shoulders. He raised his hands—glued-on black nails jutting from his fingers—growled and unseamed his lips to reveal the yellow glare of a wax glow stick in his mouth.

"That's awesome," Dave said sincerely.

"What you sink, guys?" he asked, spitting the glow stick into a cupped palm. "I scary enough?"

"You scary, man," we said. "You wicked scary!"

"Boys," Dad said. "Meet Mister Night of the Living Dead!"

"Mister Night of the Living Dead," Dave said. "You kick ass."

Soeuth looked down at the knife, raised a begnarled hand to his face—as if examining a manicure—nodded to himself and then looked up at us. "Sank you," he said.

I got the idea that Dave, Soeuth and I should study kung fu together, after we all watched *Enter the Dragon*, a Bruce Lee video that Soeuth had picked out at the video store. He had been with us for a year and a half now, and although the videos he picked were usually R-rated kung fu movies, Dad never barred any of Soeuth's selections. With the *Enter the Dragon* rental, Soeuth acquired a free, life-size poster of a shirtless, sweat-sheened Bruce Lee. After we had finished watching the movie, I helped Soeuth tack the poster up in his room, next to a blown-up photo of Angkor Wat in Cambodia.

"This guy is strong," Soeuth informed me, pointing with his face at Bruce Lee. "This guy is have lot of lives."

"Do you know kung fu?" I climbed onto the bed to right the poster.

He shrugged and bunched his hands in his pockets. "Little bit," he said.

When I suggested the next morning, during breakfast, that the three of us learn kung fu together, Dave instantaneously belched his approval and Soeuth mumbled a tepid "Okay."

After Mom called the town recreation department, she told us they didn't have kung fu or karate here in Middlebury—but they had Tae Kwon Do, which is basically the same thing, she said. The classes were held on Tuesday and Thursday nights in a brick-walled, low-ceilinged basement room of the town municipal building and drew a motley assemblage of Skoal-packing farm guys, shy, mousy women in their early thirties, a few hopped-up jock types and a lot of clumsy kids with glasses. Our instructor was Master Donnelly, a bald, stocky, vigorous man who drove a Cadillac and let out reedy whistles through his teeth, like he was calling out to hound dogs that had strayed from the pack. He would sometimes have one of us blindfold him and another hold up a board that he would then shatter with one jab of his fist. He and some former students had been featured on a 1980 episode of *That's Incredible,* demolishing an old barn in St. Albans, reducing it to planks and splinters. We learned very soon that he was a no-bullshit kind of guy who didn't answer questions twice. He would start the class by drilling: "What are you?"

We never answered him.

"You're the best a the worst, the worst a the best, and the cream a the crap!" His words burst from his mouth like drop kicks. After push-ups, he would pick out the weakest or most fatigued and ask, "Why did you do that?"

"To get strong?"

"No!" His eyes were nails, puncturing his students' answers. "Ya did that for the same reason you'd sit your ass on a hot woodstove!"

"Yessir."

"Why?" He gazed heatedly over his baffled students. "Because it feels so damned good when you get off!"

In our first class, he had taught us the meaning of the Korean phrase *t'aekwōndo*—Foot, Fist, Way of Life—by snapping out a punch and quipping, "Fist," then pivoting his body sideways and shooting out his foot and saying, "Foot," and finally bringing his hands to his sides, bowing, inhaling deeply and declaring in a soft, low voice, "Way of life."

My bully-battered ego had percolated with virginal confidence after this demonstration, and I adopted the translation of *t'aekwōndo* as a new personal credo: *You must kick ass all the time.*

But transferring those words into physical reality was not a simple task, given that my gangly, thirteen-year-old body moved with the grace of a folding ladder.

During sparring one night, Master Donnelly interrupted my match with another gawky, four-eyed kid and asked me: "Adam, what vital area were you aiming for?"

"Ah, the . . . the solar plexus, sir?"

"You were kickin' him in the arm," he said flatly, flaring his nostrils. "And nowhere on the chart of vital areas, Adam, do they list the arm."

Mom showed up early to watch the class one night. When Master Donnelly yelled *"Shi-ot!"*—rest—and we all bowed, I saw Mom standing near the door by the neat rows of sneakers, loafers and shitkickers, her arms crossed. Master Donnelly didn't like people crossing their arms—it was a sign that you were closing yourself off to the world, he had explained—and when he approached Mom with a canted smirk on his face, I wanted to warn her but knew it was too late.

"Hello, Jean," he said, smiling ravenously.

"How are you, Master Donnelly?"

"I'm great!" he barked. "Thank you for asking! Now let me ask you, Jean . . . If you were meeting your husband at the airport—say after he's been away for a long time—would you stand like you are now? With your arms crossed?"

Mom smiled slowly but did not uncross her arms. "I suppose not, Master Donnelly," she said. "But I'm not at the airport."

I never understood Master Donnelly, but he and Soeuth shared an unspoken language. Soeuth was easily the best student in the class, and Master Donnelly would often use him to demonstrate stances or blocks or kicks. When the two sparred together, they moved in a choreographed dance, arms and legs connecting in fast, blurred blows. Their eyes locked, and everything faded to a circle of fury around them.

One night when it came time for sparring, Master Donnelly walked to the center of the room, turned and said: "Soeuth, you and me."

Soeuth approached obediently and bowed. Then up went

their fists like muskets, their bodies slanting into battle position. Master Donelly lowered his gaze menacingly. Soeuth's face was expressionless. There were a few still seconds before Master Donnelly peppered Soeuth with strikes, which Soeuth swatted away like Ping-Pong balls. Undaunted, Master Donnelly shook the sweat off his head and flattened his mouth into a blade. The two were still again, for a moment, until Soeuth hopped up suddenly, so that his head nearly grazed the ceiling pipes, and spun three hundred and sixty degrees, swinging his heel toward Master Donnelly's head; Master Donnelly ducked, then raised his eyebrows, as if to say, nice execution, and shot a punch toward Soeuth's abdomen which was adroitly blocked with a sweep of Soeuth's forearm. Master Donnelly then tried a front snap kick, but Soeuth dodged that like a matador. Master Donnelly shot out another punch, and Soeuth swiveled out of its path and shrank down, accordionlike, for a moment. When he sprang up, he lanced a side kick at Master Donnelly, so that his heel stopped a few inches before Master Donnelly's face. Master Donnelly stood still and didn't blink, and after a second or two, Soeuth dropped his leg and stood before his instructor, arms at his sides, in the ready stance.

Master Donnelly, who had a fifth-degree black belt, chuckled to himself and then said to the class: "Now that's how you do it, folks." He raised his head and nodded approvingly at Soeuth.

"Soeuth," he quipped tightly and bowed.

Soeuth bowed back.

I had guessed Soeuth to be a natural athlete ever since the day at the rope swing. But he wasn't just good at flips and sparring; he easily mastered each sport he tried. Dad had to remove our diving board, because when Soeuth rocketed himself off it, he'd clear nearly the entire length of the pool, chiseling through the air and knifing into the water right next to the bright red 'No Diving!' sign at the shallow end. After only two skiing lessons, he was swerving between other skiers and hitting moguls and then clawing his way skyward, scissoring his legs in the icy air. In their freshman gym class, Soeuth and Phun were often pitted in volleyball games against five or six other kids, whom they would always trounce and who would wince at the Cambodian kids' percussive, half-court dives.

In the fall of 1985, the start of Soeuth's freshman year, he became the star of the high-school varsity soccer team. I was in eighth grade at the time and on the junior-high soccer team but spent most games warming the bench. During home games, while tearing up the grass beneath the bench with my cleats, I would follow the high school team on the adjacent field, watching my big brother outplay seniors twice his size and listening to the gasps and cheers evoked by his pyrotechnic ball-handling. Soeuth would weave through a dense snarl of lunging players, cutting to and fro, sometimes perching himself up on the ball and pivoting one hundred and eighty degrees, sometimes abruptly reversing the ball's direction in one quick zigzag of his feet. His head and feet were magnets for the ball; he could flip it up with his toe so that it would attach to his forehead and hold there. If he ever fell, he bounced up again, as if gravity had rejected him.

I had attended soccer camp for three consecutive summers but could never manage to negotiate my overgrown, size thirteen feet around the ball without spraining a tendon or somehow helping out the opposing team. We watched videos of the World Cup at soccer camp, and after seeing Soeuth play—he never came to soccer camp—I fancied him a Cambodian Pélé, one of those prodigies endowed by God with unassailable talent.

He would sometimes hold special drills for me at home after practice. He would stand before me on our expansive lawn, one foot resting on the ball, his hands rooted to his hips.

"Ball not head of bad guy," he told me one afternoon. "Head of pretty lady." And so instead of hammering the ball with all my force, I connected my foot with it diplomatically, letting my leg follow my foot, and my body follow my leg. After Soeuth served as goalie and let a few of my shots in, he declared: "Hey, man, you getting good!" Galvanized by this endorsement, I decided to drive the ball into the top left corner of the goal (a tough shot), wound up my leg and drove my foot straight into the ground. Fire shot up my leg and I dropped, my shin throbbing.

Soeuth cringed and jogged over to me. "You try too hard," he assured me. "Tomorrow. Tomorrow." But after that, I was out for the season, hobbled by my own clumsiness. He tried his best to teach me grace; but grace was as foreign to me then as English had been to him.

But Soeuth did not give up on me or Dave. Whenever he was coaching us, his patience was as sound as his skill. He would smile and say, "No worry, you getting good, you getting there." One afternoon when we were playing softball, Soeuth pitched to Dave and Dave swung heartily, driving the ball straight into Soeuth's groin. Without a sound, Soeuth sank to a crouch, as if he were bending down to tie his shoes. His face didn't even grimace or wince.

Dave ran up. "Sorry, man. . . . oh, shit . . . sorry . . . sorry." Soeuth held up his hand and croaked, "It's okay. It no hurt."

Many nights, after Tae Kwon Do class, we had a sparring clinic in the garage. When Soeuth sparred, he would imitate Bruce Lee's catlike moves perfectly, except that he never hit us. Sometimes he would let us try to hit him. At first we loosely flung our arms like we were whipping a wet towel. But after he had ducked or blocked me more than a dozen times, I tried in earnest frustration to connect my fist with his face or his chest. It wasn't that I was angry; it was more like I was a rodeo cowboy who had been thrown off the damned bull too many times and was determined to stay on for my eight seconds. But no matter how fast or hard I punched, Soeuth would dodge out of the way or knock my fist aside with the ease of Mom pulling back a curtain. He did let me hit him once, and even though I knew he wasn't really hurt, I felt bad.

He sat with me on the garage steps that night. He knew I was frustrated.

"You not bad big, man," he said suddenly, as if reprimanding me. "Like clumsy big. No, no. You good big. I see you, man—

and don't know you—I be afraid. That kind of big. You know, strong big."

I nodded and my sweat dripped, soaking into the garage pavement. "You think so?"

"Yeah, man." He stood up. "You want to, you be good fighter. "

The night Soeuth taught us how to break boards was the turning point for me. Dad had cut the boards for us; they were pine, about a foot square and one inch or so thick. Soeuth shattered three boards with one punch. I was holding the boards for him, braced against the wall. After the wood clattered to the floor of the garage, it felt like the bones in my arms were humming like electric fence wire. When it was my turn, Soeuth held a board for me. I punched it, but it didn't break and my knuckles stung badly. Dave couldn't break the board either, and so Soeuth gently set the unbroken board on the steps to the house and said: "Watch."

He held out his fist and pointed to his first two knuckles and said, "These ones the ones you hit."

He walked over to me and took my hand and closed it into a fist, folding my thumb tight round my index finger and middle finger, and tapped the knuckles belonging to those fingers. "These the ones," he said.

He stepped back. "Watch." He breathed in deeply and executed a punch in slow motion, the momentum originating in his hips, then traveling up his spine to his shoulders and finally extending to the end of his fist. That was the key, I realized: he did not swing or arc his punches, but shot them out straight and got all his weight behind them.

"Okay," I said. "Lemme try again."

Soeuth nodded and held out the board. I planted my feet on the garage floor and breathed. I eyed the center of the board. I pivoted my hips and pivoted my shoulders and struck the board straight on with my first two knuckles. Somehow the board was in two pieces and Soeuth was smiling widely.

"You do it," he said.

After that night, Dave and I broke a lot of boards, and Dad told us that we were wasting good lumber. But breaking boards is the first and only sport I'm any good at, I answered, so Dad obliged by furnishing a steady supply of one-inch-thick, one-foot-square pine boards.

Probably the only advice imparted by Master Donnelly that Soeuth ignored was the assurance that befriending your enemies was ultimately the best way to defeat them. Dave and I agreed with Soeuth. We were proud of the fact that our big brother was tough, and we religiously heeded any counsel he offered. We knew he understood certain things about toughness and rightness that eluded Mom and Dad and even Master Donnelly. He had, after all, come from a country where slavery and death and torture were routine. He had lived on his own in the jungle, eating rats. He had lost his entire family. And since we had both been persistently picked on in school—on account of my gawky frame and bug-eyed bifocals, I was a bully magnet—we were emboldened by the fact that our big brother was a bona fide badass.

In eighth grade, my most persistent tormentor was a tall, lanky, loping kid named Matt. He wasn't the worst of the bullies by far, wasn't like Big David in grade school, whose crooked grin revealed a helter-skelter set of algae-green teeth and who took great pleasure in pushing me facedown in the mud and spitting into my hair while the girls gathered in a circle around us. Matt's tyranny was mostly relegated to the verbal, standard-issue taunts like: *you four-eyed freak, you little faggot, I bet you got a small pecker, I bet you wet the bed.* But one afternoon in reading class, when the teacher had left for a coffee break, Matt surpassed his usual antics. He strode over to my friend Ronnie's desk in the back of the classroom and swept Ronnie's books onto the floor. Ronnie reached down to retrieve his books, but Matt knocked them out of his hands and said, *what a faggot,* and everybody laughed. When Ronnie reached down to pick up his books for a third time, Matt rapped the back of his head. Ronnie tried to deflect Matt's blows with a bony, upraised arm. Matt just clipped his arm aside and grabbed his hair and pinned his face to the desk and spat into his own hand and delivered a series of wet, loud slaps on the back of Ronnie's neck.

Everyone had twisted around in his seat to watch. I was sitting toward the back of the room, a few desks away from Ronnie, and I was watching, too, watching Matt torment my friend. When Matt licked his hand again before giving Ronnie another slap, I noticed that Matt's hands weren't very big—his fingers were stubby, his knuckles fat and soft and his fingernails stunted.

I studied my own fist in my lap. It had big, sharp knuckles.

I got up and walked to the front of the room.

"That's enough," I said.

Matt stopped hitting Ronnie and looked at me. "All right, four-eyes!" he jeered. He slapped Ronnie one more time, then strutted up with big, exaggerated steps to fight me. I put myself in the ready stance.

He stood close before me and formed a mock pair of glasses with his index fingers and thumbs and said: "The other faggot wants some, too."

I punched him in the face, hard, my fist connecting with his big set of teeth. He sank down for a moment as gasps wafted up from my classmates. He rose, and I could see he was mad and embarrassed. He lunged at me, and remembering some of Soeuth's sparring counsel—"Keep one foot back, man, so you kick with other foot"—I backed up and kicked him square in the stomach. He collapsed. Someone clapped. Matt whimpered.

I returned to my desk, my face flushed with victory. Just after the teacher came back with his coffee, Matt mopishly loped back to his desk. He buried his face in his arms, pretending to sleep through the rest of the class.

Dave, who was bigger and less awkward than I was, had less of a problem. But he still endured years of ear-tweaking, rabbit-punching torment from a boisterous, Skoal-chewing thirteen-year-old whose hair was soldered to his scalp by a combination of grease and styling mousse. One afternoon, while Dave was waiting for the bus, his nemesis sauntered over and pushed him. Or tried to. Dave tripped his taunter into the mud directly below the principal's office window and proceeded to pummel him for all to see—awestruck peers and sternly disapproving school administrators. He received detention, but it was well worth it.

Since he had started school in America, Soeuth had been suffering schoolyard persecution himself. Bi relayed the stories, told me how Soeuth had it much worse than I did. One encounter occurred in the autumn of his freshman year. He was retrieving books from his locker before class. Four or five boys he had never met were huddled at a neighboring locker, slinging snide looks and whispering things about him. They were all bigger than he was; most boys in his class were. Soeuth tucked his books into his book bag.

As he was zipping up his book bag, one of them approached from behind and shoved him. Soeuth stumbled, dropping his book bag, and spun around to view his attacker. It was Scott, a tall, denim-clad junior with swollen cheeks—as though he were storing up food for later—who smelled sharply of beef jerky and had a bad lisp. Because his lisp was so bad and was often accompanied by a mist of saliva, Scott avoided verbal threats and stuck mainly to physical tyranny. I had witnessed him on a few occasions raiding seventh graders' lunch boxes and tripping up well-dressed eighth-grade boys or boys wearing sweaters.

When Scott lunged again at Soeuth, Soeuth wound up and cracked him in the face with the back of his fist. Scott dropped to his knees, as if on cue, and held his face where sudden blood seeped through his fingers and dripped onto the shiny linoleum floor. Soeuth glanced up at his other taunters, but they were looking down, their arms plunged in jeans pockets.

Soeuth dealt out a lot of bloody noses in his freshman year of high school. He never once started a fight, but never lost one either. He never said anything about it to me or to anyone in our family. I heard stories from Bi and from my friends and friends of my friends, stories about the Asian kid with the name like chimney soot who could fight like Bruce Lee. By the time he was

halfway through his freshman year, Soeuth had earned a school-
wide reputation as a vanquisher of bullies and bigots.

One boy who tried to trip him had been seized by the hair
and hurled face-first into a brick wall. Another pitched a kickball
at Soeuth, only to have the ball kicked back at him, at an upward
angle, so that it struck him square in the face. In the locker room,
when a senior grabbed Soeuth from behind, Soeuth snapped his
head back, tapping a stream of blood from the assailant's nose,
then swiveled around and delivered one solid, body-folding knee
thrust to the groin.

These bullies, who strove to establish a schoolyard pecking
order, did not understand that, for Soeuth, fighting was not a
matter of win or lose, but live or die.

Unbeknownst to Mom and Dad, Soeuth and Bi always carried
their butterfly knives at school. Soeuth's was slick and shiny and
the handle was elaborately studded with fake diamonds; he had
bought it at a martial arts store in a Burlington mall. The two of
them would stand in the driveway at night, their shadows bloated
by the glow of the garage light, and practice opening and closing
their knives with quick flips of their wrists. Mom would peek her
head out and tell them to be careful, and they would regard her
with wide, innocent eyes, Soeuth calling out, "Okay, Mom," and
Bi chiming in, "But of course, Mrs. Fifield." Every morning before heading to their respective bus stops, they squirreled the
knives in the pockets of their jackets. I had seen Soeuth do this
one morning, and as he, Dave and I rode to school on the bus
and talked about the demise of Bruce Lee—Soeuth contended he
could still come back from the grave; Dave and I held that he
had died for good—I worried that Soeuth would stab someone
who messed with him and be sent away to jail forever.

They carried the knives, in part, because of three seniors who
would wait together in the hallway or cafeteria or parking lot
and whisper one stinging word at Bi and Soeuth as they passed.
"Chinks," they would say.

Bi and Soeuth heard that word, uttered collectively, one afternoon in the locker room as they toweled off after gym. They

turned to see the three seniors grinning, one of them brandishing a pair of numb chucks. Bi replied calmly, "We're not Chinese."

The seniors contorted their faces defiantly. One of them spat. "Well, then you're gooks," another said.

Bi smiled. "Do you know where the word *gook* comes from?" Bi liked to educate his taunters about the etymologies of their slurs. "The word *gook* originated from the Korean conflict. The Americans called the North Koreans gooks, and it spilled down to the Vietnam conflict." Bi pulled his towel around his shoulders. "It's a racist word. If you want to use that word, that's okay. We'll just beat the shit out of you."

The seniors' spokesperson, a tall, pasty, raven-haired kid, raised his eyebrows and snorted: "Okay, gooks."

Bi and Soeuth shot each other quick, consulting glances and then Bi said: "Meet us outside. After school. Today. Behind the junior high building."

After their last class, Bi and Soeuth strode down to the bumpy stretch of pavement outside the exit doors at the north end of the junior high school. This was a common area for prearranged rumbles, because almost everybody left the building through the south entrance, and at 3:30 P.M. it was usually quiet and unmonitored. Fifteen minutes later, the doors whined open behind them, and they spun around to see a woman janitor, scowling. "You guys come here lookin' for trouble?"

They both shrugged.

"Go back upstairs," she said, and they did.

They both were disappointed but also glad the seniors hadn't shown up. If they had shown up and had waved their numb chucks, Bi and Soeuth would have produced their butterfly knives.

Mom had placed the new computer, an enormous Apple IIE with a black screen and bright green characters, in Dad's study, between stacks of files on his desk. Although Dad rarely spent any time in there, he used it to store old files and copies of the *Journal of the American Medical Association* and *The Journal of New England Medicine* dating back more than ten years. The study smelled faintly of cat piss and was coated over with an exhaust-colored dust. With magazines and files piled everywhere, there wasn't much room to move, only a narrow path leading from the door to the computer.

At this time, I was in ninth grade and Soeuth was in tenth, and on nights when we both needed to use the computer to write papers, Soeuth would always volunteer to go second, but I would always insist that he go before me. It was still funny that way—even though he had become an integral part of our family, we all still extended him little courtesies, as if he were a long-term guest.

On the nights when Soeuth was using the computer, I would sit in the living room, just outside the study door, and read. I could hear him typing and mumbling to himself and wondered what he was writing. His grasp of English had strengthened over the past two years, but he still struggled with reading and writing.

One night, after he had finished with the computer and gone to bed, I lugged my world history textbook and notebooks into the study and set out to write a paper on Mesopotamia. He had left the lamp on for me, and the hard drive, too. And he had forgotten to eject his floppy disk.

I rose and locked the door. A coil of secret excitement wound itself tight in my gut, like the first time I had dared to peek at Dad's *Playboy* magazines. After flipping the screen on, I pulled up Soeuth's file. I read it and felt sadder than I ever have in my life.

I had six people in my family. There were my mom, dad, grandmother, my sister, my brother and me during the beginning of the war. Later, after the war was over, I had another sister—her name was Korng. She was the baby sister that I know of.

My dad's name was Saut, which I use for my last name now. My dad was a little heavy for the Cambodian people. To me, he was mean. Every time he ask me for something, if I looked straight at his face, he would hit me. This is just a tradition of the Cambodian people. Also, my dad hit me, if I did something wrong.

They believe that hitting their kids would teach them not to do it again. I was afraid of my father but not of my mother or my grandmother, because they never hurt me. They were often defend me from my father. Vat was my mom's name, and Win was my grandmother. One time both of my mother and my grandmother got a fight with my dad because of me. I accidentally stepped on soup while they sit around ready to eat. My dad was very mad and hit me with the ox's whip. That week my parents wouldn't talk to each other; mostly my grandmother wouldn't talk to him for a month. Other time my dad hit me, because I hit my little sister. I remember one time I hit my sister, and I told her not to tell dad, if she do I'm going to hurt her even harder. But she wouldn't listen—she told him anyway. So my dad took care of that. My sister was one year younger than me.

I never call her real name, Soeun. I used to call her darling
which most people call their sister in Cambodia.

Another young brother I had was Su. I never called
his name much, because I never got to see him much.

I stopped reading here and tiptoed into the living room and
listened for noises upstairs. There were none. I retrieved a Pepsi
from the refrigerator and went back into the study and locked
the door.

I was too young to understand the beginning of the
war. I remember I used to play in the village and
would climb a tree to watch the air planes drop the bombs.
The bombs were close. You could see the bombs blast
and hear the explosion. You didn't need binoculars.

A lot of people were really scared. My mom and
grandmom would be so mad at me. I wasn't afraid at
all. I was excited every time the fighting was near. I would
just go on playing, while everyone else lay on the
ground or ran down to the ditch to hide. My mom always
had to come and carry me away.

You hear the gun shots, and everybody say "Some-
body got shot!" and we run to see the body. Sometimes
the body is in front of the house, sometimes inside the
house or in the rice field, blood everywhere.

Every night I could see the light blast up in the sky.
The gun shots were very bad. It got closer every min-
ute. It came to the point where we were no longer sleeping
in the house at night anymore. Most of the people
would sleep in underground holes, so that they wouldn't
get shot. For my family, after a while, we were sick of
it, so we ran across the river toward Battambang City.
My dad, mom, and grandmom packed some supplies
for the trip. To me, they were packing too many supplies.
They filled up the oxen wagon—it had so much in it,
that we didn't even have enough space to sit. My mom

*and grandmom had to walk all the way up and down,
up and down every day, because sometimes the communists would win the fight, and sometimes the non-com-
munists would win the fight. We ran all the way to
Battambang City, when the Khmer Rouge won the
war.*

*That night, I thought the fight was still going on, be-
cause we heard the gun shots everywhere. They were
the biggest gun shots that I know of. These guns shot the
celebration of the war being over.*

*The next day, everybody went home. It was a great
loss for most of the people after the war, including my
family. We lost our house and all of the animals. After
we got back, our house was burned into dust. All the
flames were out, but it was still smoking. My parents were
very angry, but they couldn't do anything about it.
Most of the big houses in the village were burned, because
the Khmer Rouge think a big house a sign of inequal-
ity. Under the new communist order, everyone must be the
same. No rich or poor.*

*My father built a new house by the river. That's the
hut where I saw the ghost. When I wake up at three
or four in the afternoon to go to the bathroom, I went near
the bush. I saw a big man with a yellow belly, holding
his hand out. I ran inside and called my mom and said,
'I see the ghost!' We came outside, and it had disappeared. It must have been my imagination, because I just
woke up. In that time, I believe in ghosts.*

*At that time, my dad started to have malaria. It was
a really bad sickness. Every afternoon around four
o'clock, he start to get sick for about an hour. Usually he
could still talk, be he couldn't stop himself from shaking
violent from chills. We would cover him with blankets. He
would be sweating with the heat, but he would still be
shaking. There was nothing to do about it. Once in a
while, he became delirious and hallucinated that a*

neighbor who he had an argument with was coming to kill him. He would grab the shotgun and try to go and shoot her first. My mother and our near neighbors would stop him by tying him up on the bed and by taking the gun away and hiding it. Things went on like this for about three months before it went away. As soon as he stopped, I started to get sick.

When I was six, the Khmer Rouge village leader took me away to a children's work camp. I never lived with my family again.

The camp was filled with little children from ten to fifteen years old. I was the youngest. Usually the Khmer Rouge waited until a child was ten years old to take him or her away. My father let them take me when I was six years old.

I had a fight with my little sister. Now I can't remember what the fight was about. The fight made my father very angry, so he sent me to the camp. This wasn't his fault, because he didn't know what was going on. This was the first time the Khmer Rouge came to collect the children of the village. My dad and I thought that it was only for two weeks.

I was very disappointed in my father while I was at the camp, but I couldn't do anything except cry out loud. It took me two or three weeks to get my mind off my parents. The leaders make us work and told us: "If you work really hard, you will get to go home soon." So we work really hard. But day after day, you never got to go home. Finally, I realized that we were never going home again.

I closed his file and ejected his disk and put it back in its sleeve and set it on top of the hard drive. I stared at his disk for a long time and then went to bed but couldn't sleep and wondered how my big brother could.

*   *   *

Most nights after the nightly news, we'd station ourselves at the dining room table. Dave would sometimes work on his homework with Soeuth and me, but since he was still in junior high and the assignments weren't as lengthy, he would often slap his books shut just as I was opening mine and then fix himself a root beer float. With my books and notebooks and graph paper and Trapper keeper binders spread forlornly before me, I would try or pretend to work. Soeuth would dance his pencil across the page, scratching out formulas or equations or fill-in-the-blank answers. I would tap my pencil on a sheet of graph paper or doodle swords or warplanes or Camaros. At some point I'd have to relocate to my room, because I felt like a slothful dawdler in the presence of Soeuth's frenzied scribbling.

It wasn't that I was lazy, really, or a procrastinator. In fifth grade I had been diagnosed with a mild learning disability, something that scrambled words and numbers before my eyes could order them. It wasn't dyslexia, but some rogue relative of it. It struck most times when I attempted math assignments, blending and shifting numbers and shapes on the page, giving me a headache, sinking me into a swamp of bafflement.

Math was Soeuth's best subject. His assignments were handed back with accolades penned in the margins: "Great job!" "Outstanding!" "Magnificent!" My math assignments were typically marred with comments like, "See me after class." When I saw Soeuth's math assignments fanned out on the table one night with all the compliments from his teachers, I felt miserable. A Cambodian refugee was earning straight A's in algebra and geometry, and it was all I could do not to fail.

One night the power went out, leaving Soeuth and me to do our homework by candlelight. The light from the candles was feeble and fuzzy, and we both had to squint. I eventually gave up, leaned back in my chair and watched Soeuth. He was very still. Only his right hand and his eyes moved, and shadows flitted across his face. I sat very still, too, listening to my own breathing and to the light rain outside. I wondered if this was how he had read in Cambodia, by candlelight. I thought about his family's story and guessed that if my own father had given me away to a band of murderers, I could never do homework again, could never think of much else aside from that one terrible thing.

But he was doing his homework right now, here in front of me, and that thing still lived in him. Realizing this, I felt a great, slow upwelling of strength or hope or something else. I rose and brought a candle into the other room and held it up to the window and studied the reflection of my face. My cheekbones and the outline of my skull looked hard and strong, and I vowed then not to let the bad and clumsy things that lived inside me ever hold me back again.

The flick of a light switch startled me; I almost dropped the candle. The power had come back on, and Soeuth had turned on the living room light. He looked at me quizzically.

"What you doing, man?"

"Just thinking."

"Okay." He smiled and retired to bed.

Many evenings, Soeuth tutored me in algebra. We sat cross-legged on the family room rug, eating rice, and he would coach through my assignments with me. Whenever I tossed my glasses across the floor in frustration, he would put his hand on my shoulder and say, "No lock youself up, man, no lock youself." He explained algebra to me in pictures and ladders and charts and maps that he drew in my notebook. Sometimes he would transform an equation into a battle scene: X's and Y's would attack each other, and the victorious variable would emerge as the answer.

After these tutoring sessions, my first-semester report card for my freshman year bore, for the first time in my life, an unblemished column of A's and B's.

Soeuth's academic performance plateaued midsemester of his sophomore year. He continued to excel in math and science but began to flounder in other subjects, particularly English. On some nights he would slump at the dining room table for hours, shaking his head, crumpling papers, cursing quietly. I tried to help him with English the way he had helped me with math; but for him, English words were rusty barbs on a fence, catching him and holding him back.

So he relied on the tools that had always been his most reliable: his hands. He devoted himself to learning auto mechanics and was soon receiving some of the highest grades in his class. Many weekends, wearing a sweat-soiled Michael Jackson T-shirt, he would be out in the driveway all day, working on some beater car he had borrowed from the high school shop.

Grandpa Ken had taught auto mechanics and industrial arts at a high school in upstate New York and wholeheartedly supported Soeuth's career choice. He was an old-time Yankee, whose cracked, callused hands had earned him a living for over fifty years. He had complained, on many occasions, to Mom or Dad that Dave and I didn't know near enough about cars or tools or hard work in general. When we went to visit Grandpa Ken at his lakeside house in Wells, he and Soeuth would invariably retreat to the garage, discussing the pros and cons of different makes and models of cars. I could hear them while I sat on the porch, watching tourists' boats.

"You're a good egg, Suit," Grandpa Ken said brusquely one afternoon as he popped open the hood of his Ford Taurus; he could never pronounce Soeuth's name right. "You know, Suit . . ." His rusty voice was winding up for a story. "Automobiles have been in my blood since I was four years old. When I was I kid, we lived next to a Hudson dealership. I fell in love with a Saab, two-cycle, three-cylinder. Saab came out on top year after year. Ford often came in second . . ."

"Grandpa, what you think about Chevy?"

"Oh, Suit!" Grandpa exclaimed with a gruff, let-me-tell-ya-somethin'-son laugh. "Don't get me started on Chevies. Never before has such an inferior car been made."

One of Grandpa's most passionate causes, next to his support for a governmental program that would cede land to Native Americans, was his ironclad advocacy of the Ford Motor Corporation. The only people who compared to Henry Ford, in his eyes, were Abraham Lincoln and maybe Jesus. "Henry Ford changed the way we do things, boys," he would tell us whenever the topic of cars bobbed up. "He revolutionized industry and made everything more efficient. He is one of the greatest men to have lived in this century or the last one, for that matter. And he manufactured one helluva damned good car."

After my parents bought a Pontiac my freshman year of high school, Grandpa couldn't help but cuss about it. Sometimes he would utter terse comments under his breath during Sunday dinners when he visited for the day. "You can still trade the damned thing in," he said once into his mashed potatoes. Another time, during dessert as he was cracking peanuts open with his teeth, he said to me and Dave: "I hope you boys will be smart enough not to make the same mistake as your parents. I hope, when you own your own vehicles, you'll consider buyin' the best car that was ever produced—no two ways about it. I'm talkin' about the Ford, a course."

At the outset of his junior year, Soeuth bought a black hatchback Chevette. When he drove it home one afternoon after school, I began to dread the upcoming Sunday dinner. But Grandpa just ate his peanuts and held his tongue, because even if Soeuth had bought an inferior car, at least he knew how to maintain it.

He saw something else in Soeuth, I think, something he didn't see in Dave or me. Grandpa was an ardent admirer of toughness; he had long told us stories that exemplified this most vital of character traits. When he was in his early fifties, a rotten tree had fallen on his head while he was sawing through another tree with his chain saw. The force of the blow had cracked his skull and driven the whirring chain saw into his knee. He had crawled a half mile back to his house, dragging his useless leg behind him, cerebrospinal fluid trickling out his nose. He had regained the use of his leg eventually, but had lost the hearing in one ear almost entirely.

When he relayed stories like this, he would rev up his throat like an old engine and grind out all the gory details. "Thisus back when I was buildin' my house, boys." Dave, Soeuth and I sat on his lakeside porch with him one afternoon, gnawing on his home-made sour pickles. "Got this throbbin' pain in my pinkie finger. So I go down to the Jewish doctor and say, 'Doc, I'm buildin' my house and can't afford any pain in this finger. Do you think you could just have this finger taken off?' " He jabbed his arthriti-cally hooked pinkie in our direction and chuckled to himself. "Figured it would hurt a helluva lot less if it were sittin' in the trash can. But the Jewish doctor tells me, 'Mr. Fifield, if I take off your finger, the pain would move into your hand, and if I take off your hand, it would creep up into your arm." Grandpa then held his pinkie before his face and said: "Still got the damned thing. Guess the doctor was right."

By Grandpa Ken's lights, Dave and I had grown up soft. Soeuth had not, and Grandpa knew Soeuth's short life contained perhaps as many trials as his own long one. This fact bred within Grandpa the kind of respect he would reserve for the likes of war veterans and Native American tribesmen.

During the fall of Soeuth's junior year, when I was a sopho-more and Dave was in seventh grade, Soeuth and Dave would tinker on engines in the garage at home. Soeuth taught him auto mechanics, and it became clear that Dave also had a talent for working with his hands. They resuscitated a 1941 military jeep that had been under a tarp in Grandpa Ken's driveway for years, cramming its engine with enough horsepower to haul them up the logging roads in back of the Seeleys' sugar shack. I sometimes sat with notes or a book on the front steps and watched them operating on the jeep like cardiac surgeons on a near-death pa-tient, coercing life back into its frame, passing wrenches and diag-nostic opinions back and forth. The two spent many an afternoon after school together, building, rebuilding, dismantling.

Mom encouraged Soeuth to persist with academics and pressed him to apply to college. He refused, saying he only wanted a job, an income. She suggested he go to school to learn auto mechanics or business, to get a degree, but he said he didn't want any help or any degrees.

That winter, he started coming home late many nights, after everyone had gone to bed. Some nights he didn't show at all. Sometimes I'd still be up when he skulked in, studying or watching *David Letterman* or talking on the phone, and he'd walk by, reeking of cigarettes, and he'd say, hey, and I'd say, hey, and he'd go to bed.

One Saturday afternoon, after Mom, Dad, Dave and I had finished lunch and were huddling around the dining room table hatching plans for the rest of the day, Soeuth trudged downstairs, his face sullen, gray pouches under his eyes. He poured himself a bowl of cereal, and Mom said to no one in particular: "Gee, it's late—is it one o'clock already?"

Soeuth pretended not to hear and placed the milk back in the refrigerator and headed back upstairs with his bowl of cereal.

"Soeuth," Mom said.

He halted mid-staircase.

"Yeah?"

"Could you come talk to us for a minute?"

He returned to the dining room slowly and slouched at the table and ate his cereal.

"Out late last night?"

He shrugged. Dave and I exchanged worried glances.

"Jean," Dad said. "Let's not do this now."

"Then when?" she snapped.

Soeuth had not finished his cereal, but treaded to the kitchen sink and rinsed out his bowl anyway and set the bowl in the dishwasher.

"Were you at Bi's last night?"

He shrugged.

"Were you drinking?"

He didn't answer.

"Were you smoking pot?"

He lingered by the dishwasher and his angry face hung still in the bright afternoon light, and I wished Mom would stop.

"Soeuth?"

He started to leave but stopped just inside the doorframe that separated the dining room from the vestibule. Very deliberately, and with considerable force, he punched the hard wood of the doorframe.

Mom sighed. Soeuth stalked out of the room and upstairs.

He spent many afternoons and evenings at Bi's house. Bi's father, Tom, a Vietnam vet, would often give the boys beers and share a joint or two with them. Mom had heard rumors about Tom growing marijuana in his backyard and was infuriated that he could be sharing it with her son. What Mom did not know was that Soeuth had been smoking marijuana, on and off, since he was ten years old.

As spring thawed the landscape, the fields around our house filled with flood water. Mom and Soeuth's fights became more frequent. Soeuth would usually say only a few words or say nothing and seal his lips tight and keep his eyes trained on some patch of floor. He would hole himself up in his room or take long drives to get away. On the worst nights, he and Mom would both clutch their heads and empty our cabinet of the free aspirin Dad had brought home from the office.

In the summer of 1988, before his senior year of high school, when he was nineteen, Soeuth moved out.

Soeuth's apartment was a narrow, one-room box. It jutted out from the side of a sagging, one-level house, as if it had been amputated from some other structure and grafted onto this one. The cement foundation beneath Soeuth's part sloped off obliquely, disappearing almost entirely at its north end. When I saw the place, I fancied that if I watched long enough, I might see it sink an inch or two. The whole building, which was owned by his auto-mechanics instructor, sat on a random patch of yellowed grass in the north part of town, as if a wayward tornado had plucked it up somewhere else and haphazardly deposited it here.

I swung by Soeuth's new place on a Sunday afternoon in November. He still came by the house on weekends, every now and then, but this was the first time I had gone to visit him. I had a shoe box full of silverware to give him, courtesy of Mom. Inside, the place was spare and dark, a grainy semidarkness to which the eye never fully adjusts. A pyramid of Coors cans had been assembled on the countertop next to the stove. Burnt-incense stubs poked out of a tin can filled with rice. The bareness of the walls was interrupted only by his ancient Angkor Wat poster and a Heather Locklear swimsuit poster I had given him on his birthday the previous year. One pot hung over the sink, and a few red plastic plates, donated by Mom, were stacked next to some incense packets on the foldout card table. The big-screen

TV he had bought sat on a small coffee table across from the
bed. His stereo was stationed squarely in a corner on the floor,
next to a collection of his tapes and CDs: Guns n' Roses, AC/
DC, Aerosmith, Led Zeppelin, Paul Simon's *Graceland* and a few
old Michael Jackson albums.

"So, what you think? Pretty small, eh?" He sat on his bed
against the wall, resting a bowl of rice on his stomach.

"Yeah, and your decorations are a little much. Go easy on
that."

He smiled. "Close to work."

His apartment was a few wilted shrubs away from MacIntyre
Fuel Co., where he washed gas trucks and did odd jobs. He was
still wearing his blue work suit, his name stitched above the breast
pocket in bright red cursive script. Oil and grease stains spotted
the sleeves.

He had started at MacIntyre's the previous June. It wasn't his
first job: for years, he had worked in a series of summer and
after-school jobs—clearing hiking paths for the U.S. Forest Service, teaching soccer for the town recreation department, feeding
fish at the local hatchery, washing dishes at Rosie's Restaurant—
but this was the first job that earned him a few steps toward
his goal of becoming a certified auto mechanic. The stakes were
especially high, because Roch MacIntyre, the owner, was a friend
of the family and had agreed, at Mom's behest, to find Soeuth
some employment.

Soeuth was a dogged worker. He labored on engines with a
furious concentration, his lips pressed tight as a vise, his brow
knuckled up, his shirt drowned in sweat. You could never have
a conversation with him when he was bent under a car's hood—
it was as though the top half of him had disappeared into some
other realm.

At MacIntyre's, I am sure, he attacked his tasks with this same
intensity. And although he learned fast, he notched up a few
noticeable mishaps. One afternoon he climbed atop one of the
aluminum fuel tanks and secured a four-and-a-half-inch hose into
the tank's fuel socket. But when another employee cranked on

the fuel—which shot through the hose at one hundred gallons per minute—the nozzle jumped out of the socket, showering him with fuel. The worst mistake occurred when Roch asked Soeuth to wash his new Cadillac. (I had seen Roch gloating over his Sunday driving machine when Dad and I paid the MacIntyres a visit.) Soeuth innocently scrubbed it down with the same acid-based soap that he used to wash the aluminum fuel tanks, so that when he sprayed the soap off, giant bald patches in the car's paint job suddenly appeared.

Large-boned and heavy, Roch lumbered along with the gait of a man carrying a heavy crate. He had a mostly bald, shiny head and a contagious, stony laugh. When the MacIntyres joined us for Sunday barbecues, Roch would often pass out MacIntyre Fuel Co. baseball caps and tell dirty jokes. He had inherited the company from his father when it was a single gas station with only a few pumps, and had, over the years, built it into one of Vermont's largest fuel distributors.

When Roch checked in on Soeuth and saw that he had cleaned his new Cadillac not only of caked road dust and exhaust grime, but of some of the paint as well, he declared: "Anybody else would be flyin' right through the air off the end of my toe, but you don't know any better, 'cause we didn't show you, so it's our own fault. You gotta know what you're doin'."

Soeuth lowered his head and buried his gaze in the folds down the front of his shirt, something he would do a lot during his early days at MacIntyre Fuel Co.

Roch, like several of his employees, was a Vietnam veteran, and Soeuth was the first Asian person with whom he had had any significant interaction since the war. When Soeuth came to work late one morning, Roch stormed into the garage and thundered at him: "I'll tell you what—I'm gonna put you on a goddamned raft with a sail and a compass and send your ass back to Cambodia! Get your ass in gear, boy."

In the afternoons, during Soeuth's lunch break, Phun and Bi would sometimes visit for a few minutes to share a smoke and shoot the shit. One afternoon after they had left, Roch pulled

Soeuth aside and told him: "We can't have that. This is not a hangout for the Cambodian Mafia." His voice, in disciplinary situations like this, was often gloved in the stern, admonitory tone of a high school principal. Then he smiled, winked and added: "This is the Scottish Mafia, and I'm the head don, and that's it."

But Roch, even though he was sometimes impatient with Soeuth, liked him, because my brother was honest and worked hard. The same couldn't be said for others Soeuth encountered at MacIntyre Fuel Co. A friend of Roch's who owned an asphalt company up the road—and who also had served in Vietnam, in the Marine Corps—stopped by one afternoon and asked Roch outright: "What do you got that sonofabitch in here for?"

"Now listen," cautioned Roch, who had served in the Fourth Infantry Division along the Vietnam-Cambodia border and knew about the "Side Show" war in Cambodia. "This guy has been through hell, and he needs our help."

But when Roch wasn't around, some of the guys would refer to Soeuth as "poor little shit," or "little bastard," or use imitative broken English when speaking to him. They would yell out jocular taunts, like: "You wouldn't be here, you sonofabitch, if I shot your old man when I had the chance."

Soeuth, who was broiling inside—not least because these men saw him as the gook, the faceless Vietnamese, and he was not Vietnamese—would only smile and lower his head. If one of his fellow classmates said something like that to him, Soeuth would bloody his nose. But at MacIntyre Fuel Co., there were three or four of them—hefty, meat-fed men and Vietnam vets at that—and only one of him, and he also knew that Roch was a friend of Mom and Dad's and he couldn't cause a scene. Plus, he wanted to keep this job. So he withdrew into the familiar armor of reticence.

Soon his hard work and equanimity paid off. He graduated from washing trucks to helping one of the mechanics grease trucks and do brake jobs. Roch and others grew to regard him as one of the more reliable workers on hand. But perhaps his most impressive achievement at MacIntyre Fuel Co., one that he now shrugs off, was the spurring of a fundamental change in the outlook of his co-workers. The more harassment he endured without complaint, the more his harassers respected him. The gibes and taunts slowed up and eventually stopped altogether. One mechanic took him to stock-car races. The asphalt man from up the road, who was as big as Roch and twice as intimidating and whose first phrase to describe Soeuth had been "sonofabitch," regularly invited him to poker games. He once asked Soeuth a question that had been vexing him ever since he left Vietnam: "How do you eat those little bananas that grow on those little trees? In all my time there, I never did see a one ripe banana."

Soeuth smiled. "You just cut the bananas off the trees and set them aside for a few days," he explained. "Then they'll ripen."

"I'll be damned," the asphalt man said.

Now I set the shoe box full of silverware on his counter. Soeuth looked at me inquiringly, and I said: "From Mom."

He nodded, eating rice, and motioned for me to sit on one of the foldout metal chairs at his table. As I moved the chair to face his bed, I noticed the extra mattress in the corner. It was faded gray and grooved in the middle. Soeuth saw me eyeing the mattress, yawned and shook his head.

A few weeks earlier, a local high school girl who went to our church had been kicked out of her house after a fight with her parents. Soeuth knew her only peripherally; they had a few mutual friends at the high school. One afternoon she had scampered through the halls, asking around if anyone knew of a place where she could stay for the night. Someone had suggested she ask Soeuth, because he had his own place.

She was a pretty, pale, rounded girl who wore a generous amount of black eye shadow and long black shirts that gave her body a safe shapelessness. She was flirtatious but in a nonaggressive, almost self-effacing way.

When she had asked Soeuth if she could crash at his place, he had said okay, if you want, because it was not in his nature to refuse favors, even to strangers. She had stayed with him for one night. She had slept on his bed; he had slept on the mattress on the floor. A few days later, Soeuth heard that she had been spreading a rumor that they had shared the same bed that night. Whenever someone asked about him and the runaway girl and their alleged liaison, Soeuth would slowly shake his head and reply, no way, not her.

In fact, Soeuth was chronically shy when it came to girls; he had once asked Mom before a date when it would be okay to hold his date's hand—should he ask her first? Mom had said that his date would probably let him know without words, by placing her hand on the armrest in the movie theater, for instance. Soeuth, Dave and I used to joke about the lump-in-the-throat paralysis that had stricken each of us during our rare romantic endeavors, and I knew that unless the girl had managed to tie him up, drug him and undress him herself, she was—as Grandpa Ken would say—full of fertilizer.

There had been other runaways who had stayed with Soeuth, teenagers trying to unhitch themselves from authority or seeking anonymity or escape from the provincialism of Middlebury, Vermont.

The sound of a car pulling into his driveway snapped Soeuth's head up from his rice bowl. I glanced through a window to see three guys in denim jackets stepping out of an old Plymouth Duster. One of them, who had a thick film of stubble on his jaw and neck, opened the trunk and hauled out a few bulky grocery bags.

"Got some company," I said.

"Yeah." He pried himself off the bed and walked stiffly to the counter and deposited his rice bowl in the sink. I could tell he didn't want to introduce me, and so I said, "All right, man, I'll see ya later."

He leaned against the counter, watching the TV as if it were on. He finally said: "You can stay if you want."

"Thanks, but I gotta help Dad stack some wood."

He smiled, as if he knew I would go nowhere near a woodpile that afternoon. "Okay, man, see you later."

I passed Soeuth's friends on my way to Mom's Pontiac, parked a few feet from the Duster, and recognized them from the high school: kids I didn't know all that well who would hang out by the Dumpster in back of the Voc-Tech building. We regarded one another but didn't say anything. I glanced back once to see Soeuth let them in, and he glimpsed me watching him and smiled or grimaced and then shut the door.

Soeuth attracted a lot of friends during his junior and senior years, from auto-mechanics class, wood shop, the soccer team. Some of them were the same guys who had taunted him a few years earlier and whom he had trounced (Master Donnelly's counsel had, in a roundabout way, been realized). The others were a motley assemblage of misfits: truants, juvenile delinquents, foreign exchange students, kids who, for one reason or another, didn't fit into the cliques at the high school.

His apartment thus became more than just a magnet for wayward youths; it was soon a prime party spot. He worked after school and would leave his door unlocked. The parties, which started on most evenings before he came home, often lasted until dawn. The number of guests swelled sometimes to an unruly twenty-five or thirty, many of them uninvited. They would drink his beer, play their CDs on his stereo, empty his refrigerator of its contents, make out on his bed. Sometimes a hat would travel around in which beer money was collected, and most people would toss in a dollar or a few quarters, and Soeuth and Bi would have to donate the difference. When there were drinking games, almost everyone would guzzle Jack Daniel's or Jim Beam until someone puked in his kitchen sink or on his carpet or his bed. Marijuana joints would be handed around the room, and after a while, everyone was discerning shapes and faces in the static of his TV.

There was an unspoken understanding, among certain privi-
leged members of Soeuth's inner circle, that in times of hormonal
urgency his apartment was an alternative to the backseat of a car
or the bed of a pickup. They would either skip school or show
up at the odd evening times when the apartment wasn't overrun
with a brood of their peers and slink in the front door or crawl
through a window if the door was locked. If Soeuth was there—
and since he worked every day after school and all day Saturday,
he usually wasn't—he might ask them to lock up when they were
done and then drive around for an hour or two. Sometimes they
would use his extra mattress, but mostly they would use his bed.
Joe Piper, a bespectacled, tough-talking but keen-witted member
of my class, who often challenged his teachers with literary ri-
postes, admitted to me that he had lost his virginity to a foreign
exchange girl from Mexico on Soeuth's bed.

In the past year, due to my nascent social activism, Joe had
become one of my many adversaries. After being elected sophomore class president, I had spearheaded a campaign to ban smoking from the high school, an effort which spilled over into my
junior year, drew sporadic statewide press attention and cast me
as persona non grata in certain sectors of the student population.
One of those who reviled me most was Joe, who then smoked
more than a pack a day. Unbeknownst to me, Soeuth had been
smoking steadily since his freshman year and had befriended several smokers, including Joe, who considered me a straight-laced,
puritanical zealot. Many nights when Soeuth would be smoking
cigarettes and joints with Bi and Phun and Joe and others, I'd be
at home, slumped over the computer in Dad's study, writing
antismoking Op-Eds or reviewing the agenda of the next meeting
of the Vermont Lung Association, to which I had been elected
as an honorary member. When my campaign succeeded and
smoking was banned at the high school, Soeuth stopped by the
house and shook my hand and said, you do good job, man.

Bi also congratulated me on the no-smoking campaign. His
family had moved to Malden, Massachusetts, after his junior year,
but he still attended Soeuth's parties on the weekends, driving up

from Massachusetts in his old cargo van. He would come in wearing a long trench coat and sunglasses, with Serena, his dainty, freckled girlfriend, on his arm. After the beer had run out and everybody else had curled up on the floor, Bi would often fold his six-foot frame into the lotus position, close his eyes and meditate. He would let the sounds of the room—rustlings under blankets, static from the TV, occasional beer belches—dwindle to a collective hum and try to levitate into the stratosphere of his subconscious mind. Someone might wake up and, in the half-light haze between drunk and hung over, lunge at Bi, attempting to knock him down. But he was big, and his concentration impregnable, and the quixotic mischief-maker would usually bounce off him and pass out.

Phun would often show up at Soeuth's late and already half cocked, with a few buddies from his machine-trade class. An indefatigable drinker always on the lookout for a good time, Phun was often an unwitting source of entertainment. At one of these gatherings, Phun burst through the door and snatched up a wine-cooler bottle that had been used as an ashtray. He tipped it back and then, to everyone's amusement, spewed a mouthful of soggy cigarette butts.

As winter wended toward spring and graduation loomed, Soeuth tired of the ceaseless guzzling, groping, smoking and shouting. On some nights, police cars would show up on his lawn, a few people would bolt and the rest would cower together inside. After the patrol car had left, Soeuth would break up the party and go to work emptying ashtrays and collecting beer cans in a plastic trash bag.

I never went to any of Soeuth's parties. Except for Phun and Bi, I didn't know any of his friends. My friends were mostly college-bound folks I'd met in school theater activities, student government or on the student newspaper. For social activities, we'd play Dungeons & Dragons or watch Alfred Hitchcock movies or, if we gathered at my house, jaunt out to the rope swing or, on the rare occasion, pitch a tent overnight in one of Farmer

Seeley's fields. No one ever drank alcohol or had sex or smoked anything.

Next to my big brother, I was a square—I knew that. But I also knew that most of his friends couldn't possibly know or appreciate him like I did. They probably couldn't even find Cambodia on a map, I figured.

Crystal Rule, whom Phun had dated in his junior year, was a short, lithe blonde with solicitous eyes. She would occasionally brandish a bottle of Jack Daniels at Soeuth's parties and dare any of the guys—most of whom plainly lusted after her—to try and drink her down. As senior year progressed, she would often lavish Soeuth with her coveted attention. He had been warned that Crystal had had lots of boyfriends and was unpredictable, and, of course, Phun was one of his best friends. But Soeuth was stunned that the prettiest girl at the party would so much as let him light her cigarette, and soon enough, they were dating.

When Phun learned that his friend was dating his ex-girl-friend, he stopped talking to Soeuth—but Soeuth was too infatu-ated with Crystal to care. He brought her to the house one Sunday afternoon to ride the horses, and when he introduced her to us, she smiled, extending her hand to no one in particular, and squealed: "Hi! It's so nice to meet you!"

After his graduation in June of 1989, Soeuth rented a trailer in the mobile-home park that Crystal's parents owned in Vergennes and continued working at MacIntyre's. On many nights that summer when he came home, Crystal would be out drinking with friends. When he saw her, she was often withdrawn. When he asked if anything was wrong, she complained that he didn't spend enough time with her. And so the next day, after work, he packed up his things and left and never spoke to Crystal or her family again.

He stayed in Middlebury with a friend he'd met on the munic-ipal volleyball team, Mickey Holler, a hulking, affable guy with a bumbling, Jimmy Stewart-like quality. Soeuth paid Mickey a few hundred dollars in rent, even though there was still a room for him at our house where he could have stayed for free.

I knew it was more than the prospect of a fight with Mom that kept him away: moving back in would mean a loss of face.

Soeuth was drawn to Mickey because Mickey was an auto mechanic, but also because he was a grown, married man who had staked out his place in the world. The two went fishing some afternoons in Otter Creek, below the old Pulp Mill Bridge, and Mickey would catch suckers or other trash fish and throw them back and Soeuth would say, why you do that? Mickey would cock his head, a wide smile tethered ear to ear, and say, you don't want to eat those, man, and Soeuth would say, oh, they look okay to me. On other afternoons Mickey would park his Camaro by the railroad tracks, and they would sit in his bucket seats and sip beers and watch the corrugated sides of train cars slide by, and Soeuth would tell Mickey that his family in Cambodia was probably dead, probably killed and buried in a rice field, but can he be sure, can he ever be sure? Mickey had never been that close to Soeuth, but he was a transparently good-natured, unguarded kind of guy whom it was easy to tell things to. He would listen to Soeuth, crack a fresh beer and hand it to him. Are you okay, man? he would say, and Soeuth would raise his hand up so it blocked Mickey's view of his face and mumble, yeah, man, yeah, fine.

In early May of 1990, Soeuth quit his job at MacIntyre's and signed up for the admission test for the U.S. Marines. A friend he had met in high-school wood shop had promised him that the Marines would mold him into a death-defying hero and pay him for it. But the test, which was administered at a recruiting office in Burlington, had too many big words and alien acronyms, and he failed.

He soon found himself anchored to Mickey's couch, drinking Mickey's beer, eating Mickey's wife's food and worrying that he would soon be unable to pay his share of the rent.

Bi had rented a trailer, a few months earlier, in the same mobile-home park Crystal's parents owned. He lived there with

Serena—who was now his wife and pregnant with his son—and worked a few odd jobs. Even though Soeuth dreaded running into Crystal, he took up residence in Bi's trailer, paying him $100 a month for rent—money he'd saved from MacIntyre's—and slept on an extra bed in the trailer's central room. A month or so later, Phun, who had never graduated from high school and had become a drifter in the past year—he was at one point living in a tent he'd pitched in a state park—made Bi's trailer his home, too, sleeping on a mattress on the floor a few feet from Soeuth. They lived for three or four months, pressed into Bi's pinched quarters, but Phun and Soeuth said hardly a word to each other. The only time they got along was when they were both stoned.

Spurred perhaps by a reaction to Phun's listlessness, Soeuth called a friend of Mickey's, a mechanic at Ryder Rental who, Mickey said, might be able to find him some work. Mickey's friend picked up Soeuth at Bi's trailer one afternoon and drove him to Ryder's headquarters, just past Burlington International Airport, on Williston Road. Soeuth filled out a job application and then the head boss asked him to try popping open the hood of a Mack superliner in the lot. Soeuth scaled the grille of the truck and heaved the heavy hood open with a grunt and the head boss said, well, hell, he's stronger than he looks. A week later, he was commuting to Burlington every morning to pump gas, change oil and wash and inspect trucks.

In early fall, he packed up his things—which consisted of his clothes, stereo, tapes, CDs and a few posters—and migrated twenty miles north to Burlington and settled in with Sokkhan, the only other Cambodian, aside from Phun, whom he knew in Vermont. Sokkhan was stout with a square face and suspicious eyes, but he would often let out a disarming chortle once you got to know him. He had lived in Middlebury with his foster family while Soeuth had been at the Millers in 1983, but, after a quarrel with his foster brother, had been placed with a family in Burlington, where he had attended high school.

Sokkhan's one-bedroom apartment was dark, walled with fake wood paneling and adorned with a half-dozen or so plaster elephants made in the animal molding factory where he worked. Soeuth's room was dark and behind the kitchen and had barely enough space for a bed; the room on the other side of the kitchen, perhaps intended as a dining room, became Sokkhan's bedroom. Soeuth was glad that, since he was living with a Cambodian, he could once again speak his native language, something he hadn't done, with any consistency, for more than six years.

As winter enclosed, Soeuth sent a letter, addressed to no one in particular, to Cambodia. In the letter, he promised an undisclosed sum of money to anyone who could help him locate his family. Since he didn't know his family name, he listed the given names of his mother and father, Vat and Saut, and of the sisters and brother he had known as a child, Soeun, Korng and Su. He indicated the name of the village in which he had been born, Kompong Chhlang, but did not indicate its location. On the envelope in which the letter had been sealed, he wrote simply: "Kompong Chhlang, Cambodia." On the bottom of the envelope, he wrote the following sentence in Khmer: "Whoever sees this letter has permission to open it." After several months, he sent a second letter, and several months after that, a third.

In the fall of 1990, I had enrolled at Bates College in Lewiston, Maine. Dave had begun his sophomore year of high school that fall. We learned about each other's lives from cursory phone conversations, Christmas and birthday cards and the occasional bullshit session on the pool patio when we were all home for the weekend. And when we did that, I would merrily regale my brothers with inflated stories of campus life and Dave would howl and snort and Soeuth would sit still and smile politely.

When the phone rang, I cleared my throat and drew a breath. I let it ring a few times. I had started my summer internship with U.S. Senator Patrick Leahy in Washington, D.C., a few weeks earlier, and several important people—including the heads of state of foreign countries—had been accidentally transferred to me, so I needed to sound professional, composed and, if possible, disinterested when answering the phone.

I picked up. I said hello coolly, dropping my voice low.

"Adam?" It was my girlfriend, sobbing.

"Yeah, its me—what's . . . ? Are you okay?"

"I . . . I lost . . . I lost my ring," she sputtered between sobs.

"What happened?" I was leaning over, locked in an awkward embrace with my desk; one of the aides was telling a Coke-can joke about Clarence Thomas, who had been in the office just minutes ago.

"My ring . . . I can't find my ring . . . I . . . I thought it might have fallen under the stove . . ."

I listened to her sniffling; panic exploded in my chest, spread to my extremities. "He's not still there, is he?"

"No. He . . . he took my ring off before . . . maybe it fell down the stairs. Maybe . . ."

"Did you lock the doors? Just stay calm." The fluorescent light above me seemed to pulsate, flashing in sync with my heart.

"You're gonna stay with my folks," I said. "In Vermont. And I'm gonna kill that sonofabitch—"

"No," she sobbed. "Please don't."

The stalker had been calling for several weeks, breathing threats and obscenities into the phone, before he paid a visit. He had slipped through the patio screen door. She was staying at home that summer and her mother was at work when it happened. She didn't want anyone to know, didn't want to call the police. I was the only person she told.

When I heard this, numbness cocooned me—my world had been suddenly, inexplicably, rent. When I was finally able to sleep, flashes of clear, clipped violence riddled my dreams: smashing his kneecaps with a lead pipe, pulling fencing wire tight around his throat, castrating him with the snip of a pair of pliers. The weight of it displaced most other thoughts. I couldn't concentrate on work, couldn't listen during conversations, couldn't pay enough attention to cross the street safely.

A few days after the phone call, my girlfriend moved into the guest room at my parents' house. She told her mother that she just wanted to get away for a while.

I returned home at the end of the summer to be with her. One afternoon I drove down to Grandpa Ken's and told him about the stalker. I sat in his rocking chair on the porch. He lolled on the couch, listening, nodding and stroking the matted mane of his lethargic golden retriever, Murdoch. After I finished the story and confessed that I didn't know what to do, he stood up, looked around absently and walked inside the house and into his room—as if my story had reminded him of a photo in some old album he wanted to show me. He emerged a minute or so later, holding his revolver slack at his side. He set it on the coffee table and said: "It's loaded."

I didn't know if Grandpa was offering the gun for me to use, or if he was offering to pull the trigger, but I knew that neither option was a good one. That didn't prevent the visions from clicking through my head, though, like some macabre slide show; didn't stop me, when I returned to college that fall, from wandering down Lisbon Street and ducking into pawnshops to see if there were any silencers for sale. Savior scenarios still flared in my head, transmitted by some out-of-body, overhead, fish-eye camera. I would be in a bus station, video store or bar, watching some red-faced guy who was inches away, it seemed, from putting the knuckles on his wife or girlfriend, and I'd imagine pinning him to a table or lambasting him into a wall.

After my visit with Grandpa, the scenarios I envisioned of killing or maiming or castrating the stalker coalesced into a plan of action. The stalker attended a university only a day's drive from my parents' house. I would simply go down there, look him up in the student directory, case his apartment building or dormitory or fraternity house, follow his movements and isolate a time in the night when he would be alone. I would need a ski mask and gloves. I would wear sterile rubber gloves when I bought the mask and gloves so I wouldn't leave fingerprints. I would need to find a silencer for Grandpa's revolver. Having interned at the Androscoggin County District Attorney's Office during my freshman year, I knew that I could claim "emotional duress" and maybe get away with it.

I traveled back and forth between home and college a lot that fall. One Friday evening after class, I drove for six hours across saw-toothed pine swaths of Maine and southern New Hampshire, reaching Middlebury around 11:30 P.M. As I walked into the kitchen, Farmer Seeley was sipping coffee with Mom and Dad, telling them how he had had to shoot one of his cats because it kept rummaging through the garbage. I poured half a cup of cold coffee, didn't drink it and listened to a few of Farmer Seeley's barnyard stories. Before he was finished, I excused myself and plodded upstairs and sat on the little-boy's bed in my little-boy's room—seagull wallpaper, high-school-award plaques, Stephen King books—and tried to think around this thing, figure a way out. I fell asleep in my clothes, shoes and all.

Saturday morning I awoke to the downstairs sound of Soeuth's gravelly voice. He had driven down from Burlington bearing a highly detailed plaster elephant, courtesy of Sokkhan.

After a few cups of coffee, we went for a walk out by the river. It was cold already, maybe twenty-five degrees, and windy. The sky was a dull granite color. We walked together for a while, wordlessly, and halted at a place where the bank slouched into dark water.

We stood there, hands in our pockets, watching the water, and I told him that a man had raped my girlfriend and that I couldn't call the police. What did he think I should do? He did not turn to face me but answered definitively: "Somebody have to stop this guy."

"Stop him?"

"Beat him," he said. "Beat him real good. Maybe almost kill him."

"Almost kill him?"

"Not really kill him," he clarified. "Just almost. Not go to jail. That no good."

Soeuth said things like this with no particular zeal. He said them like he was talking about the advantages of buying a Chevy over a Ford. There was no glory or anger in his words, no righteous fury, or, as he would say, no big deal. I remembered sitting with him on beanbags some five years earlier watching *The Dead Zone* on TV—the scene where Christopher Walken asks Herbert Lom if he could go back in time to when Hitler was a little boy, would he kill him? Herbert Lom says he would, because he loves people—and I had asked Soeuth if he would kill Hitler when Hitler was a little boy. He had shrugged and said, I don't know, I never kill nobody yet. Yeah, maybe I take machine gun, kill Hitler and kill Pol Pot, too. I don't really want to kill nobody, but Hitler, Pol Pot different, though, because they kill a lot of people. So maybe I kill them. Yeah, prob'ly do kill them.

We had been silent for a few moments as the river purled swiftly beneath us. Soeuth dragged the toe of his sneaker through the grass and then said flatly: "If you want, I take care of it."

I watched the ripples in the water and listened to Soeuth's breathing. My brother knew firsthand that there was evil in the world—for him it had been as real, as routine, as bills and car repairs and hard winters. I suddenly envied him, because he had never learned to temper his actions with moderation. He had never learned to turn the other cheek. He had learned to hit back, so that the turning of any cheek would be that of the guy who had hit him, reeling from the force of the blow Soeuth had inflicted.

I pictured him wrecking this guy, smashing his face with a dropkick, cracking his ribs, mottling him with bruises. The thought of it gave me a head rush. I wished then, in a fleeting and shameful moment, that he and I had switched places, that I had lived through genocide, that I had been endowed with the strength that filled you with hard, easy, unequivocal power.

"No," I finally said. "But thank you, old man. Thank you."

I bought my girlfriend some Mace and enrolled with her in a self-defense class. I stowed a baseball bat in the trunk of my car along with a ten-inch knife Dave had fashioned out of scrap metal. I mustered the mettle to call the stalker and threaten him. He stammered incredulously on the other end of the line and asked: "Wh-who the h-h-ell is—is—is th-this?"

"You should have a pretty good goddamned idea who I am," I said. My hands were shaking, and my voice was, too.

"Th-this . . . this is r-r-ridiculous," he said. "I don't . . . I don't know what the h-h-h-hell you're . . . you're talkin' about."

I imagined him sprawled on a leather futon couch in his apartment, in a T-shirt and boxers, his neatly trimmed fingernails catching little white crescents of daylight, and I felt a surge of rage.

I said, "No one likes a rapist." My vision had blurred, and I was trembling very badly.

"You—you—you . . . I . . . I . . ."

I cleared my throat, but did not speak.

"This, this—eh—is r-r-ridiculous, this . . . how . . . how c-c-can you c-c-call me up like this . . . how . . ."

He began to hiss. I was speechless, frozen to the phone, until I said: "That's enough." Something had abruptly ironed out my voice. "I'm not gonna sit here and listen to you deny it. If you ever go near her again, I'll do everything I can to make you regret it. I'll come down there and tell them what you are. Tell everybody. I'll burn your life down. And if that doesn't work, I'll find out where you live, and I'll wait for you outside your apartment or frat house or wherever. I'll wait until you're alone. And I'll bring friends. You see, I just can't live with myself if I don't stop you."

I paused and listened to him listening to me.

"That's it," I said and hung up.

After my phone call, the stalker stopped calling, as far as I knew. A few months after that, my girlfriend and I were both living in a haze of denial, pretending nothing had happened. I couldn't stand it. Our intimacy became one of many casualties. Eventually we broke up.

I called Soeuth one night and told him what had happened with the stalker, and he said simply: you stop him, man, you do good.

In early March of 1992, after driving home from his job at Ryder Rental, Soeuth opened his mailbox, expecting to fish out a few bills and maybe some junk mail. But there was something else in there, something sizable, wedged in deep. He pulled out a slim, 11-by-14-inch manila envelope. It was postmarked from Cambodia. Tucking the envelope under his arm, he slowly climbed the fire-escape steps to his second-floor apartment. He set the envelope down on his foldout kitchen table and retrieved himself a beer from the refrigerator. He studied the envelope's innocuous surface, the characters scribbled on it, and wondered if the news inside was very good or very bad. After weighing it in his hands, he opened it gingerly, as if its contents were explosive. The letter inside announced that his Cambodian family—whom he had presumed dead for more than twelve years—was alive. There was also a color photograph of his parents flanked by a throng of his siblings and cousins, some of whom he had never seen. The faces of his family smiled at him: the faces of ghosts.

The letter was dated February 14, 1992. It was written in canted Khmer script on a sturdy sheet of brown paper. It read:

> *We (Kuth Saut, your father and Kuth Vat, your mother) received your letter. We were very happy we got the message that you're still alive. We haven't heard from you for more*

*than ten years. Your mother and I were very worried about
you. We had no idea of what happened to you. About us, we
returned to our native country. I had been sick for many
years. Your younger sisters and brothers are still in school,
but Su had stopped going to school now.*

All together, you have five sisters and brothers:
1-Kuth Soeun (F)
2-Kuth Su (M)
3-Kuth Korng (F)
4-Kuth Woeun (M)
5-Kuth Wuy (M)
Woeun and Wuy were just born.

*When you receive our letter, don't forget to send us your
picture. Your brothers and sisters miss you very much.*

*Before I say "Good Bye," I would like to wish you a
peaceful life. Good Bye.*

Soeuth had sent three letters to Cambodia in 1990 and early
1991. In the fall of 1991, a postman who worked in the Battambang City post office had noticed an envelope postmarked from
the U.S.A. and addressed simply to Kompong Chhlang Village,
Cambodia. On the outside of the envelope, Soeuth had written
in Khmer: "Whoever sees this letter has permission to open it."
The postal worker opened it. The letter inside listed several first
names, but no last names, and promised an undisclosed sum of
money if the reader of the letter could find these missing people.
A few days later, the postman wandered down the dusty road
that cut through Kompong Chhlang—a village six miles or so
outside Battambang City—and asked all the people he saw if they
knew a man named Saut. An old, wizened man stood smoking
on the porch of his hut. When asked the question, he answered:
"Yes, I know him—he's my brother." The man then told the
postman that Saut lived in a village a few miles away called
Ausroulab.

An old Cambodian proverb says, "To live is to hope." But
when the object of that hope seems so improbable, hope flinches

in the harsh light of reason. Soeuth never spoke of his family to any of us, never told us he was searching for them.

For years my brother never knew his family name. His legal last name, the name he had given the interviewer in the Thai refugee camp, the name that had, over the years, calcified in place after his first name, was "Saut"— his father's first name. Now he stood in the kitchen of his apartment in Burlington, Vermont, the members of his family smiling at him from a photograph, and for the first time in his life, he said his name, his real name.

"Kuth," he whispered. "Kuth Soeuth."

When Soeuth called Mom and Dad and told them that his family was alive, Mom said it was wonderful and Dad said it was amazing. They were happy for him, they said. They wanted to see the photo. Then they joked: don't forget about us.

They did not tell him that they were skeptical. They did not tell him they suspected he was the victim of an international piracy racket seeking to profit from American refugees desperate to find their estranged families. They had heard of such scams from refugee advocates and were understandably circumspect. Or maybe the scheme was less orchestrated—this postal clerk might have rustled up a haphazard collection of nearby villagers, shot their photo and sent it back to Soeuth, and now awaited his monetary reward. My parents had another reason to be doubtful: in Cambodia, it is culturally improper for a child to look into the faces of adults, even his or her own parents. What if Soeuth didn't remember their faces?

Mom told me all of this over the phone while I stood in my boxers, twenty years old, barefoot, on the cold linoleum floor of my dorm room on an overcast April afternoon. It had been just a few weeks since I had stumbled out of the murky crisis of my last relationship. I had just declared a double major, theater and political science, and was directing a campus production of *A Streetcar Named Desire*. The only other sounds, aside from her controlled voice, were the hiss of a street-sweeper truck outside and a radiator's stuttering tick.

"I always wondered," she said. "I always wondered what really became of his family."

"Yeah," I said. "It's amazing."

"It's a miracle," she said and added: "If it's really them."

"Yes," I said.

"If it's them," she said again.

"If it's them," I agreed.

I felt like I had been kicked in the stomach. I had always assumed that Soeuth's family was long dead, and, over the years, that assumption had hardened in my mind into fact. Mom might as well have told me that my grandma Dot, who had died when I was two, had stopped by for a glass of iced tea with Dad on the pool patio. Part of me, a seething, jealous part, wished that it *was* all a mistake. If these people were not his family and were just out for his money, then he would never abandon us.

I realized that I knew very little about Soeuth's life in Cambodia. It seemed strange that I'd never really considered this before. When we were older, I never asked him about it, because I figured he wanted to forget it. The stories that I heard when I was eleven, twelve, thirteen years old were now mostly grainy and unreliable, like old, moiré film clips. The only one I remembered clearly, the one I had read in his high school journal, was about his father. It baffled me utterly how he could forgive someone who had whipped and beaten him and then handed him over willingly to slave masters—but instead of saying this to Mom, I asked her if she thought he might go back to Cambodia for good. There was a pause before she said: "I don't know, Adam. I don't know what he wants."

I went for a drive. Grandpa Ken had conferred upon me his old Subaru hatchback, and it was not a good car to drive when you were anxious, not the kind of car you could gun through yellow lights. Dave had literally driven it underwater the previous summer, when Creek Road was flooded: he said he had estimated the water level at only a foot or so, but when he had stopped the car and opened the door to check, the water had spilled in up to the dashboard. Whenever I turned, East Middlebury River water still lapped at some hidden compartment above the back bumper.

I drove along a snaky road outside Auburn, the water sloshing at every swerve in the road, until I reached Lake Auburn, a man-made reservoir where boats and swimming were prohibited. I pulled into a sandy parking lot a few feet from the shore and canopied with spruce branches. I sat there in the Subaru and watched the dusky lake. There was a momentary solace, it seemed, in the enclosure of the spruce trees and the chirping of the crickets.

Soeuth had padded into my life over eight years ago, but I hadn't talked to him much in the past two years, and neither of us knew much about the other's life. What gnawed at me more than anything else was the dawning understanding that he needed something no one in my family could give him. I feared that if he returned to Cambodia, found his family and reclaimed his old life, a part of me would be erased. I wanted to call him, but I guessed that his voice would be different now, not the voice of my brother.

When it became too dark to see the water, I started the car and drove back to campus. I went to the library and plodded downstairs to the audiovisual room and borrowed a copy of *The Killing Fields* and a set of earphones.

I sat in a small, dark, video-viewing booth. It had been eight years since I had watched the film, but I understood a lot more now. I had read about Cambodia since then: William Shawcross's *Sideshow*, Gail Sheehy's *Spirit of Survival*, newspaper articles. I knew that as much as a quarter of Cambodia's population had been wiped out in a single decade by American carpet bombing and a civil war, but mostly by Pol Pot's Khmer Rouge.

About halfway through the film, I reached the scene in which Dith Pran, the film's protagonist, stands barefoot in the mud in a Khmer Rouge labor camp among hundreds of other slaves, listening to a man on a hill speak somberly through a megaphone. He was talking about Angka. I knew that term, knew it was the

Khmer Rouge organization. During the Khmer Rouge regime, it was commonly said that Angka had the eyes of a pineapple, meaning Angka could see you at all times, meaning your brother or sister or cousin could be a pair of Angka's eyes, meaning you could trust no one. Constant fear each day for three and a half straight years—how could anyone take that? How could you will yourself to life each morning when death surrounded you?

There was a shot of Dith Pran catching a lizard and pinging it on the head with his finger to kill it and then putting it in his pocket, and I wondered if Soeuth had eaten that kind of lizard. Dith Pran had welts on his legs and on his face, and I recalled seeing Soeuth's scars and realized I had never learned how he got them. When Dith Pran tripped and fell into a watery pit of corpses, I wondered how many corpses Soeuth had stepped over and then remembered his friend Phun's remarks after seeing the movie: *Movie no show smell . . . Movie no show maggot.*

What the movie did show, a world of ceaseless savagery and hopelessness, was a world my brother had escaped, and now one to which he would probably return. I knew that the Khmer Rouge had long ago been driven into the mountains along the Thai-Cambodian border and that the country was no longer a giant death camp. But I also knew that it was wounded and stunted and impoverished, and I couldn't imagine anyone ever wanting to live there, especially after more than nine years living here, in the U.S.

Dith Pran had spoken at Bates the first semester of my freshman year. I missed it; the night he spoke I had been at a Democratic Socialists of America meeting. I had joined the DSA the first week of college, when they were luring people by passing out copies of Noam Chomsky's *What Uncle Sam Really Wants*. I felt the sharp tug of regret during a meeting several months later. Our leader, a blond, bespectacled, political-science major with a trust fund, had gathered us in a circle on the floor of the student lounge to tell us that corporate oil was evil and must be boycotted. After adjourning the meeting, he trotted outside and stepped into his BMW and sped off to the mall.

We had marched on Washington in January of 1991 to protest the Gulf War, and the trust-fund Socialist leader had walked alongside me, just as we were passing the White House on Pennsylvania Avenue, and had said, "Hey, dude, it's your turn." He had handed me a pole to which was affixed a large, gold-and-red hammer and sickle flag. I had accepted it reluctantly. As dark-suited Secret Service men standing on the lawn of the White House had snapped pictures of me, I had realized that the bastards who had brutalized my brother had worshipped this flag. I had dodged out of the march, set the flag on the curb and escaped into Lafayette Park.

As I rewound *The Killing Fields,* this moment flickered lingeringly. In the past year and a half, I had been taught how to paint my ideas of the political world in the gilded abstract, to hatch theories and discourses and hypotheses, to delineate and deconstruct paradigms and hegemonies, to lunge at history by employing the prism of one French philosopher or another. But now, staring at the empty screen in the library booth, I knew that my brother had been touched more intimately by history than anyone else in my life. I ejected the tape and returned it and walked to Dunkin' Donuts and fell asleep there, facedown on a Formica-covered table.

On Friday afternoon, as the weather began, noticeably, to limp toward spring, I decided to drive home for the weekend. Over a dinner of Mom's pork chops, we pointedly did not talk about Soeuth's family. I tried to deflect Mom's concern about the major I'd declared. We discussed Dave's decision to file just one college application, to the University of Vermont. Mom raised the possibility that maybe it was time to think about selling Dave's horse, Sham, because Dave and Dad were still lugging water out to the barn for him each morning, even though no one rode him anymore.

After dinner, Dave sequestered himself in the garage to sharpen the collection of swords and knives he had forged from scrap metal in the Seeleys' dump, and Dad shut himself in the living room to listen to Aaron Copland through his headphones.

I asked Mom if she still had Soeuth's file—the one Mr. Silverstein had given her on the night of Soeuth's arrival some eight years ago. A few lines creased her forehead, and her features narrowed. She nodded slowly and padded over to the file cabinet. After peeling back a few thick layers of files, she pulled out a worn manila envelope. Here you go, she said and strolled off toward the living room.

I brewed a cup of coffee and poured a little Baileys in it and sat at the breakfast-nook table to examine Soeuth's file. Inside the envelope there were two black-and-white photos of him. One showed a small boy standing outside in the bright sun, his tiny brow wrinkled with concern, holding up what looked like a piece of fiber board with his name written in capital letters below his refugee ID number, T-800 862. In the other, he looked older and wore the glassy, unconcerned gaze of a man condemned to death. In this photo, a big white tag with the number "1" on it is pinned to his collar, as he stands in a well-lit, inside place, holding up a placard bearing the following letters and numbers: KDO1127; on the wall behind him, the following letters and numbers are affixed: 29SEP82.

Beneath the photos was his plastic refugee identification card. Beneath that were four 500 riel notes, one of which was torn in half. The notes lay on top of a beige photocopy of a faded, six-page report. I read the report. It contained the observations and conclusions an aide worker had gathered on Soeuth. The date of the interview was listed as October 11, 1982, about one month before Soeuth came to America. His address was listed as 3I 40. His date of birth: 1969; I chuckled because I knew his real birthday was approximately September 7, 1968.

I remembered then that, on what we had thought had been his eighteenth birthday, Soeuth had laughed while he had eaten his cake and told us all what his real age was. He was really nineteen. He had explained that he had lied to the interviewer in the Thai camp, telling him that he was a year younger, because this would increase his chances of settling with an American family—and Grandpa had shouted, gee whiz, Suit, you coulda voted last year, and Soeuth had smiled and said, nah, not me, Grandpa, I don't know who to vote for.

In the Thai aide worker's report, under the heading "Life in Cambodia before 1975 (Home village; province; siblings; occupation of parents, etc.)," the following was written:

> He was born at Chlong Village (Battambang Province). His house was with wood and with tinned roof. It had 3 rooms in the house. One was his grandmother's sleeping, other was the kitchen and other one was the family's sleeping room. The family usually took a bath at the river near their house. All the family usually sleep in that room. There were betal nut trees and some banana trees around the house. The village located at the countryside: It was about 15 kilometers from the national road.
>
> Father's name = Saut was a rice farmer.
>
> Mother's name = Vaht was also a rice farmer.
>
> He says he was the first child in the family. He was too young for going to school. So he only stayed at home to take care of his youngest siblings. He remembered that, he usually went to the farm when he was young. They had one pair of oxen, chickens, ducks, pigs, etc.
>
> He says he had a good time with his entire family. His village was a big one.

Under the heading "Life from 1975 until arrival in Thailand (Details of movements, activities, etc.)," the interviewer has written:

> When Khmer Rouge governed in 1975. Khmer Rouge placed his parents into the rice cooperative and then Khmer Rouge put him in the junior workforce. They forced him to dig ditches and build the dams. Khmer Rouge did not give enough food to eat. Merely 1 laddle of ricesoup a day. Khmer Rouge usually descriminated. Sometimes Khmer Rouge detained in the children team. They remained there until Vietnamese's

invasion. He fled to Thailand with other people by crossing the forest and climbing up the mountains. It took him for 2 weeks of walking across the forest. He says, he saw a lot of people were killed by starvation. He did not have enough food to eat on the way to Thailand. Then he arrived to MARK-MOUN camp.

Under the heading "Relatives (Where are they now? Any news and/or attempts to make contacts?)," the following was written:

Had never receive the news from family.

And beneath "Important relationships (Children and adults, in Thailand and/or other countries)," it said simply:

None at all.

The aide worker concluded:

He is obviously a very nice child. He will need a lot of loves and encouragement to enable him for adjusting to the new environment.
He is quiet and also gentle.

The report was signed:

Tim Sophath, 11th October, 1982.

On Saturday morning Dave woke me up early. We drove up to visit Soeuth in Burlington. When we pulled into the driveway, we could see his gaunt, shirtless form bent under the hood of an eviscerated Camaro on blocks in his backyard. A leather armchair sat on the damp brown grass next to his car. There was a six-pack of Coors in the chair. As we stepped out of the Subaru, his oil-smeared face emerged from the Camaro with a wide smile.

"Hey," we said in unison.

"Come up," he called. He dropped his oil rag and raced up his fire-escape stairs, taking three or four steps at a time. The apartment was unusually neat; his bed made, kitchen free of scattered Ramen wrappers and beer cans, carpets newly vacuumed. Soeuth went into the kitchen, and Dave and I sat on his collapsed leather couch, next to the bikini poster of Heather Locklear I had given him in high school.

"Still got that damned poster," I said to Dave.

"Yeah, well, hey, Heather Locklear's not bad."

"I guess not."

Soeuth brought some Cokes and a bowl of Doritos. He placed them down on the floor and said, "Eat, you guys," and then retrieved from his room the thin, portentous envelope from Cambodia. He sat cross-legged on the floor and carefully removed a color photo, heavily smudged with fingerprints.

"Here." He handed me the photo. "That's my family."

Dave and I studied the photo. Soeuth had carried it everywhere with him, creasing its corners. There were maybe a dozen people in the photo, grouped in front of a hut, smiling in the bright sun. I looked at the sharp, serious faces for a resemblance of my brother. It was there in the strong cheekbones, the hard eyes.

"So, who's who here?" I finally asked.

He rose and sat on the arm of the couch. "That's my father." He pointed to a gaunt man with a shriveled face. "That's my mother"—his finger slid over to a slim woman in a sarong, her hands on the shoulders of a small child.

"Who's that?" Dave asked, pointing to the kid.

"My cousin, I guess."

"And that?" I pointed to a boy-man who stood next to Soeuth's father.

"That's my brother."

"Oh," we both said.

In November 1992, when he was twenty-four, Soeuth arrived in Phnom Penh, Cambodia, setting his feet on the ground from which he had fled almost fourteen years earlier. As he plodded down the foldout aluminum steps onto the tarmac, with that familiar, dry wooden heat boxing him in, all that had separated him from this place, all that had made him unafraid, fluttered suddenly away like geese from a gunshot. His suitcase, crammed with clothing and gifts for his family, bent his body toward the pavement. As he approached the terminal of Pochentong International Airport—a flat, empty building, not unlike Burlington's roller-skating rink—he watched for signs of sudden movement behind the glass, for the silhouette of a threat inside, and thought: *I have to be careful. I hope I don't get robbed. I hope nobody kills us.*

He was glad, at that moment, that he had not traveled alone. His roommate and long-time friend Sokkhan had accompanied him. They had driven together to Lowell, Massachusetts—the largest Cambodian-American enclave on the East Coast—where Sokkhan knew a travel agent. A few weeks before they had left, Dad had given them both vaccinations for hepatitis and typhoid and medication to prevent malaria. On the plane, Sokkhan had promised Soeuth, "When we get to Phnom Penh, we're gonna have fun."

A few years earlier, Sokkhan also had sent a letter to his old village, located along the Cambodia-Vietnam border, asking for information about his father. With the letter he had enclosed a photo of himself and his first American foster mother, Mrs. Sheldon. Several months later, he had received a response from his father, asking if that pretty white lady in the photo was his wife. Sokkhan's father, a near invalid who walked with two canes, had told his son how he had cheated death when Khmer Rouge soldiers had tried to force him into the back of a flatbed truck packed with other prisoners but, at the last minute, had left him by the roadside.

Soeuth and Sokkhan were picked up at the airport by Sokkhan's stepsister, Kim, and her friend, also named Kim. Sokkhan's father lived in the countryside on the outskirts of the city, so they stayed with Sokkhan's stepsister, in her narrow, low-ceilinged apartment across from the city's frenetic central market. They wandered through French-colonial Phnom Penh—a city Soeuth had never before seen and knew only from stories—stunned by its busyness, by the motorbikes swarming through narrow streets, braiding into dizzying knots of noise and speed; by one-legged old men and orphans who clambered along the crumbling sidewalks, praying their hands, begging for money or cigarettes; by the skeletal frames of new buildings going up and the whine of their construction. The city was still militarily occupied, although this time not by the Khmer Rouge. Bright white United Nations trucks were ubiquitous, and helmeted soldiers in camouflage suits ambled through the streets, disappearing into the shadowy refuge of hotel bars. The city was recovering from old wounds, and at the same time, it seemed, bracing for new ones.

Because he had once fought in the army of the legendary Cambodian freedom fighter, Heng Samrin—who had helped the Vietnamese oust the Khmer Rouge—Sokkhan was a self-appointed expert on all things Cambodian. On their first night in Phnom Penh, they wandered into a bar near Sokkhan's stepsister's apartment, and as they sipped their pints, Sokkhan became suddenly patronizing, and Soeuth wished then that he had come to Cambodia alone. You don't know anything, Sokkhan intoned, and you must listen to me. I know people here in Phnom Penh, because I was in the army. I know what's going on. You don't know nothing—without me, you are nothing. Soeuth cast a few sharp, silent glances at his friend, who, in all the years he had known him, had never acted like this.

After two days in Phnom Penh, Soeuth awoke at 5:30 A.M., when the sky was serrated with lavender, and hired a car and driver to transport him nearly three hundred miles to Battambang, the northwestern city, close to his parents' village and also to areas of traditional Khmer Rouge presence. In the time since he had fled Cambodia, the Khmer Rouge had holed up in the northern and northwestern reaches of the country. They were still waging a low-level guerrilla war against the government, kidnapping and killing villagers and tourists in regions they still controlled. Although there was an uneasy peace in many of the cities and towns, the echo of gunfire still disturbed parts of the countryside. Some former Khmer Rouge soldiers had returned to their old villages and, in some cases, lived next door to their surviving victims.

The car ferried him north over a pocked dirt road, Cambodia's National Route 5, a segment of which he had traveled on foot almost fourteen years earlier. The road cleaved the vast rice fields. There were many huddled clusters of roadside shanties under which dogs and chickens and naked children scampered. Spindly coconut trees poked up beneath the low, mandarin Cambodian sunset that wrapped around the horizon. He saw parts of his country he had never before seen, and wondered, as these strange people and places passed him, if this was his home.

He arrived in Battambang in the evening and rented a hotel room for $15 a night. It was a big room with a black-and-white checkered floor, ants that crawled in a neat line where the wall met the floor, and a bathroom that was separated from the main room by a plywood stall door on loose hinges. There was a small refrigerator which he stocked with about a dozen cans of Tiger beer and some grapes. There was a ceiling fan, an air conditioner and a small wooden table with two chairs. There were two big double beds. His driver, a tall, quiet man, slept in the room that night, splayed across the sheets, while Soeuth slumped over the table, sipping anxiously at his beer.

As the dark condensed in the corners of the room, Soeuth sat against his bedboard, sweating, gulping beer and watching Cambodian soap operas. He wandered onto the balcony a few times, beer can in hand, and cast his gaze into the patchy darkness, wondering when he would feel something. After the city's sounds dwindled to the buzz of an occasional motorbike, he turned off the TV and lay on his bed, listening to the staccato prattle of the geckos until sleep doused him.

When morning rayed through the blinds, warming the room, he and the driver ambled down to a noodle shop across from the market and wordlessly slurped their soup, until the driver said he was going to rustle up someone who needed a ride back to Phnom Penh. The driver unfolded himself from his chair, nodded and smiled his thanks at Soeuth, who had picked up the tab, and trotted across the street back to his car. Soeuth then shambled out into the dusty heat and hailed a motorbike driver to whom he gave $20 and the address of his family's hut in Ausroulab, their village, and dispatched him there to fetch them.

He waited in his room, blasting the air conditioner, pacing back and forth, trying to remember some stories, some happy moments he could share with them. These people were shadows in his mind, and he wondered if they would accept him. As a cousin, brother and son. As a Cambodian.

An hour later, he sat against the bedboard, chain-smoking Marlboros and watching a Cambodian news program. The newscaster was talking about the upcoming United Nations–sponsored elections. Every ten minutes or so, he would go out to the balcony hoping he could spot his family on the street. It was a bright day. A white United Nations truck was parked across the street, the sun flashing off its rippled aluminum sides. Children on bicycles weaved by, their slurred silhouettes cast against the beige buildings.

As he leaned on the railing, sucking deeply on a cigarette, a man on the neighboring balcony, wearing a suit and a wreath of gold chains, shot his hand over at him and said: "Nice to meet you. We have both come a long way."

Soeuth had seen this man on the plane from JFK; he shook his hand.

Grinning in a wide, businesslike way, the man introduced himself as Ratsmey. He asked Soeuth if he had come here to see his family, and Soeuth nodded, stomping out his cigarette. The man said he might he able to help him. He was a courier, he explained, who made monthly trips to Battambang to deliver dollars to the relatives of Cambodian Americans. He lived in Lowell and charged a fifteen percent commission for his services that covered his airline ticket and hotel and earned him a modest profit. He reached into his breast pocket and extracted a business card, which he handed to Soeuth, and told him to think about it when he returned to the States. Soeuth said, thank you, he would.

About noon, he ventured to the balcony and saw the motorbike driver to whom he'd given money pull up in front of the hotel. A wooden cart was hitched to the motorbike with seven people packed into it. They were wearing sarongs, rumpled old shirts and blue-and-white checkered *khramas* wrapped loosely around their necks. Soeuth waved to them, but as they tumbled out of the cart, peering up at him, they did not wave back. He strode into the room and stood by the TV, his eyes fixed on the faded brass doorknob, wondering if these people were truly his family.

A minute later, he heard nervous chatter outside his door. His fingers slid around the doorknob, and slowly he pulled the door open. He peered into the hall, scanning a cluster of whispering shadows, until he focused on a pair of glinting, wary eyes set back in a hard, leathery face. They were the eyes of his father.

He stepped back, and they all came into the room, smiling diffidently, praying their hands. Soeuth didn't know if he should hug them or not, so he prayed his hands, too.

He approached his father, a taut, white-haired, hatchet-faced man, and said: *"Sook s'bai dey!"*—how are you?

"Sook s'bai," his father said—fine.

They all stood timidly in their ripped and grimy village clothes and rubber flip-flops, forming an awkward circle around him. He let his eyes travel over their faces until he knew who everyone was. He recognized his mother, who, like his father, was now in her mid-forties, although she looked older and feeble, as though a sudden loud noise could knock her down. Soeun, the older of his two sisters, with whom he had always fought as a kid, was now twenty-two and had a sharp, pretty face and a sturdy, competent way about her. His younger sister, Korng, had been a toddler the last time he had seen her; she was now seventeen and resembled him more than anybody else, with her round face and strong cheekbones. Su, his brother, now nineteen, was a serious, sinewy man; he looked nothing like the shy little boy Soeuth dimly remembered. He did not recognize the two quiet, skinny boys who stood next to his mother, their hands folded together tight in front of them. These were Woeun and Wuy, his younger brothers, who had been born long after he had been separated from the family and were now seven and twelve, respectively.

He motioned for them to sit on the beds. He opened the refrigerator, grabbed bunches of grapes and passed them around the room. He hoisted the suitcase onto the bed and snapped it open. The clothes in the suitcase—as many as sixty T-shirts, dress shirts and pants, which he had collected from the hand-me-down bin of a church in Burlington—were not folded but rolled up tight like newspapers. He pried a brand-new pair of Nikes out of the suitcase and set them on the bed and raised his eyebrows at Su to tell them that the sneakers were his. He then reached deeper into the bundles of clothes and pulled out three boxes containing jewelry worth over $1,300. He handed Soeun and Su boxes containing gold chains and Korng a box of gold earrings. He told them how much the chains and earrings were worth, to let them know how much he had spent. As they hesitantly drew out the jewelry, smiled, blushed and examined their new gifts with an uncomfortable caution, he unzipped his duffel bag and plucked out $1,500 in twenties and fifties, which he gently tucked into his mother's palm; she cracked a tiny smile and said nothing and held the wad of money as delicately as a timid child who has just received her first birthday present.

Woeun and Wuy stood over the suitcase and eyed its contents. Soeuth wanted to make it clear that he was not merely showing them these clothes but offering them as gifts, so he flipped the suitcase over and dumped out the shirts and pants and said in Khmer: "Whatever you want, take it."

Although he had regularly spoken Khmer with Sokkhan over the past few years, he was nervous about how he might sound. His family, too, was noticeably anxious, huddled together in the presence of this ostensibly rich and powerful American, not knowing how to act or what to say.

As everybody fondled the new clothes, Soeuth sat next to his mother on the bed, his hands still in his lap. His mother smiled quietly, her weary, wrinkled face, her soft dark eyes, telling him a thousand things.

She stared into her lap. "I didn't know," she finally said. "We didn't know what happened to you."

Soeun turned to him, her ponytail brushing against her shoulder, and told him she had had two dreams about him just months before the family received the news that he was alive. "I dreamed that somebody tied you up to a tree," she said excitedly. "And then later, I dreamed they untied you and let you down from the tree."

"I'm glad they untied me," Soeuth said.

When the veil of evening extinguished the day's heat, Soeuth ordered in some fried chicken and fried rice with fish sauce, and everybody sat on the floor and around him on the bed, spooning the food, pitching questions at him. What was America like? Who did he live with when he first got there? What were his American parents like? Was he married yet? He was single, he said, didn't even have a girlfriend. He told them America was cold and that all the people, even poor people, drive cars. He told them about our family, told them that his American dad was a doctor—an announcement that widened all eyes in the room—and that they had a big house with twelve rooms, but that now he lived with his friend Sokkhan in an apartment that had only four small rooms.

"You must be rich," Soeun said.

"No." Soeuth shrugged. "I fix trucks. I'm not rich."

His father's raspy voice floated from where he sat hunched over on the bed. "You turned out well," he said. "I'm proud of you."

Soeuth smiled in response to this comment, his mouth curling into a self-conscious crescent, his eyes hidden under the ridge of his lowered brow.

He then wrested a photo album out of the suitcase and flipped it open to a photo of our family and held it open so everyone could see.

The photo was taken by a church photographer when I was fifteen. Mom and Dad sit in the foreground, looking piously uncomfortable; Dave, Soeuth and I stand behind them, Dave and me leaning forward, as though we are about to lose our balance. Soeuth, who is standing between us, is smiling casually and is the only one who doesn't appear remotely inbred.

He guessed at his parents' internal questions as they examined these photos and scrutinized the faces of these pasty people posed around their son. Who are these people that have replaced us? What did they do to make our son into an American? What strange rituals did they compel him to undergo? Is he more like them now than like us?

There were moments that evening, when Soeuth and his father and brother Su lit up cigarettes and smoked wordlessly, and his mother and sisters and younger brothers slouched on the floor, their legs folded beneath them, waving off mosquitoes but otherwise remaining still—moments when everyone was ensconced in a heavy silence. All the things that separated him from them were too vast to allow them to live, that night, in the same world.

They all slept in his room on the beds and the floor. That was how the members of his family had always slept, together in one room. That was how Soeuth, as a child, had slept, curled like a comma on the bamboo floor. I can see them on that night, huddled together in the safety of a wordless dark, praying up all their devotions, all their unspoken questions, to the kind, impassive face of Lord Buddha.

In the morning, after a breakfast of noodle soup at an open-air place on the Sangker River, they returned directly to the hotel room. His family were country people and were intimidated by the city people with their wristwatches and their cars and their sidelong glances, and so did not want to be seen in public.

After Soeuth flicked on the air-conditioning and pulled on the ceiling fan, his family twisted around from their places on the beds to face him or plopped down on the floor in front of him. They all listened as his mother told him in halting whispers what had happened to the family after the Vietnamese had invaded Cambodia. When the fighting between the Khmer Rouge and the Vietnamese had edged toward their village, the Khmer Rouge had driven the family, with hundreds of other families, to a camp up north, on the Thai border. When the fighting had advanced to the border and the Khmer Rouge soldiers were besieged, the family had escaped and fled south. They had seen many orphans on the way, his mother said, and she had wondered if he, too, was an orphan. She had asked people, old neighbors she knew in the camp, if anyone had seen him. No one had. In the village, a few neighbors and relatives had said they had seen Soeuth but that he had left and they didn't know where he was. His mother's eyes filmed with tears when she said that she had believed he was dead.

Soeun and Su and Korng then asked Soeuth what had happened to him when the Vietnamese invaded. How did he escape the Khmer Rouge? Did he go back to the village? He glanced around at his mother and father, his brothers and sisters, still tingling with shock, still not believing that they could all sit in the safety of a hotel room and share their stories. He told them what had happened to him during the Vietnamese invasion, that he, too, had become part of a caravan driven north by the Khmer Rouge; as he spoke, he mused to himself on the possibility that he and his family could have been, at some point in time, part of the same caravan. He relayed his haphazard journey with hundreds of others, always looking for their faces. He told them he had returned to the village and waited there for them, but they had never come. His attention was fixed on their staring faces as he told his story. He realized then that he had probably missed them by a matter of months or even weeks—they must have returned to the village shortly after he had left for Thailand. He said that when he stayed in a Thailand refugee camp, he had told a camp interviewer that he hadn't received news about his family for years—and then, he said, he was sent to America.

They sat quietly after his story, as if hypnotized by the hum of the ceiling fan, their eyes trained on private pieces of wall and floor, until Soeun said abruptly: "Brother, I love you. And I've been missing you for all this time." Soeuth, uneasy with any emotional declarations, simply nodded.

Then there was silence again, until his father spoke.

"I sent you away to the camp," he said, looking at the space on the floor between his feet. "I sent you away, and I was wrong."

Soeuth sat still in the wake of his father's comment, his back curved up, his hands limp in his lap. He studied the pattern of black-and-white checkered tiles. "You didn't know," he finally muttered.

"Soeuth," his father said with sudden urgency, leaning over and clasping his son's hand softly between the callused pads of his fingers. "We need you now. We need you to support the family."

For years the knowledge of his father's seemingly unthinkable act had stoked an anger within Soeuth that was eclipsed only by the guilt of his own survival. The revelation that his family was alive did not erase the guilt, only reshaped it, etched it deeper— he was an American with a car and a job and a future; his family were peasants whose eyes widened at the sight of a pair of long pants. His father had acknowledged what he had done, though he had not apologized or told his son why. But now Soeuth did not feel he could ask him for those things. When he looked into his father's wizened face, a face puckered and shrunk by years in the sun, his anger vanished altogether.

"Now that I've found you," he said, "it's a different story. My life is changing. I will support the family."

For the next several days they all stayed in the city, spending most of their time in the hotel room. On one of those days Soeuth's cousins Khan and Pake, both his father's nephews, swung by. He gave them each $50.

Khan, a blithe, ropy man who wore the same torn Harley-Davidson tank top day in and day out, had a motorbike and often served as a one-man taxi service for people in the village. He was six or seven years older than Soeuth, but, during the Pol Pot Time had been allowed to remain with his parents.

Pake, a stocky, stubbled man whose slow grin betrayed a reassuring forthrightness, had not been so lucky; he was separated from his parents by Khmer Rouge soldiers on the same spring day in 1976 when they had taken Soeuth, and had worked, for a few months, at Wat Slar Gram, the same slave camp where Soeuth was first sent. He was also several years older than Soeuth, and after the Vietnamese invasion in 1979, had fought, like Sokkhan, as a soldier in Heng Samrin's army. Pake had picked on and taunted Soeuth when they were kids before the Pol Pot Time, but on this trip he would become his confidant, the one on whom Soeuth would rely for information and counsel. Pake told him that everybody in Ausroulab was struggling and that its families had nothing except their rice crops. He said that the villagers still feared the return of the Khmer Rouge but advised him not to bring up the topic of Pol Pot or the Khmer Rouge with anybody outside the family. You never knew who might still have relatives serving in the Khmer Rouge and who might turn on you.

One morning Soeuth brought Pake, Khan and Su to a noodle restaurant across from the city's central market. It was an upscale, air-conditioned place with potted plants, waiters in suits and bow ties and settings with napkins and chopsticks—a place where local businessmen often dined and where country people were rarely, if ever, seen. His cousins and his brother donned the new dress shirts and long pants Soeuth had given them, and Su wore his new pair of Nikes; Pake and Khan did not have any shoes and so wore their rubber flip-flops. As they ate, Pake, Su and Khan, who were not used to chopsticks—in the countryside, everybody eats with spoons or his hands—drew some tart stares from waiters and other diners. They kept on asking Soeuth if he could afford this place, and he said yes, you are my family and I have money and don't worry.

He shared a smoke in his hotel room that afternoon with the head leader of Sangker district—home to Ausroulab—who had trekked out to see him at his father's behest. He was a short, dark-skinned, serious man who tucked a gun into his khakis and wore sunglasses at all times. He told Soeuth he would arrange for his protection while he stayed in the village, and since Soeuth's father had approached him and asked for his help, it would cost only around $25 a day. He said he had four men armed with AK-47s who would accompany Soeuth on any trip after dark or into questionable areas and would guard his family's hut during the night. Do not worry, he said, but we must watch our backs. Soeuth agreed.

He then asked the head leader to accompany him to the city police barracks, where he told another serious man in sunglasses his name and whereabouts for the next ten days and paid him $10 to sign and stamp a certificate verifying that he had noted these things. He wanted the police to know of his presence in Ausroulab, but also wanted the Sangker head leader to know he had registered with the police—he was a powerful man with a gun, and Soeuth didn't know him enough yet to trust him.

Before traveling to Ausroulab the next day, Soeuth took Pake, Khan, Su, Soeun and Korng shopping at the central market. He told them to pick out whatever they wanted and he would buy it for them. The market was a maze of plywood booths and glass display cases and fly-swarmed food carts and tall shelves stacked with blankets and bright clothing. It teemed with the alacritous palaver of bargaining between vendor and customer. Near-naked children scuttled along the walkways, tugging on shirtsleeves and holding out grimy palms. Soeuth and his relatives wandered into the heart of the market, their eyes flitting back and forth at the wristwatches and dresses and sunglasses and TVs and jade Buddha statuettes and bright blue and red children's tricycles. By the end of the day, Soeuth had bought a new bicycle for Soeun, a skirt for Korng, a dress shirt for Pake, a radio for Khan and a battery-powered stereo for Su.

Most everyone returned to Ausroulab later that morning, hauled by the same motorbike driver Soeuth had hired to fetch them. Su, Pake and Khan waited with Soeuth at the hotel for the Sangker head leader, who had vowed to accompany Soeuth to the village. But by noon the Sangker leader hadn't shown, and Soeuth was anxious. He had already smoked a pack of cigarettes since morning. Do not worry, Pake said, it's not dangerous during the day, and so Soeuth trotted down to the street and hailed three motorbike drivers. He, Pake and Su perched themselves on the hot leather seats, planting their feet on the metal footrests or the tailpipes. Pake had agreed to tote Soeuth's suitcase and hugged it close to his chest; Soeuth wedged his "money bag"—a small duffel bloated with over $6,000 in American and Cambodian money—between his legs. Khan then zoomed off into the sunny afternoon's promise, and their three motorbike drivers followed.

They rode through the faded labyrinth of Battambang's jaundiced buildings and rusted power-line towers and damp garage restaurants. Before long the city had disappeared into a trail of dust behind them, and the road broke out in foot-high swells that tossed Soeuth a few inches into the air at times and dropped him hard on his tailbone. The Sangker River meandered up on the left, the current only subtly wrinkling its rum-brown surface. When the road hooked suddenly away from the river, jungle burst forth on both sides of them, swarming with vines and winglike leaves and riddled with jagged patches of shadow. Occasionally a tin shanty or bamboo hut sprang from the lush darkness, and with it, a cacophony of yipping dogs and clinking pans and grunting pigs and odors of fish and burning things. Children in tattered clothes, or no clothes at all, gnawed on sugarcane stalk and gawked at them from hammocks. Some of them waved. Soeuth waved back, and a sadness seeped into him, because he used to be one of those kids, he used to live, like them, in a place where life is distilled to its simplest, most unmerciful form.

Khan pulled off to the side of the road across from the local open-air market, a tangle of bamboo and leaf-thatched booths where you could buy—among other things—bottled water, candy, gum, ice cream, makeup, batteries and cigarettes. Soeuth's, Pake's and Su's drivers stopped, and they all dismounted, and Soeuth folded a few thousand riel into the drivers' grease-smeared hands. Pake hoisted up Soeuth's suitcase with surprising ease, his muscles billowing under his skin. Soeuth slung his money bag over his shoulder like a backpack. The four of them plodded along a path that twisted through a thicket of shrubs and banana trees, Pake leading and Khan muscling his bike along the path after Pake. When the thicket broke suddenly, they stumbled down the steep clay bank of the Sangker, Soeuth and Khan negotiating Khan's bike over the slippery clay knuckles of the bank, and landed at its lip.

An old man perched in the front of a faded sampan, smiling absently in the hot sun. Pake crept onto the boat, lugging Soeuth's suitcase, and squatted at the front near the old man, wedging the suitcase between his knees. Khan wheeled his motorbike onto the middle of the boat, propped it up on its kickstands and knelt next to it. Soeuth and Su followed and dropped onto their haunches, while the old man stood up and clutched a rope that hung low over the river, suspended from a tree on each side. He pulled the boat, hand over hand, across the river, the knobs of his shoulders rolling fluently under his shirt. When they reached the other side, Pake trotted almost sprightly up the muddy bank, despite the suitcase, and Soeuth again helped Khan with his bike.

They walked single file on a path that ran along an irrigation canal, one similar to those Soeuth and Pake were forced to dig when they had been slaves in the Pol Pot Time. The rice fields undulated around them, pulsing with a quiet breeze. The path led them deeper into the sea of rice grass, turning sharply a few times, and eventually spilled into a clearing speckled with the shade of banana trees. As Soeuth trailed Pake, he caught glimpses of dun and blue and red clothing flashing through gaps in the leaves ahead.

Pake pushed through the leaves and then suddenly they were standing before a wall of wide eyes and smiling faces. Word had spread through the village that the Kuths' American son had come home, and there were at least thirty people gathered in front of his parents' hut. Soeuth stood where he was, stunned. They regarded each other for a few moments, until Pake trudged suddenly toward the hut, his heels slapping against his sandals. Soeuth padded after him. When he reached the hut, everyone slowly encircled him, staring with hopeful reverence, as though he were a high *Kru Khmer* who could heal the village's legions of sick, weak and old.

"*Sook s'bai dey?*" he said.

"*Sook s'bai,*" they murmured in tentative unison. They bowed and prayed their hands at him the way one would to show deference to a God King, the way you would pray before King Sihanouk, and he prayed back as solemnly, as steadily, as he could.

During his ten days in the village, Soeuth would develop a mild discomfort with the obeisance everyone displayed, with the way people bowed and bent their bodies before him. If he was sweating, a woman would run to fan him. If he looked thirsty, a child would fetch him a bottle of water. If he looked tired, he was offered his pick of bamboo bed frames on which to lie. Whenever everyone gathered in the evening, elderly villagers would squat on the ground or sit on the floor of a hut and insist that Soeuth take his seat in their place on a bed frame, bench or set of stairs.

His parents' hut, constructed of bamboo, coconut leaves and the occasional plank of plywood, sat on stilts a few feet off the ground and featured two modest levels, one for sleeping, the other for eating. Soeuth followed Pake up the bamboo ladder steps, feeling the eyes on his back, and set his money bag in a corner. It was small, low and hot inside. He trod slowly around the first level, wiping sweat off his brow, the bamboo squeaking and bowing under his feet. He noted his family's possessions collected in the corners: neatly folded mosquito nets, dirty blankets, some rusty tools, a few pots and pans and a few extra pairs of sandals.

The hut was typical for Ausroulab, a small village of three hundred families about seven miles outside Battambang City. It was the village where he and his family had moved when he was six, after Khmer Rouge soldiers had burned down their hut in Kompong Chhlang, the village where he had been born. In some neighboring villages, like Kompong Chhlang, well-to-do families resided in hardwood huts with tin roofs, but in Ausroulab, almost everybody lived in bamboo huts with grass and leaf-thatched roofs and walls. His parents were subsistence farmers, like the other inhabitants of Ausroulab, and rice was their sole crop. It was a daily struggle here to harvest enough food for everyone, but what people worried about most was not the threat of starvation. Pake told Soeuth that several families had been robbed in the past year, some at gunpoint, and Soeuth knew that robberies and even murders in the countryside were not matters with which the city police concerned themselves.

The low voices murmured through the dried-leaf walls, and he stood still, trying to decipher words. But the beating of his own heart swallowed all other sounds. He closed his eyes and felt his weight pressing upon this place and waited for Buddha to tell him what he should do. He turned, finally, and the bamboo yelped at him from beneath his feet, and he forced his feet to bring him back outside. He sat next to Pake on the top rung of the bamboo stepladder and smiled at these people who had congregated to see this man who had once been one of them but was now an emissary from that great place called America.

Pake plucked two cigarettes from his breast pocket and lit one for him. Soeuth inhaled deeply and blew a tight funnel of smoke into the azure sky. "I can't believe I'm back," he said. "I can't really see myself in Cambodia again."

A few people shuffled and stammered, "I can't believe you are alive . . ."

Soeun then asked Soeuth what he wanted to eat. He said, let's go get some chicken, and she said, we have chickens—they're healthy but hard to catch. As if to prove her point, she and a few cousins scared a hen from underneath someone's hut and scrambled after it. When the team of chicken chasers swelled to ten people, Soeuth rose and descended the steps. He noticed Su was chopping wood and asked if he could borrow his hatchet. Su handed it to him, and Soeuth gripped the handle hard enough to whiten his knuckles. When the hen flapped in front of him, squawking in distress, he wound up, as if pitching a baseball, and hurled the hatchet. The hatchet spun in a blur and landed squarely on the back of the hen's head, felling it instantly. Several people asked, how did you do that? He shook his head and said, I don't know. Pake then borrowed Su's slingshot, sighted another chicken and brained it with his first shot.

Soeun and her female cousins plucked the chickens and boiled them. Soeuth, his father, Su and Pake were the first ones to eat, sitting on the floor of the hut. The women served them the chicken and bowls of rice on a big tray. They ate the meat and the insides—livers, kidneys and intestines. Soeuth quipped: "This chicken's good, better than American chicken."

"Why is that?" Pake asked through a mouthful of rice.

"Because in America," Soeuth said, "they keep the chicken in a freezer."

After dinner, he sat on the top rung of the stepladder with Pake. As the heat thinned out and the sky curdled with low clouds, questions were volleyed at him, as if he were a professor who had just delivered some vexing philosophical lecture.

"Can you park the airplane on the cloud?" Khan asked. "And then the passengers can get out and walk around on the cloud?"

Soeuth smiled and shook his head. "No, that's not true," he said. "Who told you that?"

Khan dropped his gaze into his lap. "People told me," he said.

Lon, a cousin who had worked alongside Soeuth in a Khmer Rouge slave camp, offered: "You must have traveled to the ends of the earth."

Soeuth looked at Lon and said levelly: "There is no such thing as the ends of the earth." He cupped his hands around a ball of air. "The earth is round," he explained, "like a coconut."

At some point someone asked him if he thought about returning to Cambodia for good, to which he replied: "Maybe . . . Maybe I'll start a farm."

Upon hearing this, Pake tipped back whisky from a Sprite bottle and advised: "I think you should stay in America. America sounds good. It's no good here."

When the evening shed its salmon-colored light and people drifted back to their own huts, the Sangker head leader showed up with four men toting AK-47s. The bodyguards, all veterans of the Cambodian Royal Army and in their late thirties or early forties, nodded at Soeuth, then set their guns against the bamboo bed frame and lit up cigarettes.

One night, one of the bodyguards, a dark-skinned, smiling man in a T-shirt, asked Soeuth if he knew his nephew, Sut, who had told his uncle to say hello and claimed to have been a good friend of Soeuth's during the old days. When Soeuth heard that name, a memory sprang at him, like a cobra from the rice grass. Sut was the young Khmer Rouge guard who, more than fourteen years ago, had tied his hands behind his back, forced him to his knees and kicked and whipped him into near unconsciousness. He had been his neighbor before the Pol Pot Time and was the only Sut whom Soeuth had ever known.

"I know him." Soeuth kept his eyes trained on the nearby bushes. And then, ignoring Pake's admonition not to speak of the Pol Pot Time in mixed company, he added: "He's the guy that kicked me and whipped me during the Khmer Rouge. He was a Khmer Rouge leader."

A silence eddied around the bamboo bed frame where they all sat, and Soeuth was at its center, hunched over, breathing slowly. The bodyguard hung his head and fastened his gaze onto his gun's barrel, which winked at him in the moonlight.

Nothing more was said about Sut. But mention of the Khmer Rouge cropped up several times during Soeuth's visit. Soeuth learned that an uncle of his, one of his father's five brothers, had served as a high official for Angka during the Pol Pot Time and that a second cousin on his mother's side had recently joined Pol Pot's army and was now fighting with them against the Cambodian Royal Army up north. He was disheartened when he heard these things because he knew that, even now, he couldn't trust members of his own extended family, that these allegiances had tangled together over the years and could not be unraveled into easy strands of bad and good.

After drinking with the bodyguards on his first night in the village, he climbed to the upper level of the hut, where his father sat smoking. He unzipped his money bag, grabbed $500 in tens and twenties and handed the money to his father, who did not say thank you in words but with the crinkling of his face. Soeuth called Soeun into the hut and gave her $50 and told her to buy food with it at the market. He snapped his suitcase open and told his mother that the suitcase and everything in it now belonged to the family.

He slept on a camping pad under a mosquito net that his mother had tied to posts inside the hut. After his father had lit a kerosene lamp and placed it in the middle of the floor, he and his wife curled up separately on frayed gray blankets. Soeuth lay awake for a while, watching the shadows cast by the kerosene lamp twitch along the rough leaf walls like agitated ghosts.

He awoke to the squawking of chickens. Everybody else was already up. He brushed his teeth and washed his face with rainwater from a small aluminum cistern that sat in a shady patch of dirt next to the hut, then joined his brothers inside for noodle soup. Woeun and Wuy had shed their torn, mud-caked shorts and *khramas* and donned the clothes Soeuth had given them, dress shirts and long pants. They were good boys, his mother had said, obedient and hardworking. Wuy was attending the local village school but had already begun to work with his father in the rice fields and wouldn't stay in school for long. Woeun, who helped out with odd chores and was not yet in school, would soon join his older brother in the fields.

Soeuth's family seemed content despite the Spartan nature of their lives. They had, of course, never experienced the kind of life he enjoyed, and considering this, Soeuth succumbed to a slow, saturating sadness. They had never felt the exhilaration of a first car ride, watching trees and mountains scroll by. They had never felt that hop in the throat at seeing, for the first time, a building reach as high as a plane could fly. They had never watched big-screen movies or skied or gone to the dentist or leapt off a diving board or attended a concert or listened to new CDs on a Dolby stereo or played video games or celebrated a birthday with cake and ice cream or eaten lobster with melted butter— and probably never would. Although he knew he could not provide these things, he had dispensed money and bought clothing and other little items. But guilt still lurked and eventually conspired with loyalty and compassion, and soon he was giving not only to his family, but also to the people of Ausroulab.

He started to hand out five- and ten-dollar bills and five-thousand-riel notes to villagers. Since the annual per capita income in Cambodia was under $300 at the time, word ricocheted through the village that the American was donating dollars, and a few people would soon grow into a throng of thirty or more. He would perch on the top rung of the bamboo stepladder as they pressed into a tight semicircle in the dirt beneath him; or he would sit on the floor of the hut in a corner, and they would huddle around him. The bills were arranged next to him on the floor in neat stacks, like Monopoly money. When they received the money, they would pray their hands and bow their heads and say, may Lord Buddha protect you. A feeling of power warmed him like whisky in these moments as he thumbed the damp, wrinkled bills, elated by the fact that he could share with his people the wealth he had earned in an American truck-rental shop making $8.50 an hour.

On one afternoon when a crowd had formed around him inside his parents' hut, he balled up bills in his fist and tossed them to people beyond his reach. After he flung several bills at an old woman squatting about three yards away, his aunt Him—to whom he'd already given $50—raised her voice above the murmured prayers and blessings and asked the old woman to forgive her nephew for showing disrespect and explained that he was from America and didn't know any better.

Aunt Him was his father's sister. He had last seen her when he had escaped the Khmer Rouge and returned to the village; she had lolled under her hut, regarding him apathetically, and had told him she had nothing to give him—but he did not care about that now. A brawny, broad-shouldered woman, Him gnawed on a betel nut between her words and, unlike everybody else, never refrained from issuing her opinions and criticizing Soeuth. One evening, as everyone huddled in a circle on the floor of the hut fanning himself or herself and smoking, she suggested that Soeuth bring his parents and brothers and sisters back to America with him. He stared at a bamboo post as if Aunt Him had tacked a nail there and hung her suggestion on it for him to consider, and then glanced at his mother. His mother smiled carefully and said, we have a big family, too many people, we have too many friends and relatives here, we cannot all go to America.

Aunt Him's was not the only proposition that was presented to him. He went for a walk one evening after dinner with Soeun and his cousin SeeThoul on the path that ran along the irrigation canal and arrowed through the rice fields. Easily the most loquacious of his siblings and cousins, Soeun had, in a sense, become the head of the Kuth household. Since his father and mother were older and often sick, it was now her job to raise Woeun and Wuy. The roundness of her calves and the calluses on her hands were a testament to the fact that she worked in the rice fields along with the men, tending to the Kuth family crops.

"You were always bad," she said with a sly smile. "You were always beating me up! Scaring me!"

He smiled slowly and admitted: "I was bad."

Then she remarked rather suddenly, "You're not married," and looked over at SeeThoul and added: "SeeThoul is not married."

SeeThoul was pretty and liked to wear eye shadow, makeup and brightly colored dresses. Soeun had broached this subject before, but not in front of SeeThoul; and when she broached it today, SeeThoul smiled, embarrassed, and shot Soeuth a fugitive glance.

He was attracted to SeeThoul, liked her shyness and her smile, but when he entertained anything beyond an exchange of words with her, his heart kicked at his chest and his hands went cold. He regarded her and then looked away. "You want to marry me because I live in America," he said. "Because you think I have money." After a few wordless moments, filled with the sounds of their feet thudding on the path, he added: "You're my cousin."

Despite these harsh remarks, SeeThoul remained coy and sweet-tempered around Soeuth and usually helped Soeun prepare meals for him. Later in the week, she invited him to join her at a Buddhist festival at a temple several miles from the village.

The Sangker head leader and his father both urged him not to go to the festival. It's a dangerous area, they said, full of bandits and land mines. But he wanted to experience his religion in his home country—if only for one afternoon. They would have to leave early in the morning, so he, Soeun and Su slept at See-Thoul's family's hut across the river the night before. They awoke around 6 A.M. and met the Sangker head leader, who insisted that he and his gun accompany them, and walked to a local temple, where over two hundred people were gathered for the trip to the festival. Everyone clambered aboard wagons hitched to a fleet of five tractors. The tractors revved up and rolled down the pitted dirt road, plumes of black exhaust swirling behind them. In one wagon was a traditional Khmer band that played a meandering melody of flutes and gongs and drums. As the tractors lumbered through a series of villages, plying their way deeper into the jungles of northwestern Cambodia, more festivalgoers joined the caravan, hoisting themselves onto the crowded wagons. Eventually Soeuth hopped off and climbed onto the back of the Sangker head leader's motorbike.

As the caravan wound through the jungle, the revelers spied red-painted signs that bore crude pictures of a skull and cross-bones. The signs proclaimed, in both Khmer and English: "Danger! Mines!" Children clamored along the sides of the road, some holding their hands out for money or cigarettes or candy. Old women balancing huge baskets on their hips shuffled slowly in the hot sun.

They reached the festival at noon. Soeuth dismounted from the Sangker head leader's motorbike and found his sister and the others amidst the coursing crowd. They followed the other templegoers into a clay clearing walled with dark thickets of leaves and vines. Land-mine signs rimmed the clearing. The temple, an oblong bamboo shack with walls and a roof thatched of coconut leaves, sat flatly on the ground. The monks' dwellings, bamboo boxes on stilts, abutted the temple. As they neared the temple, SeeThoul told Soeuth that there was a Khmer Rouge military compound less than three miles from here. He nodded and his eyes jumped along the string of red-painted skulls on the land-mine signs and he thought: *I cannot step beyond the weeds. I cannot step into the jungle. What am I doing here? Why did I come so close to a Khmer Rouge camp?*

Soeuth followed SeeThoul and knelt with her on the lumpy clay floor of the temple amidst dozens of others who were suddenly bobbing their bodies forward and back and praying their hands toward the orange-robed monks who sat in a somber line at the front, before the Buddha shrine. A large, gold-painted statue of Buddha wearing a shiny cloth smiled faintly over the smooth, bowed heads of the monks, and beneath the big Buddha a regiment of little Buddhas stood amongst candlesticks and wilted flowers in gold vases and silver alms bowls and quiet-rippling plumes of incense. As the worshippers shuffled and folded their knees tighter beneath them, the monks chanted, their low, droning voices a waver of toneless sounds. Soeuth did not understand the chant, because it was not uttered in Khmer, but in Pali, the ancient language of Buddhist scripture. The monks had always been a mystery to him, and he had hoped this ceremony would open the door to their secrets. But as he sat there in this strange temple in this dangerous place and watched them and listened to their voices, they did not call to him, their chant did not tell him that he had come home.

The monks had chanted just for him once, his mother had said, when the family held a funeral service for him in the spring of 1984 at a similar temple. His father had written his name on a small sheet of paper and passed the paper to the head monk, who had placed it in an alms bowl. The monk had lit the paper on fire, so that Soeuth's name had burned at the altar of the Buddha. Raising a hacked-open coconut above the alms bowl, the monk had poured the coconut's pure water onto the ashes of his name, and the water flowed, delivering down the merit that could relieve his suffering and guide him toward reincarnation. The head monk had then prayed that his spirit would not become lost in a forest of demons but would find a safe place free from desire and seduction. Then all the monks had probably chanted the following:

> *All conditioned things are impermanent*
> *Their nature is to arise and decay.*
> *Having arisen they cease;*
> *In their stilling is happiness.*

The sun sets in the west, and in the west is death; the sun rises in the east, and in the east is new life—and so the alms bowl with the ashes of his name had been carried by the head monk and set on the steps of the temple's east side, in the hope that his spirit might there find reincarnation or nirvana.

It was hot in the strange temple, and so Soeuth quietly unfolded his knees and stood up and went outside. Soeun, Su and SeeThoul followed him as he elbowed his way through the crowd to the edge of the dance space. Soeuth did not dance. He stood with his sister and brother and cousin and tipped back bottled water and watched a ritual as mysterious to him as the chanting of the monks. The dancers moved like snakes in a trance, their wrists and arms rippling fluidly, their bodies flowing with the rhythms of the jungle or the sea. But it was hot outside, too, and so he sat in the shade of a banana tree and squeezed water from his plastic bottle and ate banana-tree soup that Soeun had bought for him.

After returning to Ausroulab, Soeuth wanted to do something to commemorate his visit. He borrowed a pair of bicycles from his parents' neighbors, and he and Pake loaded the bicycles on the sampan and the old man pulled them across the river and they peddled their way along the serpentine road into the city. They prowled through the rusty tangle of downtown Battambang until they found a video store. Soeuth told Pake to pick out some videos that everyone could watch. Pake stuffed the videos inside Soeuth's money bag and they hopped back on their bicycles and peddled to a TV-rental shop, where Soeuth paid the owner $30 to rent a TV, VCR, generator and PA system and to have it all delivered to the village. They returned to Ausroulab, and a few hours later, after the TV-rental-shop owner had personally transported the equipment via oxcart, Soeuth, Su, Kahn and Pake set up a makeshift cinema in a tract of yellowed grass. They rigged the TV and VCR to the generator and wired the TV to the PA system. Later that afternoon, over five hundred people swarmed onto the field, sitting on blankets or stools, to watch the videos, which included Chinese kung fu movies with Khmer voiceovers and a few locally produced Cambodian pictures. The night unfurled its purple in the sky, and Soeuth stood up near the TV and smoked and watched the panoply of eyes and teeth gleaming in the milky flashes from the screen. He didn't watch any of the movies himself. As the shrill sounds of kung fu and the undulant murmurings of laughter washed over the village, he sauntered back to his family's hut and spooned rice and sipped a few cans of Tiger beer and eventually fell asleep in the corner under the mosquito net his mother had strung up for him. When he awoke the next morning and stumbled back out to the field, the movies were still playing and the crowd was still transfixed.

The day he left the village was much like the day he had arrived. He stood before a cluster of about thirty people outside his family's hut. They smiled at him and waited for him to speak. He rubbed the toe of his sneaker in the dirt and finally said that he had to go, the time was up. They prayed their hands and said, *lee-a-hai*—good-bye—and many of their eyes were shiny with tears and his parents' eyes, too, were shiny and his mother said that they would pray for him. He prayed his hands back at them and said, *lee-a-hai,* and he and Pake and Khan made their way to the river and everybody followed. As the sampan crept across the Sangker, he looked back once to see a flock of hands waving like tassels of corn in the wind, and then locked his gaze onto his feet and kept it there as they climbed the bank and disappeared into a thicket of banana leaves.

Pake and Khan traveled as far as Phnom Penh with him, because Khan had never been there and Pake had been there only once. But they stayed just one night, because Sokkhan and his stepbrother had made Soeuth lose face on the evening they arrived. After they had dropped off their gear in Sokkhan's step-sister's apartment, Soeuth had gone down to the street by himself for a smoke. When Sokkhan and his stepbrother thudded down the stairs and Soeuth addressed his friend by name and said hello—the way he had always greeted Sokkhan over the past nine years—Sokkhan's stepbrother shook his head and leaned in very close, as if to share a secret with Soeuth. He told him that he mustn't address Sokkhan merely by name, he must call him *borng proh*—older brother—because Sokkhan was older than he was and deserved the requisite respect. Soeuth lowered his eyes as his face flushed. He seamed his lips tight. That night he told Pake and Khan that he was sorry but that they should probably leave tomorrow.

The next morning he gave his cousins $100 and escorted them to the edge of the central market, where there was a confluence of taxicabs and motorbikes for hire. He found a taxi driver who had already rustled up three or four other passengers en route to Battambang. He handed the driver $20, nodded good-bye to his cousins and asked them to look after his family, then wended his way through a school of interweaving motorbikes and plodded slowly back to Sokkhan's stepsister's apartment.

He stayed in Phnom Penh for another nine days. One night Sokkhan and his stepbrother invited him to a club, a tawdry disco joint, where Sokkhan's stepbrother told Soeuth he could hire a girl to dance with him, and the girl would go to a hotel with him easy, cheap. Soeuth jerked his head back and forth—that's okay, man, no, thank you—and stared into the auburn dark of his beer.

On another night, he invited Sokkhan's stepsister's friend Kim to a Cambodian movie. His heart ticking, he clasped her hand during the movie, and she squeezed his hand back. Kim was a pretty, chatty woman who wore lipstick and liked to pose for pictures. She lived with Sokkhan's stepsister and sold sweet coconut soup on the street in the evenings.

The next day Kim showed him around Phnom Penh. They visited Boeng Kak Lake, Wat Phnom—the city's main temple perched atop its only hill—and the grounds of King Sihanouk's royal palace. As they ambled hand in hand on a sidewalk skirting the palace, glancing at the spires and the orange-tiled roofs that jutted over the gate, he wondered at the possibility of bringing her back to Burlington as his wife.

That evening they talked, as Soeuth slouched at the kitchen table and Kim wrung clothes in a bucket on the floor.

"What do Americans do for fun?" she asked.

"Stay home, watch TV."

At some point she announced: "You must be rich."

Soeuth shrugged and pursed his lips, a reaction he had practiced over the past two weeks when this statement was pitched at him. "I'm not rich," he muttered. "I have a car, but I'm poor. I'm a mechanic."

She smiled: a typical reaction to his answers. She had told him several times during the days and late evenings they spent together that she had always dreamed of living in America.

The morning of his departure, Soeuth gave Kim all of his remaining clothes, leaving him with just the T-shirt and pants he was wearing. A few days before that, he had presented her with a quid pro quo proposition: if she would consider living, for a short time, with his family in their rice village—a test of loyalty, he figured—then he would arrange for her to come to America and live with him. Yes, my love, she had said—anything for you.

The only item Soeuth had to declare, as he filed through Customs at JFK, was a bag of dried fish. He had an empty duffel and $75 in his wallet. The guards asked him, where are all your clothes? He said, I gave them all away. What country were you in? one of them asked. Cambodia, he said, and the guards exchanged a few puzzled looks and then waved him through.

Back in Burlington, as the drone of his work resumed, the reunion with his family assumed the texture of a dream. We all wondered if he was considering moving back to Cambodia and rejoining his family. He told me over the phone that he was thinking about it, but in Cambodia, he would probably have to be a rice farmer. Here he had a good job—he was a mechanic.

Within a few weeks of his return, he left Sokkhan's place and moved in with one of his coworkers at Ryder, James Riopeel, whom most people there called "Rio." Rio was paunchy and contagiously easygoing, the kind of guy you could watch a whole afternoon of football with and, even if you didn't like football, find yourself pleasantly munching beer nuts and reclining deeper and deeper into the couch. Soeuth rented a room for $250 a month in the house Rio shared with his girlfriend and her teenage son and daughter. He usually ate dinner with them, but when Rio's girlfriend and her kids started to fight over curfews and weekly allowances, he and Rio would fetch a backyard blackjack table at a local gambling joint or drive out to Rio's garage and sip a few beers while working on one of Rio's Camaros. Rio became one of Soeuth's best American friends, in whom he confided all his fears and hopes about his family in Cambodia. When he joked that Rio should accompany him back to Cambodia someday, Rio said, hey, if they have McDonald's, I'll go.

Just after moving in with Rio, Soeuth had written to his family, informing them he'd returned safely to America. At the bottom of the letter he had scrawled Rio's telephone number. A few weeks later, his parents and brothers and sisters had all jaunted to Battambang City via motorbike cart to call him collect. Soeun had prattled on for a good fifteen minutes, asking Soeuth to send her money for a new bicycle, because the one he'd bought her had been stolen, and money for a motorbike so she could rent it out to people in the village and earn some money. She also told him the stereo he'd bought for Su had somehow been broken, as well as a camera he'd given them.

A week later, Soeuth called Ratsmey, the money courier he'd met at the hotel in Battambang, whose office was in Lowell. Ratsmey said he was traveling to Cambodia that Saturday, and if Soeuth produced some cash by Friday, he would deliver it to his father in Battambang the following week. Soeuth drove down to Lowell Friday night and met Ratsmey in a parking lot adjacent to some Cambodian food stores. Ratsmey flashed a grin when Soeuth approached and seized his hand in both of his and pumped it eagerly, like a politician floundering in the polls. Soeuth handed him $1,500 in cash, which Ratsmey promised to personally present to his father. Soeuth then passed him an envelope containing $225, Ratsmey's fifteen percent commission.

A videotape arrived in the mail a month later. The tape showed Ratsmey and Soeuth's father standing in Ratsmey's hotel room in Battambang, facing each other, his father smiling timidly. Ratsmey then briskly handed a wad of bills to his father, who counted them carefully—so that Soeuth would know it was all there—then turned toward the camera and said, I have received the money you sent, thank you, and may Lord Buddha protect you.

The videotapes were part of the package Ratsmey provided to all his clients, and Soeuth would accumulate a half dozen of them. Every two to three months, he would wire a money order to Ratsmey in Lowell and Ratsmey would deliver the money as promised and then mail Soeuth a videotape of the transaction. Over the course of the next year, his parents would receive a total of over $7,000—including the first $1,500 he'd sent—from their American son. They would also call him frequently, always collect, and his phone bills that year tallied to around $2,500.

His mother and father never asked for the money and always wrote him deferential thank-you letters or thanked him over the phone. But he received other letters, dozens of them, from cousins, aunts, nieces and others who sometimes politely, sometimes artlessly, sometimes with veiled references, asked for American dollars. He obliged, meting out close to $3,000 to members of his extended family that year. He sent $500 to Pake to help subsidize the building of his new hut; $500 to his cousin Lon to cover the costs of his wedding; $500 to Soeun so she could buy her motorbike; $500 to SeeThoul so, like Soeun, she could invest in a motorbike to rent out to other villagers; $100 to SeeThoul's mother so she could afford meat at the market; and $30 each to a number of other relatives who needed the money for miscellaneous reasons. He received a collect phone call sometime in late winter from SeeThoul's sister, who, for some reason, was stranded on the Thailand border with no money, and so he sent her $500 via Federal Express.

His hourly wage, after he returned from Cambodia, increased from $8.50 to $9.00, and he started bringing in $450 a week. He bought stock in Ryder which earned $3,000 after six months, at which point he sold it and collected the cash. Since he ate at Rio's free of charge, he managed to whittle his personal expenses down to rent, beer and cigarette money and an occasional gambling allowance. Gambling, he figured, was another avenue to harvest cash for his family. But on at least one occasion, when he and Rio drove down to Atlantic City, he lost over $1,000; the following week he signed up for as many shifts as he could get to compensate for the loss.

As the letters deluged him, he was soon working double shifts nearly every day of the week and weekend, bent into oily engines or tethered to fuel pumps, pulling in money, sending it away, pulling it in, sending it away. His hands became blunt, callused implements, no different from his wrenches and clamps, seizing metal, wires and rubber, seizing a miracle Buddha had given him. If he finished work in the early hours of the morning, he would often climb up into a cab of one of the trucks, splay himself across the leather seats and sleep there. One afternoon, after several such nights, while working beneath one of the trucks, he stood up abruptly and hit his head on the axle. He blacked out and collapsed onto the hot, oil-stained asphalt. When he awoke sometime later, rivulets of his own blood intermingled with puddles of leaked oil. When he crawled out from underneath the axle, a couple of guys loading a nearby truck trotted over and offered to take him to the hospital. He wiped the blood on his sleeve, smiled and said, no, thank you, I don't want to have a bad record. After stumbling to the men's room behind the garage and throwing enough water on his face to stanch the bleeding, he went home.

In early April he received a letter he'd long been anticipating and one that did not, in outright terms anyway, issue any monetary requests. Dated March 17 of 1993, it read:

> *To my darling—*
> *My love, many months have passed and I have not re-turned your letter. I miss you so much and please consider how much I love you. You are the only one who I love and respect for my whole life. I will always wait for you, and I'll never forget you. For the best of our future, I will try to live with your parents for a while; it wouldn't be that difficult for me. You told me to live in Battambang with your parents; I'm not happy about it, but I will go anyway. Trust me, I would not want you to worry about it. But I'm afraid that*

your parents and the whole family don't like me. Anyhow, I will have to go, my darling, but would not want to go at this time. I will go after New Year. Then I will give it a try. If they don't like me, I will come back to Phnom Penh. I will let you know what will happen. Please don't be angry with me of what I have spoken to you so far. I'm told you all this because I'm not sure of myself. One thing, is that I miss you very much, and I also miss my mother, who is very old now. Another thing is that I'm living alone here. I will be very happy if your family likes me.

Before I leave I pray to all the sacred things to be there with you. May you be happy and peaceful forever.

From,

Kim, Waiting for you, always

But Kim never traveled to the village. She would mail other letters, apologizing and asking outright for money. But she hadn't kept her word, and so she never got any money, and he eventually stopped writing her back.

Toward the end of summer, the tenor of the letters began to sour. Some relatives complained that they were loyal to him but were not receiving as much money as others who, they alleged, were not as loyal. Cousins accused other cousins of squandering the money. All vied for Soeuth's exclusive favor.

In September a letter arrived from his mother informing him that his brother Su had been shot at with an AK-47 one afternoon outside the family's hut; he had ducked the spray of bullets and had scurried safely under the hut. But another letter from his mother soon followed, telling him that the family had been robbed of several hundred dollars' worth of gold by armed bandits who had then beaten his father, almost to death, with the butt of a rifle.

He knew that the thugs who had done this were probably people to whom he had given money in the village or people who had at least witnessed him handing out ten- and five-dollar bills outside his family's hut. And he knew that, had he been more discreet, this might have been avoided. His family was now in mortal danger, however, and this knowledge fueled a scorching guilt in him.

The night he received the letter, he translated it into English for Rio. His friend went out and bought a case of Coors Silver Bullet, and the two sat on his couch and drank themselves into a numbing wordlessness.

Sometime in the fall of 1993, he received this letter:

> To Soeuth,
> On September 20, 1993, I received a letter from you and I received another one on October 5, 1993.
>
> First, from a distance, I would like to ask about how are you doing? How is everything there? Please let me know because I already received letter from you, which you never mention about how you are doing. About the money, I received all the amount you sent. You told me to deduct $100 to give to my father; I already gave it to him. Thank you very much for your support. About my father, when he received the money, he thought that he's now has some money to spend on the coming Pchum ceremony just like everyone else.
>
> Next, I would like to tell you about the people who broke into our house before. They had calmed down now because a number of them were caught and shot to death. Therefore, it's more peaceful here now. Cambodian people who have money to invest in business try very hard to be successful. Uncle came to me and asked me to join him to make a ship to make some money, but I had not responded to him yet because I have not finish building my house. When I finished building my house, some day or next year, when you have some money, I would like to borrow a small amount to make a living.
>
> Next, I would like to tell you about the bad guy you were asking me about. He used to joke around with [your brother]

but took it seriously and tried to shoot [your brother] without [him] knowing it. What I told you is true, but I had told our uncle about everything. Right now I'm trying to find a way to kill him; he wouldn't let us live peacefully, so we should not let him live; for what? Your family is like my family, we cannot buy guns.

I apologize for my writing, please forgive me for such mistakes. Good bye for now.

Pake

At first Pake's suggestion intrigued him. He could send Pake a few thousand dollars to hire someone to kill the men who had robbed his family and bludgeoned his father. There would be no legal consequences, since in the village, there were no police, no written laws prohibiting such actions, virtually no governmental structure at all—except for the village council, who were known to openly sanction, even sponsor, vigilantism. But he also knew that if he financed the killing, it could touch off a chain reaction of violent reprisals and possibly put his family in even more danger. And so in December of 1993, he dispatched to his parents just over $3,000 to enable them to build a new hut in a village closer to Battambang City.

That was the last time he would dole out money to anyone in Cambodia, he vowed to himself. He stopped mailing letters, too, and threw out many of the letters they had written to him. He had hoped that when he found his family and his country again, he would somehow know who he was, where he belonged. But as he continued his routine of emotionless tasks, he understood that it had all been an illusion. He had tried to resurrect himself, who he once was, contriving an identity from broken bits of language, a few photos and a well of fragmented memories.

In January he moved out of Rio's and rented a motel room without a telephone, where no one could find him.

On Sunday afternoons I would meet Francis, a thin-lipped, erudite, IRA-sympathizing classmate of mine, at what he claimed was the oldest pub in Dublin. There we would discuss assigned readings from *Ulysses* over pints of Guinness. It was sometime in May, near the end of the semester, when we reached Molly Bloom's monologue, a sixty-page, one-sentence chapter at the end of the book. Each time I tumbled headlong through Molly's unpunctuated meanderings, my heart rate would quicken and beads of sweat would collect on my brow like flies on a carcass. I had journeyed to Ireland in January of 1993 to study Anglo-Irish literature at University College Dublin, and there were only a few weeks left before I was due to go home, and Molly Bloom's monologue was the last hurdle I had to clear.

On my way to the bus stop to meet Francis, I would pause to make my routine call home from a pay phone outside the wrought-iron gates of a gloomy, moss-stained cathedral that was flanked by rows of wilted flowers on each side and whose dark, yawning entrance beckoned the occasional contrite congregant. On this particular Sunday, as the tolling of another cathedral's bells echoed in the distance and some errant seagulls flapped overhead, Mom gave me the latest news on Soeuth. She spoke in furious fragments, her voice edging between sarcasm and rage.

"How much . . . money . . . do they think . . . he has?"

"I know, Mom. I know."

"Here he's found his long-lost family. A miracle. And all they can do . . . is drain him—"

"Mom," I interrupted. "I know, but you have to look at it from their perspective. I mean, to them, Soeuth's wealthy beyond belief. They have nothing, I mean—"

"Adam, don't lecture me on Third World poverty."

"Sorry, it's just that it's impossible for us to understand where they're coming from."

"I understand where Soeuth's coming from, Adam. He can hardly afford his rent. He breaks his back every week. For these people."

"He certainly does."

"Adam . . ." Her voice quavered. "These people may be his family, but that's not how you treat a family member. That's not how you treat your long-lost son."

PART FOUR

I was watching a video of *The Graduate*, because I had just graduated, when tires crunched over the gravel in our driveway. Dustin
Hoffman had just checked into the hotel to meet Mrs. Robinson
and told the front-desk clerk that his only luggage was his toothbrush. I turned the VCR off and tromped toward the door, past
the heap of my luggage, musing on how easy it would be if I
showed up on San Juan Island—part of an archipelago in Puget
Sound, where I would be starting my job as a local newspaper
reporter in less than a week—with just a toothbrush. I pulled back
the curtain and glimpsed Soeuth stepping out of his blue '85
Grand Marquis.

I opened the door and jogged down the steps. People I did
not know were climbing out of Soeuth's car. There was an older
man wearing sunglasses and gold chains, a small woman, a teenage boy in baggy jeans with bangs that hung well below his eyes
and a younger boy beside him.

"Hello," I said, and everyone swung around, and Soeuth
smiled widely and said, "Hey, man."

"Come in."

We all sat on the patio, sipping iced tea, as Soeuth explained
to me, Mom, Dad and Dave that he would be moving to Long
Beach, California—home to over sixty thousand Cambodians—
with a Cambodian neighbor from Burlington, to whom he referred simply as the old man. The people with Soeuth today were

the old man's stepson, the stepson's wife and the old man's two boys. The couple had flown in from San Jose, Soeuth said, to help the old man and his family prepare for their trip west. The old man and his wife had stayed in Burlington today, but would meet their family tonight to pack their belongings into a Ryder truck Soeuth had rented. Soeuth would drive his Grand Marquis, and the old man's stepson would drive the Ryder truck, and they would try to reach California in under a week.

As Soeuth spoke English with us and Khmer with this Cambodian family, he seemed like a distant friend, the kind who stops by every couple of years unannounced, with a car full of kids and a cooler, headed to Montreal or Quebec. In his translations or asides to the Cambodian man and his wife, there were inflections and little chuckles and smirks that we were not meant to understand.

What we also did not, could not fathom was that this new migration was merely a variant on his last one: Soeuth was still searching for his family, hoping this time to find them not in one nuclear unit, but rather in the deep-flowing, culturally familiar currents of the Cambodian-American community.

After the iced tea, Mom invited the old man's stepson, his wife and the old man's two boys on a tour of the house. Dave brought out a twelve-pack of Coors, and we three reclined on lawn chairs, facing the sun.

"You got a girlfriend?" Soeuth asked me, flipping a tab on a can of beer.

"Nope."

"Dave, how 'bout you?"

"I did," said Dave flatly. "But she ran off and found Jesus"—which wasn't far from the truth. "What about you, Soeuth? Is there a lady in your life?"

He didn't answer at first. Then his brow furrowed. "Nah," he said. "Not me."

"Well, hey, California girls," I offered.

"Yeah." He swigged his beer. "Except American girls—they sleep with everybody. I need Cambodian girl."

Dave and I laughed. "Yeah, me, too," we said, almost in unison.

When they left, Soeuth had donned his sunglasses, too, and he and the stepson lingered by the car with their sunglasses and their family. I wondered if I would ever see him again.

"See ya later," he said, and they all climbed into his Grand Marquis. The engine growled and he waved and pushed up his sunglasses and then they were gone.

The old man had a friend in Long Beach whom Soeuth called the old lady. She wore a sarong and a T-shirt and her smile revealed betel-nut-reddened teeth. They all stayed in her close-quartered apartment for several months. Soeuth and the old man's older son, who was fifteen and lugged his skateboard everywhere, slept in the old lady's extra bedroom.

It was hard to sleep at first, because the searchlights of police helicopters stabbed through the window at night and the sounds of gunfire between Cambodian and Latino gangs echoed in the streets outside, and after the gunshots, often, sirens wailed. Soeuth would sit up some nights and talk with the old man's older son, whose name was Tuu. I don't like my father, Tuu told him one night, flipping bangs out of his eyes. He's mean, and he's always bragging and he don't know nothing.

Within the next few months, after Soeuth and the old man's family had moved into their own place, Tuu's typical teenage gripe would prove to be valid, even understated. If Tuu didn't pass the soy sauce fast enough, the old man would reach across the table and whack him on the side of the head, and a silence would ensue. Everyone, including Soeuth, would keep his or her head down and carefully continue eating. As summer drifted into fall, the old man would grow progressively more infuriated, as if his temper were building toward some unavoidable zenith. His face would redden and he would tremble. He would slam his fist on the table and tell his wife and sons they were stupid and slow and no good.

While the old man raged, Soeuth would usually slip up to his room. The old man did not lose his temper with Soeuth, not at first anyway. He would often share an afternoon beer with him on his couch, while he, Soeuth and his boys watched *Tom and Jerry* and other after-school cartoons.

"When I was your age," the old man intoned one afternoon, "I was strong—nobody can catch me, nobody can fight me."

Soeuth nodded and kept his eyes on the TV.

"I used to kill a lot of people," the old man said, slurping his beer. "When I was in the army."

Soeuth remained silent.

The old man then proceeded to tell him about his days as a Khmer Rouge soldier in Pol Pot's army. "The Khmer Rouge are patriots, they fight for the country," he said wistfully. "There are bad Khmer Rouge, but I was good Khmer Rouge. Sometimes I help the civilians, give them rice . . ." He chuckled to himself, as if reliving a fond memory. "One time I have to prove to people I'm tough. So I cut the liver out of the dead body, and we cook it and eat it."

The old man told him other stories on other afternoons, and Soeuth never said anything, never unfastened his eyes from the TV. Even after his patriotic act of cannibalism, the old man once said, the Khmer Rouge leadership had still distrusted him. One day they had tied him to a tree, and he had known they were about to kill him. He had asked for a last cigarette and, when they untied him, grabbed one of their guns, he said, and beaten them all in the head, beaten them dead. On another afternoon he explained to Soeuth how he had lost his eye. He had been hiding behind a dead tree while the enemy—presumably soldiers in the Cambodian Royal Army or the occupying Vietnamese Army, although the old man didn't specify—had tried to shoot him. A bullet had hit the tree and a piece of wood had broken off and lodged in his eye. He confided, on yet another afternoon, that he still had relatives fighting for the Khmer Rouge to whom he frequently sent money.

Soeuth had heard similar stories some seventeen years ago, when he had been a child slave, stories of murder and cannibalism. These stories leaked now into his thoughts. He remembered the faces of the demons who had kicked and whipped him. The old man had been a demon, too, had done far worse than kick and whip. But the old man was now frail, and Soeuth knew that, if necessary, he could knock the old man down and kick out his nicotine-stained teeth. The old man was, however, his only acquaintance in Long Beach, and he was determined to stay there at any cost and so he tolerated his boasts and retreated into a cocoon of silence.

In late September he landed a job at a three-bay garage owned by a Cambodian man and was glad that, for once, he was employed by one of his own people. He worked from 7 A.M. to 4 P.M. with six other Cambodian mechanics, changing oil, doing brake jobs and general engine work. His co-workers were cordial, but he never got to know them, because by the end of the month his boss owed him $500, and he quit.

He had done some auto-mechanic work free of charge some months earlier, just after arriving in Long Beach. The old lady had told him one afternoon that her monk was having trouble with his car—would Soeuth mind looking it over? Soeuth had mumbled, okay, for the monk. The monk, a slim, middle-aged man, had been waiting in the driveway. He had directed Soeuth to a small garage adjacent to the temple and nodded toward a Pontiac sedan parked inside. As he shuffled back toward the temple, the monk's orange-saffron robe blazed in the sun. After popping the hood, Soeuth had spotted a leaky gasket, which he had replaced. He had changed the spark plugs, too, and then had glanced up to see the monk standing a few feet away.

"Do I have to pay you anything?" the monk had asked, smiling weakly.

"No," Soeuth had replied.

The monk had rubbed his hands together and then had said in a low, teacherly voice: "When you are on temple property, you must take off your hat."

Soeuth had quickly reached up for his black, greasy Ryder cap, as if it had suddenly caught fire.

"It's a Cambodian tradition," the monk had explained. "You must not forget that."

The Ryder cap crumpled in his hands, Soeuth had lowered his head. "I'm sorry," he had mumbled. "I lived with Americans a lot of my life. I forgot my traditions."

The monk had answered sympathetically, "You did not know."

The closest Soeuth got to his traditions, while in Long Beach, were the Chinese and Cambodian poker games the old man often hosted on the floor of his living room. Soeuth, who had a practiced hand at poker, would usually win $20 or $30 from the old man or the three or four other regulars. The old man, who always acted as dealer and who owed most of the men money, would sip Budweisers and speak bombastically of his days under the Khmer Rouge, telling stories Soeuth had heard many times before.

One night, after a Cambodian five-card game had ended and the men were stubbing out their cigarettes, one of the players, a tall, well-muscled man in his forties, complained that the old man hadn't paid him his earnings.

"I did pay you," the old man said dismissively. "Check your money."

The man said again, "You did not pay me."

The old man glanced up from the pile of money he was counting. His face went red, and his lips quivered. He stood up abruptly and slammed his fist on the table.

"I will kill you!" he screamed, giving each word equal emphasis and pointing a withered finger at the man. "I will rip your heart out! I will rip your liver out! And I will eat them . . . raw!"

The man who hadn't been paid put on his coat and left quietly.

Despite these outbursts, the old man was still a respected figure among the men—all except Soeuth—who attended his poker games. Soeuth never understood why these men were willing to overlook the fact that the old man was a murderer and a cannibal. Maybe the old man attracted younger fellows who were just a little bit afraid of him and who admired his version of Cambodian patriotism. Soeuth played along, drinking, smoking, shuffling cards and searching for his next chance at escape.

One of the old man's poker buddies was an insurance agent who sold policies to Cambodians in Long Beach and San Diego. One evening he mentioned that he had to travel between the two cities and that it was a long, lonely drive. Soeuth, not having a job and not wanting to spend his days with the old man, volunteered to be his driver. The insurance agent paid him a few hundred dollars here and there for his chauffeur services and for his help inputting data and filling out paperwork at his "office," a small room he rented from the old man, not twenty feet from where Soeuth slept. An amiable, bespectacled man, he promised Soeuth that he would train him and eventually hire him to sell policies.

The insurance agent had a friend and client visiting from Cambodia, a magician who was performing in San Diego. After Soeuth had been introduced to the magician, he was soon selling tickets for him, without pay. The magician, a tall man in his early fifties with a thin, sharp voice, played almost exclusively to Cambodian audiences. He wore a suit and a top hat, and his act consisted of tearing up dollars into tiny shreds and producing them again as whole legal tender, pulling flowers and other predictable objects from his sleeves, or untying his sleeves—after an assistant had knotted them together—without using his hands.

During his southern California tour, the magician was accompanied by his daughter, a light-skinned Chinese-Cambodian, who was apprenticing under her father. One day over lunch, the magician told Soeuth he was looking for someone to marry his daughter so she wouldn't have to go back to Phnom Penh. Soeuth's heart jumped when he heard this. She was a quiet woman, who smiled in answer to questions, with big eyes and long dark hair— a good candidate, at first glance anyway, for a wife. She had once offered to show Soeuth some of her magic tricks but never did. Since he didn't have $10,000 to pay for a proper Cambodian wedding, he shrugged whenever the magician brought up his quandary and told himself that this girl was just a wild card Buddha had slipped in, that he would wait until he knew his hand was sound before he played it.

Soeuth arrived home late one night after a trip to San Diego with the insurance salesman and nudged the door open carefully. The old man was sitting at the kitchen table, a Budweiser in his hand.

"You cannot stay out late," the old man said.

Soeuth stood in the doorway and fixed his eyes on where the shadows at the end of the hall convened into a V. "I can't be staying home," he mumbled. "I'm going with this guy to help him."

The old man's eyes darkened, and his hands shook like he was an alcoholic who had gone days without a drink. "This is my house!" he roared. "You will not talk back to me!"

Soeuth stood still and said nothing.

The old man slapped his hand on the table and pointed at Soeuth. When this elicited no response, he bared his teeth and growled. Soeuth, fearing the old man would bite him if given the chance, turned and left.

He slept that night in his Grand Marquis. The saberlike searchlights of police helicopters punched into the car, rupturing his sleep.

For the next several weeks he slept on the couch of one of his poker buddies, who had also had a falling-out with the old man. Soeuth's new host was a neat, bespectacled, potbellied man, always wiping the counter or putting dishes and saucers away or rearranging drapes and couch pillows that seemed out of place. He lived off welfare and volunteered at a local youth center, working with Cambodian-gang kids. He informed Soeuth one evening, as the two sat at his foldout table eating bits of dried fish with their hands, that although he now received his income from the government, he had been the richest man in Cambodia before 1975. He had owned a commercial ship, a bank and a casino and had accumulated lots of gold. When the Khmer Rouge invaded Phnom Penh in April of 1975, he had fled to Thailand with an entourage of armed men who had carried all his gold; but when they had neared the border, a band of Thai thieves had ambushed him. I wish I'd known you then, Soeuth joked, and the richest man in Cambodia before 1975 smiled obligingly.

Bi had tracked Soeuth down a few months earlier, calling Mom to get his number. What the hell are you doin' down there? Bi had asked over the phone, and Soeuth had mumbled a feeble reply. Bi had then said brusquely, you will come live here for free and find a job and get your shit back together.

Bi had joined the Army shortly after Soeuth had moved out of his trailer in Vergennes, had been stationed in Germany for two years and was now at Fort Lewis, outside Tacoma, Washington, where he had earned the rank of sergeant. When he had extended his invitation, Soeuth had said, thanks, man, but I stay here. Soeuth had migrated to Long Beach for three things—a wife, a job and his culture—and he vowed not to leave until he had found them. But now, his time marked only by the light that filtered through crooked venetian blinds as he slouched on the couch of the richest man in Cambodia before 1975, smoking and watching soap operas and not drinking beer—because he had money only for cigarettes—he felt steeped in a familiar, stagnating self-pity. And so one day he called Bi and said, okay, man, I come.

San Juan Island was peopled, in part, with Luddites, conspiracy theorists, anarchists, barnacled fishermen and other eccentrics who regarded technology as a form of contagion. The "San Juan expats," as they called themselves, would refer to the mainland as "America," a place you would go only to get supplies—because if you stayed too long, you might contract *mainland disease,* an ailment, they allege, that glazes your eyes and scoops out your soul like a melon, one dollop at a time. The other sector of the island's population was comprised largely of real-estate developers, small-business owners, small-fry bureaucrats and seasonal tourists. These were the people with whom, as a reporter, I spent most of my time.

My job consisted mostly of covering somnolent meetings of the school board or town council or county commission and occasionally writing perky, sycophantic profiles of local businessmen. I lived alone in a circa-1970s fiberboard-walled apartment in a leafy, fenced-in complex called Wisteria Court—though the only evident wisteria clung languorously to the fence and looked withered or dead. Sometimes I plodded down to Herb's Tavern to upend a few pints and listen to the fishermen gripe about the Canadian beer on tap; mostly I drank at home.

Afternoons after work I would swing by the harborside Front Street Cafe, to meet Paul, a serious, chiseled man in his late thirties whose deep-set eyes winked motes of paranoia. Paul, who had dropped out of an elite neuroscience program at the University of Washington, worked at a local bookstore and maintained that the end of the world was imminent. We usually sat at a table by one of the ceiling-high windows, sipping cappuccinos and watching ferries disgorge streams of cars. The Holocaust, Paul said, was not a thing of the past—it was now, we were living it. When I asked for examples, he relayed a close encounter with a black helicopter one afternoon on the island's rocky southern shore. He was fishing, when he glanced up to see one of the sleek, silent machines suddenly hovering just a few yards from him, with big guns fastened to its sides and trained on him. The windshield was a mirror, he said. The helicopters were part of a government conspiracy to create an Orwellian state where the forests would all be clear-cut, personal freedom extinguished and dissenters either jailed or killed. To give me further evidence of this doomsday design, Paul drove me to the island's slate quarry one afternoon to show me a set of four almost perfectly straight scarifications in the rock. We stood on a steep, sandy incline peering up at the grooves in the rock. He turned slowly to face me, sending pebbles down the slope and into the water, and said simply: "Lasers."

I knew Paul viewed the world through a lens tinted by grandiloquent delusion, but he was also exceedingly well read and, unlike many who harbored similar views, was not a racist. He became a friend and confidant, and some fantastical, latent part of me indulged in his ramblings.

We spent many evenings on South Beach, grilling oysters, watching the occasional fins of a pod of orcas. One evening we straddled large driftwood logs, which had been bleached bone gray by the sun, and Paul stoked the coals of the grill and told stories. I stared across the strait of Juan de Fuca at the spine of the Olympic Mountains hued pink in the low evening light. As Paul's halcyon voice undulated, I became fleetingly convinced that the mountains were but a prop that would be plucked up after night had mantled the sky, that all the contours and boundaries would ever so discreetly be plucked out of existence, so that when I awoke, the world would be one immense beach covered in driftwood.

"Do you understand?" Paul asked finally, like a father speaking to his son.

"Yes," I said. "I think so."

The phone rang at 7 A.M. one murky morning in February. I stumbled down my hall, expecting my editor's panicky voice to lunge at me through the receiver.

"Hey, man." It was Soeuth.

"Jesus . . . Soeuth?"

"How you doing, man?"

"Hangin' in there." I coughed. "Are you in California?"

"No," he said quickly. "I got out of that."

"So, what—are you in Vermont?"

"Tacoma."

"Tacoma? That's just down the pike."

"Yeah . . . I'm staying with Bi. At the army base."

"Well, hell, what are you doing this weekend? You wanna have lunch? In Seattle? Maybe we could get a few piercings."

He chuckled obligingly. "Yes," he said. "We have lunch."

We met at Pike Place Market in front of the fish-throwing kiosk. Salmon and monkfish sailed over beds of ice, hurled by guys with dreadlocks and caught by guys with shaved heads. Soeuth looked older; his face was leaner and inscribed with wrinkles. He was wearing his black Ryder jacket with his name stitched above the breast pocket, a pair of dark khaki slacks and shiny Red Wing work boots. He was holding the hand of Bi's four-year-old son. Two women with crew cuts walked by, a bright silver chain swaying between them, hooked from nose ring to nose ring. A few teenage boys with scrubby goatees played hacky sack next to a newsstand. A man in a glossy beige business suit, slurping coffee, almost walked into Soeuth, said, "Sorry, dude," then veered away.

Bi lumbered out of a gaggle of people with his wife, who

cradled his baby daughter, spotted me and yelled: "Hey, man. You like Grizzly Adams and shit!"

We ate lunch at a seafood place on the pier, crammed into one of those tiny, no-slouching-allowed booths, and all ordered lobster. As Bi gently broke apart the claws and tail for his son, he asked me about the island. Soeuth stared raptly at his plate, as if reading a map. I knew he didn't have any money but also knew he hated to be perceived, in any remote way, as a freeloader, so when the bill came, I slipped him a twenty under the table.

When we filed out to the street, Bi's son broke away and skipped down the dock. Bi and Serena chased after him. Soeuth and I were left standing by a streetlamp, our hands in our pockets.

"You like Seattle?" he asked.

"Yeah, but I don't spend much time here. You know, I'm up on the island."

He nodded, glancing at a cluster of dock pilings where a seagull had alighted. "You the big shot up there," he announced suddenly. "The reporter."

"I ain't no big shot, old man. Big loser, maybe."

"Nah," he said harshly, as if reprimanding me. "You no loser. You got a job, man, you got your own place, you no loser." Then he added, "Maybe I'm the loser."

"No, no," I said.

It was the only reply I could conjure. I took a deep breath and rocked a few times on my heels. "Guess it didn't go so hot down there in Long Beach."

"I can't find a good job," he said. "I can't find no job here neither. I can't find nothing."

"You didn't meet any women?"

He glanced at me sideways, as if I had made an offensive remark.

Then he mumbled: "Your life sound good. It sound real good."

Soeuth was squinting at something in the harbor, his crow's-feet sharp and distinct. I looked at my brother and he did not look at me and I wondered how he could take it, being cut adrift of all moorings, living in two worlds but belonging in neither— and I felt selfishly relieved that the stakes had not been set so high for me.

In early spring of 1995, Soeuth drove back east. It took him just three days to traverse the continent in his Grand Marquis. A conscientious driver, he made sure his speedometer needle rarely crept past sixty-five. A thermos full of ice cubes had been propped against the passenger seat, so that if he nodded off, he could tip back a mouthful of ice. He slept twice during the trip, for two three-hour stints. When he stepped out of the car once at a rest stop to stretch, his knees faltered, so he climbed back into the car and chewed more ice and pulled back onto I-90 East and tried to keep the white lines on the road from sliding out of focus. He crossed the Massachusetts border around midnight on the third night. Spotting an exit sign for Malden—an industrial town ten miles or so north of Boston where Bi's parents, the Fishers, live—he let up on the gas and coasted down the off-ramp. He rolled into the first gas station with a pay phone and called the Fishers. Bi's brother-in-law, Hung, drove to the gas station to meet Soeuth and led him back to the house.

He moved into a musty, ceiling-slanted room in the Fishers' attic and found steady work as a mechanic at a two-bay garage, Patsy's, a block away from Dunkin' Donuts. His days were spent in the garage, his nights in his room. He didn't know anyone in Malden, didn't have much in common with any members of Bi's family, the Fishers—all of whom were Vietnamese, except for Tom, Bi's father, who was a Vietnam vet—and so his life distilled into the almost ascetic, two-tiered routine of day and night, work and sleep. He put in for overtime often, because he hadn't worked in months, and the less free time he had, the less useless he felt. He lived this way for several months, unfastened to future or past, walking down the stairs to work, up them to sleep—until one night, while he helped Bi's mother, Thuy, with the dishes, she joked to her son-in-law, Hung, who slumped at the table sipping a Budweiser, that Soeuth would someday be her son-in-law, too. Knowing Thuy referred to her second eldest daughter, Mai, the last member of her family to remain in Vietnam, Soeuth said, nah, I can't marry nobody, not me.

For the next several months, Thuy persisted in raising the topic of her unwed daughter. Finally, one afternoon, Soeuth said to Thuy, let me see the picture. When Thuy handed him a framed photo set behind glass of a demure woman glancing side-long over folded hands, he said to himself, she's pretty in the picture, and then told Thuy, okay, and betrothed himself to his best friend's sister without ever meeting her.

I had come back east in August of 1995 for an unpaid editorial internship at *The Village Voice* in New York. Soeuth called me one night, at the Brooklyn apartment I shared with a cadaverous Irish pothead, to tell me about his wedding plans.

"I saw the photograph," he told me. "We talked on the phone."

"But, old man . . ." I didn't know if I should tell him how sketchy the proposition sounded. "Are you sure about this?"

"I feel like nobody want me." His voice had the slack, deflated tone of someone who is trying to explain why he has just willingly accepted a demotion and pay cut. "This girl and her family, they want me."

In political terms, for a Cambodian to marry a Vietnamese is like an Israeli marrying a Palestinian. The two countries have feuded for centuries. Cambodia's king, Norodom Sihanouk, who lost a number of family members to the Khmer Rouge, proclaimed shortly after Vietnam withdrew its troops from Cambodia in 1989: "The Khmer Rouge are tigers. But I would rather be eaten by a Khmer Rouge tiger than by a Vietnamese crocodile, because the Khmer Rouge are true patriots."

But Soeuth didn't care about any of that. What mattered to him more than anything else was that this woman was Asian. "A white girl—now that would be different," he half joked on the phone. In America, he knew that he and his wife would share similar lifestyles, eat similar foods, both be Buddhists—and that few Americans would be aware that they came from different ethnic groups anyway.

When Soeuth informed Mom and Dad of his intention to marry a woman he had never met, they swallowed their reservations and gave him their support. What concerned them most was that this marriage had been orchestrated for strictly practical reasons. His new bride could step off the plane and tell Soeuth, thank you very much, but I don't think it's going to work out— and he would be left used and broke. We all understood, however, that he had, in some ways, chosen this family over ours. I knew that they gave him something we could not, that comfort, on a rudimentary level, came with sameness.

We had known the Fishers before they had moved to Massachusetts, when they had lived in a one-level ranch house perched on a knoll over Middlebury's Otter Creek, but had never really been friendly with them. Because Tom would roll marijuana joints for Bi and his friends, Soeuth's spending afternoons at the Fishers had, of course, been the genesis of many a fight between him and Mom.

At six-foot-two, Tom was a rangy, long-limbed man who shambled along with a rickety lunging gait, as though he had been loosely assembled with a box of rusty, ill-fitting screws and could collapse, at any minute, into his individual parts. He supported the family, working as a night security guard at Children's Hospital in Boston. The few times that I had seen Tom in Middlebury, he was amiable and droll. Dad and I had stopped by one evening to pick up Soeuth and had noticed Bi sonorously slamming the front fender of his run-down cargo van with a sledgehammer in the driveway. Tom had plodded over to our car and had said flatly: "Hey, Bill, hey, Adam, sorry for the noise—Bi's just doing some fine-tuning on his van."

Tom's "office" was tucked into a corner of his attic, a few dusty file cabinets and a loosely hung curtain away from the room in which Soeuth slept. Hanging on the wall over his desk were a half-dozen black-and-white photos of Saigon street children he had snapped while serving in Vietnam in 1969 and 1970. In the top right-hand drawer of his desk was a collection of artifacts from the war, including a shoe box of old Zippo lighters with various profane and cryptic engravings and a dozen or so bent and dented U.S. Army pins. Affixed to a paint-chipped space of wall over his marijuana plants was an old red-and-black cork dartboard. In the summer of 1995, Soeuth spent a few evenings with Tom in his "office," smoking unfiltered Lucky Strikes and winging ice picks into the dartboard.

Tom's wife, Thuy, was a small, shy woman whose presence in a roomful of her family members was so faint that you might not have noticed her, until she rose to fetch a diaper for a wailing grandchild. She kept the house in order and took care of her entire extended family, all of whom lived either in the house or nearby (Bi and his wife were the obvious exceptions, residing at Fort Lewis in Tacoma).

Tom had met Thuy in November of 1969, during his first week in Vietnam, at the Monkey Bar, a small, smoky Saigon dive across the street from his barracks—a French colonial hotel that the Army had converted into GI housing. He had been assigned to serve as a night-duty officer at the Army's Military Assistance Command center in the city. He had soon moved in with Thuy and her four children, three girls and a boy. In June of 1970, she had given birth to Tom's son, Bi, her third child fathered by an American (the father of her eldest daughters, Mai and Tram, was Vietnamese). Five months later, Tom had been relieved of duty. He had asked Thuy to be his wife and vowed to be a father not only to his son, but also to her four other children; they would all walk through American Customs as a family. But she had refused, and Tom had gone home to Vermont alone. He had sent Thuy money every few months so she could provide for the children. They lived in her paltry apartment, all six sleeping on the same bed. Thuy had sold fish sauce on the street to supplement Tom's installments.

After the fall of Saigon, the new government had sifted through its populace to weed out traitors. When North Vietnamese officials had discovered that Thuy had consorted with several American servicemen and was now caring for their children, she had been sentenced to a year in a prison camp. While their mother was incarcerated, Mai's older sister, Tram, who was seventeen, had sewn clothing in the apartment and sold it on the street; Mai, who was fifteen, had stayed home to take care of her three younger siblings.

After Thuy was released in 1976, she had worried about the kind of lives her three Amerasian children would have under the new Communist government and had reconsidered Tom's offer. She had applied to emigrate to America through the Orderly Departure Program—a joint U.S.-Vietnamese initiative created in 1979, in part, to reunite Amerasian children with their American fathers—and many years later, in 1983, had been granted an exit permit. The government would permit Thuy, however, to bring with her only her three Amerasian children, Bi, Lan and Louis; Mai and Tram, since their father was Vietnamese, would have to remain. On February 7th of 1983, their mother and siblings boarded a plane to America, and Mai and Tram waved goodbye and then returned to their mother's apartment on a tiny, squalid street in Saigon, now renamed Ho Chi Minh City.

But Mai already had a back-up plan in the works. Many years earlier, in November, 1979, her boyfriend, Thanh, had befriended the captain of an oil rig, who had agreed to stow him in the cargo hull and let him off in any country that would take him. Thanh had promised Mai that once he arrived in America, his final destination, he would sponsor both her and Tram's daughter, Nuon, who was born earlier that year. In December, after a circuitous trip around the globe, the ship had docked in Italy. Thanh, after he had made it known that he was a Catholic, had finally been allowed through Customs. Tom Fisher had agreed to be Thanh's sponsor, but the Immigration and Naturalization Service had, at first, refused Tom's petition. But Thanh, who enlisted the advocacy of a Catholic non-profit in Rome, somehow managed to persuade the INS to reverse itself. Once he had arrived in New York, Thanh filed a sponsorship petition with the INS for Mai and Nuon, listing Mai as his wife and Nuon as their daughter.

But four years later, and a year after Mai's mother and younger siblings had escaped Vietnam, there still hadn't been any movement on Thanh's petition. In the summer of 1984, when her desperation peaked, Mai had paid a smuggler $1,000 in gold to ferry her, Tram, Nuon and Mai's friend Hang in a small open motorboat into the choppy waters of the South China Sea. After two full days, they reached an island where more than a hundred Vietnamese and Chinese escapees had been assembled. Mai had been told they were waiting for a cargo ship, in whose hull they would hide among crates of coconuts. Then the ship would take them to freedom.

Before the cargo ship could reach the island, however, it had been intercepted by the Vietnamese coastal patrol. The escapees were immediately transported back to Ho Chi Minh City and interned in a re-education camp. Everyone except for Tram's daughter, Nuon, who was then five years old, had been strip-searched. They were herded into a communal prison cell with more than 30 others. Because Nuon was a child, she and Tram were released after a month, but Mai and Hang would remain in the camp for a year. Most detainees had worked in the rice fields, planting or harvesting, but, since her sister had paid bi-weekly visits to bribe the guards, Mai had been spared field work and, instead, assigned kitchen duty. Privacy had been a luxury; those who had missed the scheduled bathroom trips outside had to defecate in plastic buckets in the main cell. There were meetings every week, at which they were told that Ho Chi Minh was a god and they were all his servants.

In the summer of 1985, just after her release, Mai had learned that Thanh had tired of waiting for his sponsorship petition to clear and had married another Vietnamese woman he had met in New York.

After arriving in Vermont in 1983, Thuy had filed a petition to sponsor Mai, Tram and Nuon. But since she was not yet a U.S. citizen, her petition, like Thanh's, had become lodged in the amber of INS bureaucracy. Tom had not been able to file the petition on Thuy's behalf because Mai and Tram were not his daughters. In 1990, INS officials finally acted on Thuy's petition, contacting Vietnamese officials, and the two sisters had been called for interviews. Tram had immediately been granted an exit permit. But Mai's files had indicated that she had two sponsors— one, her mother, and the other, her husband—and a daughter, and so her exit permit had been denied. Tram had departed for America by herself in the fall of 1991, leaving her daughter, Nuon, with Mai. Thuy had filed another petition for Mai and Nuon, knowing it could be another seven years before it was processed.

When Soeuth moved in with the Fishers in the spring of 1995, Thuy saw an opportunity. Here was an eligible Asian-American bachelor, soon to take his citizenship test, who could travel to Vietnam to marry her daughter and, as a citizen, get a sponsorship petition noticed by the INS in no time. But the wedding was also a gamble: While Thuy's petition was still pending, the wedding would have to be kept a secret from Vietnamese officials—no one wanted a repeat of the debacle created by her and Thanh's dueling sponsorship forms. But if the Vietnamese government remained unaware of the wedding and denied Thuy's petition anyway, Mai could, at some later time, produce a certificate showing her marriage to an American citizen, and that, hopefully, would finally free her from the clutch of Communist Vietnam.

In September, Soeuth took his citizenship test—something he'd been putting off for years—and passed it on the first try. He would not be qualified, however, to act as Mai's sponsor until he had undergone an INS interview and been granted his citizenship certificate, which wouldn't be for another nine months. But he couldn't wait. In December, he journeyed to Ho Chi Minh City and became a married man. When he came back to Massachusetts alone, there was nothing for him to do but wait for her and work.

In March of 1996, lolling on the Fishers' lumpy, beer-stained couch, warm cans of Budweiser wedged in our crotches, Soeuth and I watched the video of his wedding. The video was produced professionally by some outfit in Ho Chi Minh City and was full of over-the-top graphics and fades and images that spiraled across the screen. It opened with a string of acknowledgments—including one for Mom and Dad that spelled our name "Fifiela"—typed in neon pink, that clicked by to the beat of techno-pop music.

The techno-pop music continued during a shaky succession of hand-held shots of wedding gifts on platters—teas, cakes, betel nuts, apples, oranges, grapes, mangoes, fried chicken, sticky rice. The screen then showed Soeuth and Tram's husband, Hung, a bushy-haired, broad-faced man, in Soeuth's brightly lit beige hotel room. They were draping red cloths over the wedding gifts, which were set out on a table. Soeuth was wearing a stiff, charcoal-black, pin-striped suit and had a white corsage pinned on his lapel.

It is customary in a Vietnamese wedding for the groom's family to prepare gifts in the groom's quarters—in this case, Soeuth's hotel room—for the bride's family and then to march, bearing the gifts, in a solemn procession to the bride's quarters. No one had explained any of this to Soeuth. When he had arrived in Ho Chi Minh City with Thuy and other members of Bi's family, he had given Mai $1,000, with which she had bought her own wedding gifts. She then had dropped the gifts off at Soeuth's hotel room. Soeuth's groom procession consisted of Mai's English teacher and several of her male friends. The camera focused on the teacher, a short, avuncular man wearing gold-rimmed, eye-inflating glasses, leading the procession. Soeuth followed the teacher, and following him were Mai's friends, young, serious guys in khakis and white dress shirts.

Mai and her family and female friends were waiting in a line on the street outside when the groom procession arrived. Mai was wearing a frilly wedding gown, white lace gloves, lipstick, rouge and eye shadow. She was very obviously pretty but also stern and nervous, and it was hard to get a sense of her through all the makeup.

After the groom procession greeted its way along the bride line, the video cut to Soeuth and Mai standing together inside her apartment before her ancestor shrine. There was a small Buddha statuette on the shrine and a few vases and half a dozen candleholders. The ceremony ostensibly began when the teacher, who served as the matrimonial agent, poured a cup of tea and set it gently on the shrine. There was a close-up then of a pair of hands holding a cigarette lighter, which was supplanted by a shot of the teacher waving the wicks of two red candles over the lighter's flame. He then turned toward the ancestor shrine, lifted the lit candles, clasped between his praying hands, and bowed several times. He pivoted away from the shrine and handed one of the candles to an old, round woman in a multicolored dress; he and the woman approached the shrine and inserted each candle into one of the candleholders and then stepped back and watched the candles. The purpose of the candle-watching was to determine whether or not Mai's ancestors would give their blessing to the wedding; if one of the candles went out, that meant no. There was a close-up of the candle flames fluttering, clinging to the wicks in what might have been the breeze of a ceiling fan. The camera focused again on Soeuth and Mai, who both appeared relieved as the flames straightened, fighting off the breeze.

It was unclear in the video at what point Soeuth and Mai

were formally pronounced man and wife, but in a shot soon after the candle-watching, they exchanged rings. Soeuth had a hard time slipping Mai's ring around her lace-gloved finger. Then Lan and Tram affixed earrings on Mai, and Soeuth watched intently, as if maybe he should help.

Abruptly, the video cut to the bride and groom sitting in a canopied boat on a lake. There was no sound at this point, though it appeared that Mai was pointing out to Soeuth rock formations and trees and legs of land jutting into the water. Soeuth sat beside his new wife on the boat, nodding, sweating, as if he were a soldier listening to instructions for a risky mission.

The reception was held in the Huong Sen Hotel restaurant, a dark room with a dozen tables. There were candles on the tables and their light shivered in the reflection of champagne glasses. A Muzak version of "Black Magic Woman" swelled as the camera swung onto Soeuth, Mai and the teacher, who stood at a microphone.

The teacher swiveled toward Soeuth and said: "Here comes the speech designed by the groom. Very short, and he'll speak in English."

Soeuth cleared his throat and leaned toward the microphone. There was a clumsy grin on his face. "Um, I would like to thank you all who show up here tonight . . . and . . . thank you very much." He stepped back and then leaned in again, abruptly, and uttered one of the only Vietnamese words he knew: *"Ca'mon"*— thank you. There was a smattering of applause.

Several people in the audience rose, lifting their glasses. During a round of toasts, all in Vietnamese, husband and wife stood awkwardly side by side like two kids coupled at a square dance. A shiver ran through me when I remembered that, at this moment in the video, it was just a week and a half since the two had first met. After the toast, everyone chanted, *"Hon! hon!"*—kiss! kiss! The camera hovered on Soeuth's sallow, sweating face. He turned toward his bride, who regarded him with wide, wary eyes. He leaned in then to kiss her, and she flinched, backing away. His pained face split reflexively into a wide smile. Amid ripples of laughter in the audience, he took her shoulders and tried again. Still tense, she did not move but allowed herself to be kissed.

I glanced over at Soeuth, who sat in a La-Z-Boy chair across the room. He shrugged. "She's shy," he said. "We practice kissing. She's okay now." He then wearily trained the remote at the TV and clicked off the VCR, banishing these images to some safe place behind the static. I watched the static, and Soeuth watched it, too, for a while. The woman in the video, the woman who had become my sister-in-law, was nothing to me but a woman in a video. I felt nothing for her, except maybe a pang of resentment.

The next morning we drove to the garage, where Soeuth had to work on a few cars. The place reeked of motor oil and cigarettes. On the far wall hung a *Playboy* calendar next to a velvet painting of Jesus. Soeuth hoisted open the hood of a Toyota with a grunt. For the past few months, he had been working virtually every waking hour so he could send his new wife money in Vietnam and build a bank account to support her when she arrived. His hands were stained with oil and chafed from constant use, covered with calluses that resembled scales. In the milky morning light, it looked as though his hands had been charred over a flame, as if the blackened skin could be peeled off in the pinch of two fingers to reveal the shiny pink meat underneath. He had told me that he couldn't even wash his hands now, because the soap stung too much.

As he tried to wrest loose a rusted bolt, I leaned against a nearby workbench. I listened for a while to the sound of his work. The image of his wife flinching from him in the video was indelible—the barbs in her eyes, the silent, circumspect admonition: stay away from me, I don't know you.

I hadn't foreseen my older brother getting married before me, and I knew I wouldn't be married for some time. Neither of us had enjoyed much success on the female front. I had had only two serious girlfriends up until now, and Soeuth had had only one. A few weeks earlier, he had kidded that maybe I should get an arranged marriage, too, like his—it was better than nothing, he had said. And Asian girls are better than American girls, anyway, he had added seriously—more loyal. Given the outcome of my last relationship, I had chuckled and said I couldn't disagree.

My eyes swung over to the exhaust-coated windows on the garage door, and a memory subtly slipped itself in place. It's Seattle, around 3 A.M., and I am lying on my side, awake, on a futon in a dank basement room. The voice of Billie Holiday floats up to mingle with plumes of incense smoke and the flickering shadows of candles. On the far wall there is the occasional spoke of a headlight from a passing car outside; I keep wishing I were in that car, wishing I were anywhere but here. Four or so feet away from me, she is curled up facing the wall, facing Billie Holiday, whose voice croons from a stereo speaker just over her head, whose voice has paralyzed me and sent my heart drumming madly in my chest.

"Welcome to the dungeon," she had joked when first showing me her basement room, and lying there on the futon, I couldn't help but think that was what this place was. She was a tall woman with very thin wrists, brownish-blond hair and almond-shaped eyes. She was from California. Whenever I came down from San Juan Island to see her, it was always the same: Billie Holiday, candles, incense, paralysis.

She had tried to explain to me one night why she had slept with a friend of mine—to whom I had introduced her. "It's his fault just as much as it is yours," I had droned repeatedly, while she had wept; finally she had asked in a kittenish, falsetto voice: "Can you forgive me?" And I had, because I hadn't been with a woman since my sophomore year of college and was afraid that if I let her go, I would be forever consigned to some purgatory of celibacy. Within a few months she had broken up with me, explaining that she was locked down by the heterosexual construct—that maybe she would start dating women again. That's okay, I had mumbled, I can understand. I had trudged down to Herb's Tavern, chain-smoked nearly a whole box of Swisher Sweets and got drunk enough to have myself thrown out.

Something heavy clanked on the cement floor. I pushed myself away from the workbench, and my head seemed to shrink and expand at the same time—the way it does when you wake up into a hangover—and I inhaled a big gulp of grease-laced air. Soeuth was wincing and shaking out his thumb over a wrench he'd dropped. I cracked my neck, and before I knew it, I asked him: "Why did you agree to marry Mai, even though you'd never met her?"

He stopped shaking his thumb, was still for a moment. Then he lifted his head slowly, as if a cinder block were strung from his neck. He did not look at me. His low, serrated voice cut against the room's stillness. "I feel like I'm useless," he said. "Like I'm still a kid."

He placed the wrench on top of the battery case next to him, and I thought about telling him, no way are you a kid, you weren't allowed to be a kid, you were a man when you were nine years old—but before I could speak, he continued: "Everybody . . . everybody has a better life than I do."

For the next few moments there was silence, and we both tried to abide by it by not breathing too noticeably. "I need some-body," he finally said. "When she comes . . . I will be in the good soil. My life will be okay then. I waited long time for my life to be okay. Not perfect, but okay."

After everyone had retired to bed, we sat on the Fishers' porch on a bamboo couch that was surrounded by boxes and rusty file cabinets. The pale light of a streetlamp reluctantly crept across the porch's back wall. The only sounds were crickets and the din of distant traffic.

Soeuth was wearing shorts and had removed his socks and shoes. When he lit a cigarette, I glimpsed the scars spotting his legs—scars I had fancied to be bullet wounds when I had first seen them nearly twelve years ago.

"Old man . . . how did you get those?"

"Hmmm?"

"The scars on your legs. You never told me that."

He chuckled and said, "Abscess. Working in fields. Infected. Get abscess."

He took a deep drag on his cigarette and then held up his thumb. "Most thumb-big," he said. "One, right here . . ." He indicated the meaty place just above his elbow. "Big like golf ball."

"Man, it smell bad," Soeuth continued. "Real bad!" He contorted his face for effect.

He extended his foot to show me the missing toenail on his second toe. "This abscess, too. Toe swole up big. Worms in it, too. It really hurt."

"Damn."

"Ahhh," he intoned dismissively. "A lot of people got it worse than me. Worse scars than me."

He lit a new cigarette off his old one.

I asked, "Ya still gambling?"

His eyes squinted against my question. "Once in a while."

"Atlantic City?"

"Where else."

"How do you do, usually?"

He nodded to himself, running figures in his head. "I won around five hundred dollars last time."

"That's my rent," I said. "What were you playin'?"

"Blackjack—my favorite."

"Does Mom know about this?" After I asked the question, I knew I shouldn't have.

He made a sarcastic hissing sound. "Mom love it," he said. "Sometime she come with me, play roulette. Sometime we go drinking."

I laughed and looked over to see his eyes shining fiercely in the light of the streetlamp. His smile, wide and toothless, seemed for a very small moment the slightest bit sinister. But then he started laughing, and I could see his teeth catching light, and what I'd seen just before was gone. Then he became suddenly silent, all too suddenly, and his breathing was foreign and loud, drowning out the crickets.

"Hey, man," he began dryly. "I didn't tell you about my sister."

"What about her—is she available?"

"She's dead."

Silence.

"She's what?" I didn't know if it was a joke.

"Dead." His eyes were pure black and still. "She's dead."

It felt as if everything inside me had suddenly collapsed, and I was just skin wrapped around emptiness, around shame.

"Soeuth . . ." His name, with my voice wrapped around it, arced out into the night and seemed to come boomeranging back at me. "Jesus . . . I'm sorry."

"It's okay."

"What happened?"

His face seemed to darken all of a sudden, as if all the blood in his body had been brought into his head with one great pump of his heart. "She die last summer of some sickness. Nobody know why."

He told me about another letter from his parents that had arrived several months ago, informing him of his sister Soeun's death from an unknown illness. The letter also claimed that his parents had been forced to sell the new house they had built with his money in order to pay her hospital bills. They had never even told him she was sick, leaving him powerless to intervene. After reading the letter, he had set it on his desk. Then he had opened the shoe box that was full of letters from his family. He had found the old letter Soeun had sent after his visit in 1992 and had slouched on his bed, her letter in his lap. *Please forgive my writing*, she had written. *I never wrote a letter before; don't mind me (your younger sister Soeun), but I wrote it by myself. p.s. Please sing for me.*

His throat had swelled hard as wood as her voice shimmered in his ear: *Please sing for me.*

"She was twenty-five," he mumbled. "And she took care of the whole family. Now she's dead. And I'm mad."

"There's nothing you could have done."

He nodded. "If I gave more money, maybe . . ."

"No, Soeuth," I said. "No."

Why hadn't I known about this earlier? I was his naive American foster brother, tripping over my stupid condolences, not knowing, not understanding anything.

"I want to go back," he mumbled suddenly.

"Go back?"

"To Cambodia." He lit another cigarette. "Wanna go with me?"

I didn't answer at first. "I . . . well, it's expensive—"

"Have a beer," he said and passed me a Bud Light; the can floated toward me in a slow, watery motion, suspended from his fingers.

I cupped the beer in both hands and didn't say thank you or anything else, because I knew the talking that night was done.

We wouldn't say another word to each other until we sat crooked over the counter at Dunkin' Donuts the next morning, eyeing traffic, the wagging tails of exhaust.

"Hey, old man."

"Yeah?"

"I hope this works out." I slurped up coffee. "With Mai, I mean. I think . . . it could."

"Yeah." His eyes trolled after the crumpled fender of a passing hatchback. "I hope so." He finished his coffee in four or five gulps, then announced abruptly: "Hey, man, I passed."

"You passed," I repeated meditatively, not wanting to betray the fact that I had no idea what he was talking about. "You passed?" I said again.

"My citizenship interview."

I stared at him for a few seconds and then extended my hand. "Holy shit!"

He smiled. "I get my certificate this fall."

"That's terrific."

"I know." He pumped my hand. "I feel good about it."

"That must be one helluva relief."

"It is."

I fake-punched his arm and joked: "Well, I guess all you gotta do now is change your name to Freddie or some other goddamned generic thing and you'll be one hundred percent American beef, just like Sokkhan." When Sokkhan had secured his citizenship in 1989, he had changed his legal first name to Peter. Phun, too, had shed his Cambodian name, although not legally, and now asked most people to call him Johnny.

Soeuth smiled faintly and said: "Yeah, right." Then he crushed his coffee cup with a slow fist, frowned and added: "People have no face when they change their name. They don't know who they are." He tossed the cup, spinning through the fluorescence of Dunkin' Donuts, into the trash bin. "I know you kidding, man, but I keep my name."

In the fall of 1996, Thuy received a letter from the INS. Her second sponsorship petition, filed in 1991, had somehow surfaced, and the INS had contacted the Vietnamese government, and Vietnamese officials had called Mai and Nuon for interviews, and they were soon granted exit permits. It was the end of a murky, twenty-year ordeal. Ultimately, Soeuth's marriage to Mai had been an unnecessary measure, like a lifeguard thrashing out to sea to rescue a drowning swimmer, only to discover that the swimmer had been hauled up by sport fishermen. But he still considered this woman to be his wife and only hoped that, when she landed here, she would embrace him as her husband.

Mai and Nuon flew in from Ho Chi Minh City in November. Soeuth called me in New York the night after their arrival. When he tried to give Mai the phone so she could say hello, she refused. "She's shy," he said. "But don't worry." He raised his voice for her benefit. "She can't hide from my brother."

He promised to bring her to the house in Vermont at either Thanksgiving or Christmas, when Dave and I would both be home. When he called a few days after Christmas and said they would be coming the next day, I tried to make a picture of his wife in my head, tried to see her smiling in his arms. But the picture that filled my head, the one ineradicable image, was of this unknown, uncomfortable woman flinching from my brother during his wedding ceremony, and his startled, pained face.

★   ★   ★

I woke up at ten o'clock, trimmed my beard, put a kettle on the stove and paced around the house until I stumbled upon some drawings in the parlor Dave had brought down from the University of Vermont. Dave, who had once joked, "I like college, all right—just not the academic part," had recently finished the first semester of his junior year and had declared studio art as his major. He was capable of realist renderings but preferred abstracts, the more sarcastic and morose, the better. When assigned to do a self-portrait during the second semester of his senior year, Dave would draw a macabre charcoal likeness of himself, with a gray face, black holes for eyes, and giving his viewers the finger. The drawings propped against the wall of our parlor were epileptic amalgams of distorted faces and cartilagelike strands of color that annexed my eyes until the kettle whined from the kitchen.

Soeuth showed up around 11 A.M. I was sipping my second cup of coffee when tires crunched over our driveway.

Mom skimmed by the table, her eyes lidless and alert, and scooped up my eggshells. "They must have left at six-thirty this morning," she said, pitching the shells into the compost bin. "Where's your father and brother?" Her eyes were aimed toward the sound of car doors closing.

I shrugged, and she flitted toward the stairwell.

I finished the coffee in one gulp and went to fetch Grandpa Ken in his "apartment," a few rooms on the south side of the house that Dad had renovated for him when he became too blind to drive a year or so earlier.

Grandpa and I shuffled toward the back porch and Grandpa asked me if Soeuth's wife was a blonde and I said, I don't think so. When we got to the coat rack, I could hear footsteps on the crusty snow outside. We all huddled into greeting formation in the parlor, while the tops of their heads, shiny in the sun, and then their down-turned faces bobbed up behind the glass of the back-porch door. The door screeched open, and they spilled in from the cold, wide-eyed and smiling. We clustered into an eager

crescent around Soeuth and Mai and Thuy, and after a few seconds of clumsily cross-wired smiles, there was a jumbled volley
of hellos.

Mai was petite, engulfed in her blue winter parka. As she
stood in the crook of Soeuth's arm, he, for once, seemed tall.
She was disarmingly pretty in person. Black hair hemmed her
pale round face like the ebony frame of a portrait. Her eyes,
smooth and black, peeked up from beneath her bangs and rested
on the safety of Soeuth's face. As Soeuth told Mom about the
trip up from Massachusetts, the windy route over the mountains,
Mai smiled tentatively.

Mom laced her hands together. "The roads must have been
awful!" she said. "I'm glad you could make it."

Mai's eyes clipped back and forth between Soeuth and Mom
before she suddenly chirped: "Sick crazy driver!" (It took Mai a
while to pronounce Soeuth's name correctly; at first, "Sick" was
the closest she could get.)

Soeuth shrugged, as if to say, I can't argue with that.

Grandpa then made a show of removing his Ford cap—which
he'd pulled on only a few seconds earlier—and tipping his head
down in a modest attempt to bow. "Welcome to the Fifield home-
stead!" he declared.

Soeuth smiled and informed Mai: "That's my grandpa."

Thuy followed Mom into the kitchen and Dad took Grandpa
by the arm and sat him at the table and Dave and I moved his
paintings over by the piano. Soeuth and Mai were left standing
by the door. I heard her whisper to him: "Your momma, your
family, very nice."

"Yeah," Soeuth answered. "My family good to me."

An involuntary smile took my face when he said that. I
couldn't remember Soeuth ever referring to us as his "family."

He very gently put his hands on Mai's shoulders and led her
into the kitchen. The last time I had seen Soeuth with a woman
was in the summer of 1989, when he had brought Crystal to his
high school graduation party on our back lawn. Crystal had been
affectionate with him, in an effervescent, adolescent way, and he

had tried to reciprocate, but even though they had dated for six months, he had displayed a clumsy cautiousness around her—as though her daddy were lurking somewhere with a shotgun, waiting for him to make the wrong move. Maybe it was because she had been his first real girlfriend or because he had never been comfortable with American dating rituals. Or maybe it was just that, like Dave and me, he had been plain petrified of intimacy. With the exception of Kim—whom Soeuth hadn't even dared to kiss—Mai was the first woman he had been with since Crystal. Seeing him with her now, I couldn't help but think that some obstruction had melted away, that he had suddenly, in the space of a month, crossed over from the jitters of boyhood romance to being a husband at perfect ease with his wife. Those painfully stilted scenes in the wedding video might as well have taken place ten years ago.

Shortly after Mai's arrival, her sister Tram had apparently advised her to dump Soeuth and find a Vietnamese man. Mai would later admit to me, "I used to think all Cambodian ugly, until I meet Soeuth." But Mai forcefully promised that she loved Soeuth and would never leave him. She could be stubborn about some things, Soeuth would tell me—curtailing his smoking and beer drinking and keeping a tight reign on their finances—but her loyalty to him, like her occasional censoriousness, would prove, in the next year, to be unbending.

We were seated around Mom's oak dining room table for a lunch of Chinese takeout. Mai picked the chicken out of her portion of sweet and sour chicken—which left her only with rice and a few clumps of syrupy broccoli—because after finally escaping from Vietnam, she had engaged in a meat fast as a gesture of gratitude to the gods. We all ate our food carefully, politely, and Mom filled the silence, telling Mai about Soeuth's athletic prowess during high school. After Dave and I had cleared the table, Soeuth nodded at Mai and she nodded to herself and then told us all her story of escaping Vietnam. She ticked off each disheartening episode with an unlilting offhandedness, blinking a few times after each completed sentence.

When Mai had finished, Mom was crying. Soeuth rose and padded around the table and stood behind Mom. He looked toward Mai and asked flatly: "Honey, what you think, we look alike?"

Mai didn't get the joke, but Dave and Grandpa laughed. Then Grandpa leaned over to me and remarked, loud enough for everyone to hear: "Well, she may not be a blonde, but she isn't hard to look at."

During dessert, Grandpa adjusted his hearing aid and bellowed at Soeuth: "So, Suit, what are ya drivin' these days?"

"Cadillac," Soeuth shouted.

"So you're movin' up in the world!" announced Grandpa, impressed.

"No, Grandpa." Soeuth laughed. "It's just a 1985 El Dorado. Nothing much."

"Well, I'm sure it's better than that damned Pontiac Jean drives," he said, coughing out a few chuckles.

"Oh, Grandpa," Mom said.

After lunch, Soeuth and I rode Grandpa's four-wheeler through the mud fields in back of the house. He drove. I held onto his shoulders as he raced down the Seeleys' access road, closely skirting the barbed-wire fence.

"You see that?" he shouted.

"What, that bluff?"

"Yeah," he said, shifting into higher gear. "I'm gonna jump it."

"Oh, shit." My shoulders tightened.

He laughed as we sped toward the bluff, the wind lashing us. "Hold on!"

The bluff rose up in front of us like the back of a breaching whale. The four-wheeler shot up it and lifted for a terrifying moment into the bright afternoon sky. We howled as the hard ground approached.

When we hit, the impact sent me a foot or two off the backseat and then let me crash into a joint-racking affirmation of gravity. Numbness overwhelmed as we eased to a stop. We sat silently in the open, muddy field for a minute or two. Our breathing layered over the engine's raspy sputtering.

Soeuth shut off the engine and asked innocently: "You okay, man?"

"Yup." I coughed. "Fine."

He dismounted from the four-wheeler and walked toward the fence. Leaning against a fence post, he stared toward the purple-and-brown vastness stretching south. "It's nice here, man."

"It is."

"I love coming out here."

I climbed off the four-wheeler. "Remember fishing for the first time, right over there?"

He grinned slowly. "You guys eventually got good."

"Well, I don't know if I ever got the hang of it." A gust of wind swept up my words; I raised my voice. "Maybe we could go fishing again. Maybe this summer. Maybe before our trip."

He looked at me seriously. "You really want to go?"

"Fishing?"

"No, the trip."

"You bet," I said and joked: "Maybe find me a wife, too." I rocked on my heels in the mud. "You know, I really like Mai. I think she's a real sweetheart. Really."

"Thanks, man. She's good for me."

"I'm really happy for you, old man."

He walked toward me, his hands in his pockets, until he stood facing the house with me.

"You know," he said, "I feel like I almost get there."

I squinted against the wind. "I think you almost have."

After a long silence, Soeuth reached into his pocket and fished out the four-wheeler keys.

"Here," he said. "You drive."

With seats reclined, hands in our laps, we sat silently. The sunlight clung to his face, so that he was merely a silhouette, a shadow cast against the wall next to me. The murmurings of other passengers enveloped us, and it felt like we were the only ones on the plane not talking.

The seat belts around us clicked hurriedly, almost simultaneously, into place—as if everyone except us somehow knew that all the passengers were about to be ejected, catapulted up over Jamaica Bay—and a stewardess parked her cart in the aisle next to us. She cocked her head and smiled sympathetically and handed me two sets of headphones wrapped in plastic; I wordlessly passed one to Soeuth. Then she waved her hand across an array of newspapers laid out on her cart, and I pointed to the only newspaper that was in English. She plucked a copy from somewhere inside the cart, passed it to me and swung her smile over at Soeuth. "Sir?" He shook his head. Then, as she left, her eyes passed over us one more time, quickly, perhaps trying to decipher if the two of us—a tall white man with big hair and a short, dark Asian man—had a reason to be sitting together or were merely strangers assigned neighboring seats.

Soeuth clamped on his headphones, and I wondered at the circumstances that had put me on a plane to the Far East with a man who had become one of the most important people in my life but today seemed as distant as the Korean man flapping a newspaper at his granddaughter across the aisle.

Before boarding, we had sat with Dad in the Korean Air waiting area and he had reviewed with professional precision all the medical precautions we should be prepared to take and, several times, had asked if we were sure we had had all our vaccinations and medications for malaria, hepatitis, typhoid, dengue fever—as if he would administer them right there on the spot if we hadn't—and we had said yes, Dad, yes, we're sure. Mosquito net? Got it. Snake-bite kit, you know what to do with that, right? Yes. Cold compress, Ace bandages, Ceftin, syringes? Yup. Then a snatch of Korean over the loudspeaker, the rustle of people folding their coats, stuffing things into their carry-ons, patting their pockets to make sure the tickets were still there. We stood up.

"Okay, guys, good luck."

"Thanks, Dad," I said.

"Thanks," Soeuth said.

There was an awkward moment when we all stood tethered in a tense triangle, heads bowed—as if Soeuth and I weren't merely leaving for a month, but were being sent off by our father to some distant theater of war. At some point Dad reached for both of us suddenly and hugged us. He let us go and looked down before mumbling: "I love you guys."

Soeuth put his hands in his pockets and I adjusted the shoulder strap of my backpack and then we both stammered simultaneously: "I love you, too." We turned away and filed into the line of passengers, and as we shuffled toward the metal detector, I heard Dad zipping up his duffel bag and remembered him saying, a few days back: "God . . . Cambodia . . . I've never been any place like that. You guys just stick together."

The trip had been looming before us for more than a year. We had waited until the last minute to buy the plane tickets, to plan everything. When I had asked Soeuth if he thought we would have any trouble finding his family, a slow, defensive smile stole its way onto his face.

"Could they have moved to a different village?"

"Where would they go?" he had muttered. "Unless they won the lottery. No. They stay put. Or . . . unless they died."

"You don't think—"

"I would be sad." His voice was suddenly sharp, poised. "Don't worry, we find them."

He had told me months earlier that he would write them a letter announcing our visit. But it wasn't until a week before we left that he had admitted the letter was still in an unaddressed envelope on his dresser. He hadn't written to or spoken with them for more than two years, since his sister's death, since the money he had given them had been stolen, since he had cut off all communication. Anything could have happened to them in that time, and I knew he didn't want to think about it. And I knew that this trip would once again force him to confront the tangle of events that had pried him away from them on that spring day in 1976, the events that had made him a child slave of Pol Pot and that, paradoxically, ultimately had given him the freedom they would never have.

The first thing he said on the plane was, "They can't dunk."

I looked over to see him smirking, and he pointed with pursed lips to the movie screen, which showed a game of Korean basketball. "They're too short. Just like me." He mimed dunking a basketball. "I can't dunk either."

"I can't even dribble," I admitted. "But you know, I bet Jackie Chan can dunk, and he's what, five-five, five-six."

"Jackie Chan is the king," Soeuth said.

"Do you think you'll ever take up Tae Kwon Do again, old man?" I chopped at his arm.

He knocked my arm away and fake kidney-punched me. "No, man," he said. "No time, no money."

We landed in Vietnam ten minutes short of midnight. After a stiff, boyish Customs official went through everything in our bags, holding up magazines and books and microcassettes with the tips of his fingers like they were contaminated, we fought our way through a wall of heat and taxicab drivers to Mai's friends,

Hang and Ut, who had agreed to meet us at the airport. We dropped our bags, and Soeuth took Hang, a stocky, smiling woman in a baseball cap, by the shoulders and hugged her. She gave him a Southeast Asian hug in return, tentative fingertips on his shoulders.

"You look good," he said.

"No!" She laughed and pinched her cheeks. "I'm fat."

Hang hailed a cab. We climbed in and the car raced off into the murky night, palm-tree leaves, amputees on crutches and the shining spokes of cyclos every so often flashing under the formaldehyde light of fluorescent streetlamps.

Hang's apartment overlooked a narrow, busy street about three miles from downtown Ho Chi Minh City. It was a shanty with a corrugated tin roof sitting above her mother's antiques shop. The place was cut by sharp angles and shadows, arranged haphazardly on two levels connected by rickety steps. Above the refrigerator on a porcelain tile shelf was a plump Lucky Buddha statuette surrounded by vases in which incense sticks burned absently.

We sat on a bed in the central room and drank Cokes until Soeuth whispered to me that I should take a shower. The bathroom was a slim stall on the lower level with a tile floor sporting rectangular holes big enough for a small child to fall through. The shower consisted of big barrels of water and a red plastic bowl.

After a dinner of pig intestines with soy sauce, we roosted on stools on the balcony and watched the current of motorbikes and mopeds and cyclos choking the street below, surging like a flock of anxious blood cells down one crowded artery. TV antennas and telephone wires made a crazy pattern in the evening sky, like stick figures throwing fishing nets. On the sidewalk, which intermittently gave way to rubble or dirt, a one-legged man swung himself on crutches toward the pale blue light of a Tiger Beer sign. The din of bleating horns and buzzing engines filled the damp air.

Soeuth dug out one of his photo albums, featuring Mai shoveling snow in front of their apartment and shots of her and

Soeuth posing in front of her mother's house in suburban Massachusetts.

Hang laughed at the sight of her friend in these cold, American places. She ran her fingers over the surfaces of the photos and then started to cry.

"Sorry," her quavering voice managed. "I . . . I miss Mai."

Soeuth later informed me that Mai and Hang had been closer than sisters and had known each other since they were very young. "At first I thought they were gay," he said.

On the walls of Hang's apartment were several blown-up photos of Mai, one from the wedding. A few months after joining him in America, Mai had asked Soeuth to marry Hang as well so she could come to America, too. He had refused.

Soeuth set his hand on Hang's shoulder. "Don't worry," he said softly. "We come back to Saigon to visit, Mai and me, when we have money . . . maybe in two years."

Hang wiped at her eyes with a tissue. "Sorry," she said again, stood up and went inside. Soeuth followed.

I was left sitting with Ut, a tall, delicate woman with childlike bangs, who spoke hardly any English. I smiled and she smiled back, betraying brownish teeth. "One minute," I said and ran inside to get my Vietnamese-English dictionary.

We sat side by side on the stools, perusing the dictionary for words such as "spring roll," "tasty" and "humid." She giggled when we stumbled across the phrase "to be intimate," and shifted her stool closer to mine. I moved mine closer to hers. Before long, our shoulders were touching. She found the word "handsome" and pointed to me. I found the Vietnamese word for "pretty" and nodded at her. She noticed I was sweating and wiped my brow with her palm.

After about fifteen minutes, Hang returned to the balcony with more Cokes and proclaimed brightly: "You like Ut!" She sat across from us and giggled some Vietnamese at Ut, who smiled abashedly.

"You like?" Hang hooked her thumb toward Ut.

I cleared my throat. "Ut . . . I think she's very pretty . . . and nice . . . but . . ."

They both giggled, and I lit one of Soeuth's cigarettes and prayed he would return from the bathroom or wherever the hell he was.

Before bed, I asked Soeuth what he knew about Ut. He said she was thirty-seven, had been married before, but had fled her husband because he beat her. She had been pregnant once but had lost the baby.

At Hang's insistence, Soeuth and I slept in the "good bed," which was in the central room under a fan, and I slapped my arms all night even though there were no mosquitoes and let the growling of outside motorbikes pummel me into fitful sleep.

In the morning we set out into the city. I rode on the back of Hang's bike and Soeuth rode with Ut, because I was "tall-big" and Hang's bike was bigger than Ut's. We joined the throng of motorbikes, some carrying whole families, three people or more, and sped through the faded concrete suburbs of Ho Chi Minh City, down dizzying alleyways and back streets, past fly-covered fruit stands and children running after us for money, under the compact French colonial balconies where women wrung clothes and men smoked. We were the only men riding on the backs of our motorbikes; young male drivers leered at us, their girlfriends or sisters or daughters clinging to them as we all zoomed into impossible densities of rubber and tailpipes and dangling feet.

Hang wanted us to see the Vietnam War Remnants Museum. We rolled into a parking lot full of tanks and artillery guns and fighter jets. The exhibits inside included grisly photos of the My Lai massacre and dismembered and napalm-burned children. Further in, on a modest table, were dead babies deformed, allegedly, by Agent Orange, stuffed into jars of formaldehyde.

Ut clasped my hand as we ambled through this hall of American atrocities. We halted to study a photo of an American soldier holding up the mutilated remains of a child, feet loosely connected to a head by tiny sinews and shreds of a shirt. Ut shook her head and waved her finger at me in a scolding gesture.

I offered weakly, "We did some very bad things here."

She smiled, not understanding a word.

When we turned away from the photo, Soeuth was standing behind us. I don't know how long he had been there. He leaned in and asked in a whisper, "Where the photos of the Vietcong?"

I shrugged and Ut shrugged, too, even though she didn't know what he had said. We made our way toward the exit arrow and passed a photo of American troops proudly displaying the decapitated heads of Vietcong soldiers.

As we stood outside waiting for Hang to buy some Cokes, Soeuth murmured flatly, "I don't know, man—I think this museum is one-sided." He had told me that after Vietnam toppled the Khmer Rouge in 1979, he considered the Vietnamese soldiers to be heroes. They had ended the nightmare that had devoured three years of his life and indeed, by keeping their troops in Cambodia throughout the '80s, had prevented the return of the Khmer Rouge. But in 1984, the Vietnamese government had imprisoned Mai, her sister and her niece after they tried to escape the country, and after her marriage to Soeuth in December of 1995, they had kept her from joining him in the U.S. for nearly a year. He had reasons to love and hate this country, and the only comfortable place for him between these two polarities seemed to be a cool skepticism.

In the afternoon we visited the zoo. Ut held my hand as we walked past children throwing rocks at the crocodiles. We shared a Coke, two straws, and Hang snapped a photo of us.

Hang took us window-shopping downtown, past women chipping at blocks of ice on the sidewalk and children sitting in circles playing cards and upscale hotels whose neatly capped bellboys smiled brown teeth and beckoned us into their sparkling lobbies. I stopped to buy another Coke from a street vendor and said, "No ice, please," and so she gave me my Coke in a plastic Ziploc bag. I was sweating profusely, so Ut bought a packet of Kleenex and wiped my brow every few minutes. She held my hand and

pointed out uneven places in the sidewalk—there were many—
so I wouldn't trip. When Hang suggested to Ut that I had a
headache, Ut poised her thumb and forefinger over the space
between my eyebrows and pinched the skin with her nails. It left
a purplish mark. Later, while studying the mark in the mirror, I
understood that it was more than a headache remedy—it was a
mark of ownership, indicating that while I was in Vietnam, I
belonged to her.

Ut was pretty, in a shy and wounded way. Often when I
tried to communicate with her, she would smile and proclaim
enthusiastically: "I don't know!"—one of the only English phrases
she had mastered. She had taken time off from her job at a
bamboo wall-hanging factory—where she worked to support several members of her extended family—to help Hang show us
around. She had just met me, yet she doted on me gratuitously.
I wondered at the awful things she must have endured in her life.

Before Soeuth and I left for the airport, we all ate a breakfast
of squid and noodle soup in a narrow restaurant that used to be
a garage. Colorful calendars featured pretty Vietnamese girls in
conical hats and silk *ao dais* smiling from the walls. A fan
hummed absently. Sweat crawled down my brow and dropped
into my soup.

As Soeuth and I smoked and searched for the rest of our
dong to pay the bill, Ut and Hang were consulting. Ut waved at
me coyly with two fingers.

Suddenly Hang slapped the table. "Adam!" she barked. "You
like Ut!?"

I coughed and Soeuth looked at me with wide, accusing eyes.
"Yes," I said.

"She want you marry," said Hang.

"She what?"

"Ut you marry," declared Hang resolutely.

I stubbed out my cigarette and coughed; I couldn't stop
coughing. Soeuth patted me on the back. "Uh, look, I—"

"No," Soeuth said. He slid some dong out of his wallet and

folded it into the bill. "No marry. He can't marry her, Hang. He's too young."

I was stunned; Soeuth rarely asserted himself like this.

"He's my brother, Hang." Soeuth grabbed my shoulder.

Hang and Ut exchanged whispers.

Hang reached across the table and seized my hand. "Okay." She patted my hand. "Maybe you Ut friends?" she offered, her eyes soft and conciliatory.

I took her hand in both of mine and smiled at Ut. "Yes. Friends."

"You write her?" Hang asked.

"Yes," I said. "I will write to her, tell her that. But I can't marry her." I glanced at Soeuth, whose gaze was fastened to the far wall. "No marry."

"No marry," they both repeated in unison.

While we were packing our things and Hang was calling on the phone for a taxi to the airport, Soeuth warned: "Don't get too close."

I zipped up my camera bag. "Sorry."

"Just don't get too close. She's a friend of my wife's and you are my brother, and I don't want anybody to get hurt."

But in a few weeks, on the first night we returned from Cambodia to Vietnam before leaving for New York, I was in bed with her. I had promised myself that I would follow Soeuth's warning. But I hadn't been with a woman for more than a year, and when Ut clenched my hand and pulled me down to the bed with her, my heart, or something else, mutinied.

She kissed me and mimed slipping a ring on my wedding finger. I held up my hand. "No marry, okay?"

"No marries," she acknowledged. "Friend, okay?"

"Okay, friends, yes, friends."

Her gaze locked onto mine. She unbuttoned her blouse and put my hand on her breast. I let it rest there, and she began to take off her underwear. I stopped her and held her until she fell asleep or pretended to, because I had only just met her, could hardly communicate with her and didn't have the Vietnamese-English dictionary to look up the word for "condom." I lay under her, sweating, hoping the beating of my heart would not wake her. When she rolled onto her side, I got up, went to the balcony and smoked until dawn.

In the morning she and Hang joined me on the balcony with the Vietnamese-English dictionary. We sat on stools in a circle like summer-camp counselors planning a parents' barbecue.

"Hang, can you tell Ut I'm sorry?"

Hang told her. Then she plucked the pen from behind my ear and scrawled a sentence on a sheet of lined notebook paper. It read: "Ut want you not think bad her."

I gripped Ut's hand in both of mine before I realized the gesture might be misconstrued. "Tell her . . . I think she's a great lady. But I'm going back to New York, and I don't plan on marrying anyone, not for a while."

Hang communicated this to Ut in short bursts of explanation. Then Ut said something in a small voice.

"Ut want me tell you," Hang said. "Here Vietnam very hard." She opened the dictionary. She pointed to the word "shortage." Then she flipped some pages and pressed her thumbnail down beneath the word "affection."

I mouthed the words: "Shortage of affection."

"Life Ut very hard," Hang explained. "She married, but husband hit her. She left husband, and for long time no one. Then she meet you."

I looked at Ut. She shrugged, embarrassed. In a brief flash, I thought about it, about bringing her back to New York with me. I would take her out of the dirty alleyways and crowded markets, out of this place of shortage. I would encourage whatever uncultivated talents she harbored, whatever ambitions had been smothered by this place. As for me, she would at least be faithful, my romantically battered ego suggested. She wouldn't play mind games, because we could barely communicate. I imagined us sitting on the plane together, Ut sniffing my cheek and feeding me Korean dumplings, me clumsily flipping through the Vietnamese-

English dictionary. Then I saw us sitting in my shoe-box studio in Manhattan, riffling through want ads—she would have to get a job—and me chain-smoking while she lathered me in pleas and vows I could not understand. Eventually we would have to move to some place near Boston, near Mai's in-laws, near people with whom she would be comfortable, and I would have to find a job somewhere, anywhere, at a local newspaper, and she would be slicing mangoes for me when I came home, and I would smile at her and then stare up at the Buddha shrine she had built over our microwave and ask if this was it, if this was my life, now and forever. I found some solace in the thought that if I agreed to it, Soeuth and I would, for once, be on the same side of a cultural barrier: non-Vietnamese men with Vietnamese wives.

I offered a fragile smile. "I'm sorry."

Then I grabbed both their hands. "Friends?"

"Friends," they said.

Soeuth came out onto the balcony, saw us all holding hands, smiled, lit a cigarette and turned away to watch the traffic.

Neither Soeuth nor I wore sunglasses when we stepped onto the tarmac at Pochentong International Airport in Phnom Penh, and the whiteness of the afternoon assaulted us. I swabbed the sudden sweat on my brow and squinted at the ground as we lumbered toward the terminal, my eyes led along the asphalt by the soft brownness of female ankles.

It was somehow hotter inside the terminal. A delta of sweat had already formed on the front of my shirt. When it was our turn to show our visas, the Customs official asked Soeuth for some money for his family. Soeuth turned away from me and shrugged, as if consulting some invisible, imaginary counselor, and swiveled back around with a $5 bill in hand. He passed it to the Customs official, who prayed his hands and said: *"Au khun"*—thank you.

We lugged our bags toward the entrance and a swarm of taxicab drivers. Soeuth sighed and said half sarcastically, half wearily: "Welcome to Cambodia."

A few days before we had left New York, I had met my friend Gary for a drink. Gary was a freelance journalist who had traveled in Cambodia and Thailand this past January. He read the wires every day and, if prompted, could recite the latest news in any given country. He had handed me an inch-and-a-half stack of Associated Press and Reuters articles about a variety of events: the Hun Sen coup d'état on July fifth and sixth that had people

fleeing Phnom Penh, much like they had on April 17, 1975, when
the Khmer Rouge seized the city; the jungle show trial of Pol Pot
in July; the murder of Hun Sen's opponents after the coup; the
Hun Sen government's alleged involvement in drug smuggling
and clear-cutting. The articles portrayed a country still pinned
by Pol Pot's legacy, struggling under a mass of political, social
and economic ills.

As we prepared to leave, Gary had blown smoke at the ceiling.
"Cambodia," he had said, "is the Wild West."

I had expected Phnom Penh to be a city on the brink. I had
anticipated panic and gunfire and mortar blasts. As we rode into
town—past sunlit billboards advertising Mild Seven cigarettes,
past teenage boys who trucked huge blocks of ice and pigs in
baskets on the backs of bicycles, past children in blue uniforms
on their way home from school—I kept expecting to see funnels
of black smoke on the horizon or hear the grinding of armored
vehicles crushing street-side restaurant tables as they plowed
over sidewalks.

But Phnom Penh was quiet. There was, of course, the ever-
present buzz of motorbikes and the tinkering of bells on ice-
cream carts and the aggressive yammering of street-side vendors.
But once my ears got used to them, an eerie silence predomi-
nated. It wouldn't have seemed so quiet, I guess, if all I'd read
and seen about Cambodia hadn't lacquered my impression of
the place with images of mass evacuations and bombings and
general chaos.

Soeuth said the city was quieter than it had been in November
of 1992, when he had last visited. At that time Cambodia had
been swelling with the hope of democracy advertised by the
United Nations. At that time many people believed that the de-
cades-long curse on their country might be lifted. But after the
recent July coup—in which as many as ninety people had been
summarily executed, allegedly by Hun Sen's troops—that hope
had again been smothered by fear.

"In my heart, I hope Cambodia will be all right someday,"
Soeuth said as our taxi wended through Phnom Penh's worn,

dusty streets. "But I believe it's not going to be all right until somebody teaches them a lesson. Even after the next election, it's not going to be all right. Somebody is always going to be taking over. I hope I'm wrong." He paused and nodded to himself. "Here's what the UN should do: take all the leaders out of the country and then leave the country alone."

In our room at the Tokyo Hotel on street 278, Soeuth and I lounged on our beds and chain-smoked 555s, and Soeuth asked me to read out loud some articles from a local English-language newspaper, the *Phnom Penh Post*. I turned to the police blotter:

Da and Oun, beergirls, were seriously wounded by a grenade explosion at Taphol village in Siem Riep Province . . . Neng Borath, 25, a pimp, was arrested by police after they received a complaint from a victim's brother. The victim said that she was sold to a brothel in June for $50 by a moto-taxi driver after he raped her. At a Toul Kork brothel the victim alleges she was forced to accept 6 to 8 clients per day and she received nothing except food . . . Keo Vannang was killed, and his wife died after going to hospital, by Sam Yana, a military policeman who shot them after they had an argument with each other . . . Neang Pheap was seriously injured after a cruel husband burned her with petrol at Thnal Thmey village, Kampong Thom province. A source said that their family was too poor, living with no house with three children. On that day the husband came back and took all his wife's clothes to burn them. When the wife saw that she cried and said why didn't he burn her if he was burning her clothes because she had only these clothes. Suddenly the husband took the petrol and poured it onto her and lit it. She survives by help from the neighborhood.

I handed the newspaper to Soeuth. He folded it and placed it beneath my notebook on the dresser. "This country is hopeless," he said.

We walked downstairs and the hotel clerk, a thin, graceful girl named Tien, smiled and asked us how we liked our room. Soeuth said it was okay. Tien answered the phone and unleashed a stream of Khmer into the receiver, saying, *"Jaa . . . jaa . . . jaa"*—yes, yes, yes—in between every few breaths, and I watched her fine lips, like her fine epicanthic eyelids, curl around her syllables. I asked Soeuth to ask her if we could interview her once she got off the phone. He did, and she agreed. She was twenty-two and had recently returned to Phnom Penh after living with her two sisters in a refugee camp in Thailand for six years. When the hotel hired her, she was afraid they would force her to be a prostitute as well as a clerk. As of yet, they hadn't. If she had wings, she said, she would fly to America.

"Pretty girl," I remarked as we stepped outside.

"Yes," he said. "But don't tell her that. Don't get too close. Unless you want to be her wings to America."

We hired two motorbike drivers who took us to the U.S. Embassy, where we registered as visiting American citizens and were both handed photocopies of the following travel advisory:

> The U.S. Embassy in Phnom Penh reports that the potential for violence and criminal acts remains high. During periods of political tensions, violence directed against foreigners, including American citizens and facilities, cannot be excluded. The U.S. Embassy advises American citizens to remain vigilant about their personal security.

Ever since we had stepped off the plane, Soeuth had been vigilant, if not fanatic, about our security. He had instructed me to keep my money in as many different places as possible—my camera bag, shoes, backpack—and not to carry my wallet in my back pocket, something I hadn't done ever since I began living in New York City. Our passports and plane tickets were stowed in an interior pocket of my camera bag; Soeuth told me to sling the bag over my shoulder and hug it close at all times. He said to trust no one and not to go anywhere without him, except for the Lucky Supermarket, which was only about thirty yards from the hotel. A week before we had left for Cambodia, he had muttered over the phone one night: "You will be my responsibility."

And then he had added: "If you don't leave Cambodia, I don't either."

After we returned from the embassy, we smoked on the hotel balcony and surveyed our environs. Below us in the adjacent lot, a father and son sang a song together while washing the family car with red plastic buckets of concrete-colored water; two old women sipped tea and played cards in the shadowy, vine-veined balcony across the street; a young woman lit the incense sticks of her Buddha shrine in a shanty on a neighboring rooftop; a few teenage boys played hacky sack with a piece of fruit in the hotel parking lot; a sinewy girl, her head wrapped in a blue-checkered *khrama,* hauled a wooden cart ladened with rice sacks on the street below.

"You think you could ever live here? You know, if the fighting ever stop?" Soeuth asked, leaning against the balcony railing.

"Me? Well, if I got a job at one of the English-language papers, I think I could live here. For a year or two anyway."

"Really?"

"It's different. There's a lot to write about, I guess. And I haven't seen a single No Smoking sign."

"Well, I can't live here." His eyes consulted something on a distant rooftop. "It's not just fighting. A lot of Cambodians hate Vietnamese. My wife is Vietnamese. Maybe we could live in Vietnam."

"Some Vietnamese aren't too fond of Cambodians either, old man."

"Yeah," he said. "Vermont probably the best place to live, when we have money for the house."

It struck me then, more than ever before, that his identity had been whittled to the one choice, which wasn't really a choice: he was an American.

Mai had originally planned to join us on this trip, and I think we'd both been relieved when she decided, at the last minute, not to. Animosity for the Vietnamese was still widespread and virulent here. So far, the country had been anything but hostile, although I knew that would have been different had a light-skinned Vietnamese woman accompanied us.

Since our arrival, many people we had met had smiled brightly and energetically enunciated, "Welcome to my country!" Soeuth advised me: "Everybody seems nice, because you're a foreigner and because all the tourists are gone and because they want your money." I felt myself being whipsawed between wariness and curiosity, and was eventually pulled by Soeuth closer to wariness.

Soeuth had also stressed we shouldn't leave the hotel after dark, and it was only after insistent prodding that he agreed one night, at a charcoal-gray 6:30 P.M., to go out for dinner at a Vietnamese cafe tucked into a crumbling concrete building around the corner from the hotel. We sat outside in plastic lawn chairs. After some spring rolls, we swigged Tiger beers and observed three military policemen wearing helmets, AK-47s slung over their backs like guitars, search a group of teenage boys who stood, hands and legs spread, against a wall on the opposite street corner.

Within a few minutes, the police were gone and the boys were chuckling to one another, as if they had just been caught smoking in the bathroom by the school principal. As their motorbikes sped jauntily into the moist dark, I was reminded of the time British soldiers had stopped me on a deserted street in Belfast, Ireland; I had been shaking so badly that I had dropped my passport twice.

Soeuth had finished his sandwich and was absently wiping at the corner of his mouth with a paper towel while regarding a brightly lit balcony across the street upon which a few young girls in red sequined gowns were decoratively perched. They were waving to two fat white guys, in shorts and dress shirts, plying their way drunkenly down the sidewalk. One of the girls, tall with long arms, blew a kiss and rubbed her fingers together. The men stopped and consulted each other. One stroked his mustache and fiddled with his watch and looked up at the girls and looked back at his friend, who shrugged. Then the one with the mustache shook his head and held up his hands in apology and they left.

Soeuth nudged me and pointed with his chin and pursed lips to a short, stocky girl in high heels attempting to climb from her balcony to the balcony of a neighboring building where another fat white man was grinning at her and vigorously rubbing his belly.

We watched the girl teetering for a few seconds on the balcony railing, and then Soeuth rose suddenly, so that he blocked my view.

"Let's go," he said.

We ate breakfast at a place on Preah Sihanouk Boulevard that sprouted blue table umbrellas with Mild Seven and 555 logos. A fat woman sat cross-legged atop two or three chairs in the back, barking orders at the help, slurping noodles and picking her toes. A miniature collie panted in her lap.

I ordered the chicken, and Soeuth got the crab. Our waitress, a big-boned woman who wore heavy eye shadow, sat down at our table after she had brought out the food. She asked Soeuth questions in Khmer, and he answered casually while picking apart his crab, as if he had known her for some time. He was usually reticent with people he didn't know, but since we had arrived in Phnom Penh, he had held sustained conversations with a random assortment of strangers.

Our waitress said we were handsome, Soeuth told me. She then advised us that Vietnamese girls have AIDS, watch out. My wife is Vietnamese, Soeuth replied, and our waitress laughed, as if to say, that's funny. When she waddled away to fetch our bill, Soeuth whispered that she made $24 a month. I removed my wallet, and he said: "What you doing?"

"Just gonna leave her a few dollars."

"Don't do that," he snapped. "They don't leave tips here. They'll think we're stupid."

When Soeuth rose to leave, I told him I had to tie my shoe. Then, while he stood waiting for me on the sidewalk, I wedged a few dollars under a saucer. The gratuity reflex was too ingrained. But as we walked back to the hotel, I knew he knew what I had done, knew it from the way he looked just past me when I spoke to him. I guiltily chattered on about Hun Sen and Sihanouk and resolved to myself that, from now on, I would heed his advice and trust it, all of it. Because this time, I was on his turf.

And so the next morning, when he appointed himself keeper of our money, I didn't protest. I consulted the *Lonely Planet* guidebook while he slouched on the edge of his bed, counting out all of our cash and travelers' checks into two neat stacks. He slipped each stack into a small manila envelope. The thicker of the two envelopes contained the cash; this envelope, he decreed, was never to be drawn from in public.

"And don't keep money in your wallet today," he said, crushing an empty 555 pack. "Only enough for the museums."

"You got it." I carefully culled ten singles from the cash envelope and passed the envelope back to him—he had, after all, agreed to visit the "museums" with me, and I knew he didn't want to.

The road to Choeung Ek billowed beneath us like a lake gone choppy in the wind. In about fifteen minutes the bustle of Phnom Penh had tapered, and we were riding past straw huts and people slumped at picnic tables in the shade and chickens that spilled onto the road. Old women vendors eyed us from behind their stands, the fruit and candy and Fanta they were selling displayed like forlorn objects in a still life. The car slowed to a crawl when the road developed craters more than a foot deep in places, and children tumbled out of huts and shade and waved to me, shouting "Hello!"

Soeuth smiled. "You're a foreigner," he said.

The car rounded a curve in the road and suddenly there were expansive rice fields all around us. Bright in the sun, the tips of grass resembled lean, little blades. After turning onto a dirt path, the car halted in a sandy clearing. We stepped outside, and children swarmed out of nowhere, holding their hands out. I kept my hands in my pockets.

The guide at Choeung Ek spoke good English and blinked a

lot. He was young—late twenties, early thirties, Soeuth's age. We followed him to a three-story glass tower packed with skulls, eight thousand of them, he said. They were arranged according to age and gender; above the bottom shelf rested a sign that read, "Juvenile Females."

"This one pickax," the guide said and held up a small skull with a hole in its temple that looked like a coin slot. "You can touch."

I felt its smooth, chalky surface. The guide turned to Soeuth, who briskly shook his head.

The guide picked up a sledgehammer from underneath the shelf. "Khmer Rouge smash the skulls." He pistoned the hammer up and down with both hands.

He then led us on a narrow path that skirted overgrown craters in the earth, each about five feet deep. On the edge of one of the craters was a stupa-shaped, fiberboard sign that leaned precariously and read in Khmer and English: "MASS GRAVE OF 166 VICTIMS WITHOUT HEADS." The guide jabbed his chin at the sign, glanced at me and quipped, "No heads." He then knelt and picked something out of the dirt. After blowing dust off whatever he had procured, he held it, between his thumb and forefinger, close to my face; it was a human tooth. "Bones still in the dirt," he explained, shaking the tooth in his palm like a die.

Halfway around the next grave pit, the guide stopped and reached up to grasp the serrated edge of a dead palm-tree branch jutting just over our heads. "The Khmer Rouge use the palm branch to cut off the heads," he said, sawing the air with his hand.

After we had completed the tour, the guide stood with us and wordlessly shared a cigarette. We were the only visitors.

"I sleep here one night," he announced abruptly, his voice cracking. "Over there, in the little house." He pointed to a small pavilion about fifty yards away.

Soeuth and I exchanged inquiring glances.

"I hear the ghosts crying at night," the guide said. Then he looked at me in silence; his eyes were hard and black.

I glanced at the ground to avert his gaze and cleared my throat. "What were they saying?" I finally asked.

"They ask the Khmer Rouge please don't kill them."

In the car, Soeuth said he had chills. On returning to Phnom Penh, our taxi driver took us straight to the S-21 Genocide Museum. It was an old school building in the city's Toul Sleng district that had been used by the Khmer Rouge as a prison and torture center. We were the only visitors there, too, and as we entered, children screeched enjoyably in a neighboring yard, playing boccie.

We wandered haltingly through the old school hallways, me leading the way, Soeuth following. The classrooms, which had been used as torture chambers, featured grainy, blown-up photos of burned and bloodied prisoners. Every time I ducked into one of these rooms, Soeuth lingered by the door.

All of the rooms were basically the same: bloodstained tile floors, rusted torture devices, dilapidated bed frames on which shirts and other articles of clothing lay rumpled and stiff with age. There were no ropes keeping you from these exhibits, no signs saying: "Please don't touch." But everything appeared untouched, as if the place had just been evacuated of its prisoners the day before. When the Vietnamese had discovered S-21 in 1979, they had made a point of leaving it just the way it was, not cleaning anything up—except the corpses. When Soeuth's old friend Sokkhan had volunteered as a soldier in Heng Samrin's army, he had inspected S-21 before the bodies were removed. The bodies had lain gashed and rotting, he said. Pulled fingernails and clumps of hair had been scattered across the floor. Of the fourteen thousand or so people who had been detained here, only seven were known to have survived.

In one room, my eyes fixed on a bloodstain that spread over a few squares of the white-and-gold tile in the corner. It looked as innocuous as a grape-juice stain on the linoleum floor of a suburban kitchen. I stood very still, wondering whose blood it was—a child who had openly grieved for his parents? a woman whose husband was found to be a former government official?— and it suddenly felt as if something forbade me to speak or move. After a few seconds, I heard Soeuth's Nikes scuffing down the hall, and I was able to stumble out of there.

The second part of the museum consisted of a series of large rooms with hundreds of head-shot photos pleading mutely from the walls. They were photos of the prisoners who had been detained here. They had been snapped by Khmer Rouge officials just after they had removed their victims' blindfolds. Virtually everyone in the photos was brought, at some point, by his captors to the killing fields at Choeung Ek, told to kneel at the edge of a mass grave and struck in the head with a hoe, hammer or pickax.

Our eyes scrolled past the hundreds of faces, men, women and children, all with the same dazed look, the look of someone roused suddenly from sleep. We stopped once before the photo of a little boy. Soeuth stood inches from this photo, as if studying the features of his own face in the mirror. Soeuth's face was concentrated, clenched. But then it softened a little, and his eyes widened, and his face seemed to imitate the boy's face. He knew that that boy—whose eyes did not ask any questions, whose life already seemed to be over—could have been him.

In the last room of the museum, mounted on the wall, was a map of Cambodia made entirely of human skulls. We took photos of each other standing before the map. "My country," Soeuth mumbled, eyeing the skulls.

We left the museum both drenched in sweat. It was hot, near one hundred degrees. As Soeuth fished a few thousand riels out of his pocket and handed the money to two legless veterans in front of the museum, I noticed he was shivering.

We plodded silently down the dusty street until Soeuth said: "They need the money, man. They prob'ly fight the Khmer Rouge. They prob'ly . . ."

His voice evaporated mid-sentence. He was holding his hands together to keep them from shaking.

Soeuth hated inconsistency, and I knew he didn't want me to think that he was a hypocrite for giving money to these men when he had told me not to give out money before. But something in that museum had hit him hard, brought him back to a place where the skulls and bones weren't part of an exhibit. When he slipped the ex-soldiers just enough money to buy a meal or a few packs of cigarettes, maybe he was telling them, thank you, thank you for losing your legs, thank you for doing your part to stop those bastards.

"Let's get a drink, old man."

"Okay," he said. "Good idea."

That night we went to the "naked dancing" club. Our motorbike drivers waited for us outside. The place was dimly lit, as swank as some strip clubs in New York. When we sat down, a nearly nude, very pale woman took shape before us in the warm dark, her arms and hips and breasts coalescing together like shapes in a kaleidoscope. She leaned toward me, her dusky eyes sliding past mine, and sat down suddenly, sending a breeze across my face. She pressed up flush against my side, then clenched my hands and cupped them over her breasts. I slid my hands down to her flat belly. Another woman, tall with a bowl cut, sat next to Soeuth, but he wouldn't let her touch him. We were the first customers there.

As other men filtered in and took their seats around the circular stage, I asked Soeuth if he would translate an interview. He said, go ahead. I asked how old they were. The woman next to me was twenty-six; the one next to Soeuth, twenty-five. I asked how old they were when they started doing this. When Soeuth muttered the question, they both giggled and batted at the air dismissively, like sorority girls coyly waving off a come-on. They then confided that sometimes they get tips, sometimes they don't; if a man hands them $5, they are obligated to sit with him all night. Are you afraid of the men? I asked. They nodded slowly, yes. Then the woman next to Soeuth sat upright and pivoted toward me. She drummed her fist in three quick whacks into her palm and gave Soeuth some hard words in staccato succession. He cleared his throat and mumbled to me: "They have to do whatever the men say."

When the woman who had sat with me was dancing, swiveling her hips and breasts to a song that went, "Sha la la la la, sha la la in the mooorning, sha la la la la, sha la la just for you-ooo," she blew me a kiss. I nodded back. When she came to sit with me again, I asked her, through Soeuth, to write her name on my cigarette box. Her name was Ly. I asked her where she was from. She said Ho Chi Minh. She told Soeuth she liked me because I was afraid. Then she kissed me and sniffed my cheek and pulled my arm snug around her shoulder. The jasmine smell of her hair was pungent.

After a few beers, my imagination percolated. I envisioned Ly lying on her back on one of the tables as a gaggle of blond boys take turns with her. Their heads bob in the flashes of a strobe light. She clutches the table. Her eyes are seamed shut. They cram $5 bills into her mouth as she gasps for air. Then I storm in, the tails of my trench coat flicking in a phantom breeze. I snatch a fourteen-ounce bottle from a table, flip it into the air and catch it by the neck. Then I smash it, and the shards float and flicker like fireflies. The men whip around, stunned. *As of right now*, I say, *she doesn't work here anymore*. Then I hold out my hand. Ly sits up and her shiny eyes meet mine. She spits out the $5 bills and runs to me. I cover her with my coat and escort her in dreamy slow motion into the swampy darkness beneath the exit sign.

My consciousness stuttered back on like an old light in the horse barn when a bespectacled, middle-aged woman plopped herself down across from me. She raised her eyebrows inquisitively. "This girl you like?" she asked. "Forty dollar. You sleep her. Bring her hotel." I glanced at Ly, who blew me a kiss. Then I shook my head, no. At the table next to us, a naked girl no older than eighteen was sprawled across the laps of three men who were grabbing her in various places hard enough to leave dark bruises. I held Ly close to me. She rubbed her face against mine. I wanted to keep her away from the men, from the dance floor. I gave her $30. She sniffed me, put her tongue in my mouth, stood up and said, "Go dancing."

While Ly danced, her eyes hovered just over my head, and her face hung still in the pink neon light as her body twisted beneath it. She was moving almost mechanically, as if some remote transmitter sparked signals in her brain, swinging her hips. The light refracted off her face like it would off something metal. Her eyes were moored deep in her face, empty and unmoving, not unlike the lifeless eyes that had gawked at us from the walls of S-21. When we had left the museum today, something had followed us out of there, something that had kept Soeuth's hands shaking all the way back to the hotel, had injected a silence between us and had now fixed itself in the steely vacuum of Ly's eyes.

Another girl straddled me suddenly and tried to unzip my pants. I grabbed her hand away, and she seized my other hand and tried to rub it along her crotch. I shook my head and gently pushed her away. Soeuth leaned in so that no other girls would straddle me. He explained through the listing smoke of my cigarette: "A lot of Cambodians don't know where to go. Live in the street." He put out his cigarette as if to punctuate this statement. "This the only job they make money. Boom-boom all the time."

We finished our Tigers and left.

After we landed in Battambang, we stood outside and watched a small boy skip and jump across the sun-battered tarmac, pushing a bicycle tire. Three oxen tied to a shed next to the airport terminal picked weeds out of a stubborn patch of dirt. We stood wearily, our luggage at our feet, as the taxicab drivers advanced.

"Taxi! Hotel!" A cherubic man was jogging toward us.

After we checked in at the International Hotel, our very friendly driver chauffeured us to the Neak Poan restaurant. Tables were arranged among palm trees around an open-air stage. On the stage was a man singing a melancholy tune. Some instrument that sounded like an underwater flute rippled eerily in the background.

As we were seated, a flock of nine or ten beer girls descended upon us. They were wearing beauty-contestant banners with beer logos, Heineken, Budweiser, Stella Artois. Our driver informed us that the idea with the beer girls was to pick the girl you liked, not the beer. Even though I found that idea just shy of repugnant, I ended up going with the Heineken girl—although I wanted Tiger beer—because she was prettier. Soeuth had Tiger beer and our driver drank Stella Artois. Our three beer girls hovered around the table as we ate, refilling our glasses even if they weren't empty, until they were drawn away by other customers. If we liked one of these girls, our driver said, it was only $20 to bring them to the hotel.

The Stella Artois girl pulled up one of the plastic chairs and sat next to Soeuth. She looked very young. She began to ask him questions in Khmer, and he nodded, and in response to one question—her last question—he smiled, shook his head and held up his wedding ring. Then he began to ask her questions. She answered abashedly, swinging her bangs in front of her eyes. When Soeuth offered her a cigarette, she refused politely, rose, bowed and left. As she strolled away, carrying our beer cans clumsily in her plump arms, Soeuth said: "She's only eighteen. She came to Battambang because her husband in Phnom Penh hit her."

"How old was she when she got married?" I asked.

"I don't know." His eyes followed her making her way around a neighboring table, collecting beer cans. "She became a prostitute when she was sixteen. When she make enough money, she go back to her family's farm near Phnom Penh and give them the money."

At the hotel, Soeuth collapsed on the bed and said: "You know, it's so sad, only twenty dollars—those beautiful girls, wasted."

He propped himself up on his elbow and stared intently at the ashtray, as if his gaze could nudge it across the bureau toward me; I was lighting a cigarette. His head hung heavy between his shoulders, and the contours of his skull were prominent under his skin. Then he muttered almost inaudibly: "Cambodian girls are cheap."

His words hovered in the room for a moment, until they were dispelled by the clack-clack of the geckos. I inhaled deeply and blew the smoke out slowly. My eyes followed the curls of smoke as they rose to the ceiling, as if in their ephemeral ascent I could find a response.

"Old man," I said, "it's not because they're Cambodian—it's because Cambodia's been so royally fucked by almost everybody. Everybody here is so damned poor . . . but you know all that."

"It just make me sad." His eyes followed a bug crawling on

the wall. "If I have money, I give to them enough, so these girls can go home, stop being prostitute." Then he sat up with the suddenness of a catapult. "Do you think you will marry a girl from Cambodia?"

I shrugged and pulled a blanket across my legs, even though it was hot. I was too tired for questions like this. "I don't know," I said. "Who knows? I thought you said I was too young to get married."

"Well, not now," he replied. "But if you ever decided to marry a girl from Cambodia, I want it to be good. Because you're my brother, and I'm a Cambodian and she's a Cambodian. I want it to be good."

"Thanks," I said. "You never know."

"You never know," he repeated and picked up a wooden Lucky Buddha I had bought at the market. He held the fist-sized Buddha close to his face, so the two shared eye contact. Then he said, "Only Buddha know."

In the morning our driver said yes, no problem, he could help us find Soeuth's family's village, fifteen dollars, no problem. We left in the early afternoon, rolling down Battambang's pocked streets, past children playing soccer with a sandal, past tiny faces peering from dark doorways, past shops with amputees on crutches posed out front like partially disassembled mannequins. Once we were out of the downtown area, the city slumped into a series of tin-roofed shanties and lopsided buildings. As we neared the city limits, a military truck lumbered slowly by, tired teenage boys with AK-47s crowded in the back.

After an hour or so, the car turned off the road onto a narrow path running through a thick gauntlet of banana- and coconut-tree leaves. We emerged into a modest clearing flanked by a few straw huts on stilts and some crumpled sheds. The car stopped.

We sat still as faces surrounded us and eyes invaded through the glass.

"Okay," Soeuth said. "We're here."

We climbed out. Three little girls in skirts and no shirts giggled and pointed at me, and tiny cries of "Hello!" echoed from everywhere.

A cry of great joy or grief rang out from underneath one of the huts. Smiling gold teeth, a small, middle-aged woman emerged. She stood before Soeuth in awe. He prayed his hands. *"Sook s'bai dey,"* he said.

She prayed her hands back, answering, *"Sook s'bai."*

He said something in Khmer and indicated me. Then he said to me, "This is my cousin."

She walked over to me, seized my hand in both of hers and gave me her big gold, twinkling smile. She was the daughter of Soeuth's aunt Pai, a frail, wispy woman who watched us from inside the hut.

We drank coconut juice under the hut and his cousin with the gold teeth paddled a sampan across the river to tell his mother and father that their son was home. What would they think?— after their reunion, Soeuth and his family had once again drifted apart. They hadn't heard from him in more than two years. And now here he was, unannounced, barging into a random, unremarkable afternoon. And his tall, white American brother was with him.

A boy with long matted hair, in a tattered white sport coat, lay a chessboard on the bamboo bed frame in front of me. He and the girls who had giggled at me began to set up the game pieces, which included a coarsely carved king and queen, seashells, and bottle caps. The four of them took turns playing against me, wailing in enjoyment as they cleared my pieces off the board. I hadn't played chess in a while. I lost.

Soeuth finished his coconut juice and set his cup audibly down on the bench. He rose, looking out over the river, and I noticed the sampan returning, carrying over a dozen people. A flurry of hands waved at Soeuth. They reached the shore and tumbled off the boat, dazed children, young and old women, a teenage boy.

I shambled down the bank after Soeuth. He motioned me over to a shy, stout woman balancing a baby on her hip. The resemblance—the strong cheekbones, the defiance etched in her brow—was unmistakable. He placed one hand on my shoulder and one on hers. He looked at me levelly and said: "This is Korng, my sister." Then he turned to her and said: *"Bpa-oan proh ra-boh k'nyom"*—my little brother. Her dark eyes roamed my face. Then she smiled, a small, private smile, as if she, too, had detected some resemblance.

Back at the hut, Soeuth tenderly led a slight woman in a white shirt and blue *khrama* by the arm over to me. "This is my mother."

I prayed my hands and bowed. She put her hands together very carefully so just the tips of her fingers were touching and raised them close to her face, as if to relieve me of some curse. The careful creases in her face, the deep weariness in her eyes, told of the things she had lived through, things that had taken her eldest son out of her world and put him in mine.

Soeuth was tossing a Frisbee with a taut, handsome boy. "Adam," he shouted and whizzed the Frisbee to me. "This is my brother Wuy."

I threw the Frisbee to him. "Good catch," I said. He grinned widely.

When the game was over, Soeuth had me take their photo together, Soeuth standing in back of Wuy, his hands on his shoulders. Wuy stared boldly into my camera, tiny bayonets fixed in his eyes, as if to say: "You can't take my brother away from me, buddy . . . not just like that."

After I put away my camera, I looked up to see Soeuth and Wuy walking together down the bank toward the river, Soeuth's arm slung over his shoulder, two brothers laughing over some joke I did not hear and would not have understood anyway. They stood by the river's edge, and Wuy told Soeuth things that required full-bodied gesticulations. I lingered on the stubbled rim of earth that hung over the river and watched them. As the gaggle of people behind me prattled about me in Khmer, I felt weightless and awkward, as if the slightest breeze could knock me over and send me tumbling.

*   *   *

We all boarded the sampan. It bobbed across the grayish-brown Sangker River, a boy no taller than three feet muscling it forward with a bamboo paddle. We climbed the bank single file and children's faces peeked from the shadows of huts. Chickens squawked and dogs barked and children shrieked, and when we came to a dirt road, the line dispersed and formed a throng around Soeuth and me. All eyes were on us.

"My family's house." There was a wooden hut raised seven or so feet off the ground by heavy posts. "It's a new house, better than their old house," he said. "A lot better."

It turned out that this was the house his father had built with the last $3,000 Soeuth had sent him, after he had been robbed. They had written to him that they were forced to sell it, and when I asked him later why they had done that, he looked at me askance. We both knew why.

We padded up the steps and set our bags down on a porch that skirted two sides of the hut. I bent down to grab my camera, and when I glanced up, Soeuth was bowing. Emerging before him from the shadows was a frail man with a shock of white hair and a clenched face that looked, at first glance, like a piece of dried fruit.

"This is my father."

I was frozen for a moment, kneeling on the porch. I tried to match this man, who appeared as benign as an ancient monk, with the stories Soeuth had written about him: the beatings and whippings and the day he had sent Soeuth into the hands of the Khmer Rouge.

I rose, praying my hands and bowed. *"Sook s'bai dey."*

"Sook s'bai," he answered, bowing gently back.

"You got the cigarettes?" Soeuth asked.

The three of us sat in a circle on the floor and smoked and Soeuth and his father talked. After a while Soeuth turned to me.

"A lot of people are sick," he said. "He's sick."

I looked at his father. He smiled. He looked easily seventy-five years old, but I later learned that he was only fifty. The average life expectancy for Cambodian males, at that time, was fifty years. I wondered then, as I watched him inhale deeply on the Marlboro I had given him, how many years he had left.

Soeuth's voice slackened. "Since I was here in ninety-two," he said, "five people in my family have died."

"Jesus."

"My sister Soeun was one of them."

"Who were the others?"

"Cousins. And my uncle."

"What from? How did they die?"

"Sickness."

"What kind of sickness? Does he know?"

Soeuth asked his father; he didn't know.

His father exhaled and whispered to his son, changing the subject. Soeuth shrugged, mumbling an answer. Then his father grasped Soeuth's shoulders and softly uttered a few more words. There was a moment of smoke-filled silence.

"What did he say?"

An involuntary smile claimed Soeuth's face. "He ask why I didn't write to him for three years." He stared into a thicket of banana leaves abutting the hut. "I told him I had no money, couldn't send him any more money. He said that's okay. He said I'm his son, and please write to him, money or no money. He said he want to know if I'm okay or not."

Grinning, his father clutched Soeuth's hand and held it for a very long time.

After a communal lunch of rice and dried fish among the men, Soeuth and I strolled through Kompong Chhlang village. A tide of children, a dozen or more, surrounded us, eyes and smiles and little reaching hands.

"They like you," Soeuth said. "You're the foreigner. The white man."

"Hello!" they chirped. "Hello! Okay!" These were the only English words they knew and they uttered them excitedly, as if they belonged to some wonder-working recipe of which I was the central ingredient—a recipe that would bring them shoes and medicine and new clothes.

Other children squatted in the dirt and mud and cow manure, chewing on sugarcane stalks, playing with discarded plastic syringes. They had big, searching eyes, matted hair and beaming smiles, even though some of their teeth had already turned brown. Their tiny galloping forms and the anxious patter of their feet gave the village its life. As we walked with them, it felt as if some great current were directing us, and the farther we went, the more children it pulled into its wake.

Smoke and dust mingled and crept among the huts, and the stink of rot and shit and fetid fish was ever-present. A few rusted bicycles leaned against the sides of sheds, the only hint of something not preserved in precolonial time. The leaves of coconut and banana trees arched limply like the broken wings of prehistoric flying things.

The force of gravity was greater here, it seemed, pulling everything toward the hard dirt: the haunches of old women squatting, the heavy hulls of hammocks, the sagging roofs of thatched huts. It appeared that the higher one's hut sat off the ground, the more social clout one commanded. There was a ceaseless struggle to fight gravity, to stay upright, to ward off the squalor that drew one toward the mud, the fragmented coconut husks, the decaying detritus of life.

Kompong Chhlang was the village in which Soeuth had been born. It was located six or so miles from Battambang City and was not on the map, not the one I had anyway. Seven hundred families lived here, and the one occupation shared by all of the village's inhabitants was rice farming. Some families, like Soeuth's, who owned a few extra acres of land, had a small grove of orange or banana trees and maybe an acre or two of corn or cassava. The village appeared to be better off than other rural Cambodian villages, if only because no one here seemed to be starving. But no one seemed all that healthy either: many children were seriously stunted with distended bellies. The tiny boy who had paddled the sampan across the river, and whose age I had guessed to be five, was at least ten years old, I later learned.

Soeuth's family was one of the more prosperous in the village. Their hut was built of hardwood two-by-fours, not bamboo, and their roof was made of tin instead of grass and leaves. His father owned more land than most other villagers. When Soeuth came here in 1992, his family had lived in Ausroulab, about two and a half miles from here, where the land was scarcer and the threat of banditry higher. They were as poor as everyone else then, living in a thatched bamboo hut on stilts, with rice their only crop. Before our trip he had assumed the worst, envisioning his family robbed of all the money he had given them, perhaps living in a hut that sat directly on the ground, with no crops, no livelihood. Upon learning that they had been able to move back to Kompong Chhlang and build a new hut, and later receiving a tour of their new fields, he had felt proud indeed; in the time since he had seen them, their standard of living had increased two or three fold, mostly because of him.

What plagued this village, what had killed Soeuth's sister, what had taken the lives of adults and children alike, was sickness. Death from disease here was numbingly common. A friend of Soeuth's family, a woman who had lived across the river near his aunt, died one day while we were sitting on the floor of the family hut eating breakfast. She had been emaciated; her flesh had evaporated off her bones in a matter of months. No one knew exactly which diseases were causing the deaths. A few people had mentioned tuberculosis, but malaria, particularly in densely wooded, mosquito-infested areas of the countryside, like this one, was at least as great a threat. Everyone seemed resigned to the fact that anyone could get fatally ill at any time. The village could receive mail from anywhere on the globe (allowing sometimes for several months' delay), but because medical care was scarce and relegated mainly to urban areas and because medicine was prohibitively expensive, its residents could not get vaccinations or treatment for diseases that had been preventable for over thirty years.

On our way back to Soeuth's family's hut, a gaunt woman

whose polka-dot shirt clung to her, accenting the sharp angle of her collarbones, motioned us over to a bamboo bed frame in front of her hut.

After a greeting, she clutched my arm and led me toward a small hammock tied between stilts under her hut. As we approached, I could see a lump of something inside, maybe a sack of oats or a bag of dried fish. But then, suddenly, we were standing over it and I saw it was a child, a boy no older than two, sunk deep and still into the folds of the hammock.

The woman gestured wildly, an urgent entreaty issuing from her crumbling teeth, her words like the plucking of steel strings, her fingernails sharp on my arm.

She pivoted and shot a fury of words and spit at Soeuth. He nodded and then cut his eyes into the side of her hut, his face wan, downcast.

"Her baby's sick," he said thickly.

A few more words from the woman. Then she stopped abruptly and sighed, her polka-dot shirt crumpling like a sail that has lost its wind.

"She asks if you know what's wrong with her baby," Soeuth mumbled, looking intentionally away from me because he knew I had no answer.

I leaned over to examine the child, hoping a diagnosis would somehow miraculously occur to me. He could be dead already, his tiny, lifeless fingers tucked piously under his chin. I shook my head.

The polka-dot woman smiled softly, turned away from us and slowly rocked the hammock.

Soeuth and I bowed good-bye and walked down the village road. I lit a cigarette. "Is that child dying?" I asked him.

He turned away and lowered his head, as if to say, don't ask me questions like that.

Right then, I felt like the worst kind of impostor, the American voyeur who had come with his Cambodian foster brother to see what life was like in the old village, with no answers, no hope.

"C'mon, man," he said, and the village current took us up again and brought us and the shrieking children past some oxen tied to a small shed, over a wooden plank that bridged a dry gully and deposited us before an elderly woman with open arms and a sturdy, toothless smile. A gruff greeting, her hands firm on Soeuth's shoulders. She was chewing absently on a betel nut between her excited words, and pink-brown rivulets dribbled down her chin. She hooked a finger at me. *"Sa-at!"* she barked.

"She says you're handsome," explained Soeuth. "This is my aunt Him, my father's sister."

I prayed my hands.

She said, *"Goo-ee,"* and motioned for me to sit on the bamboo bed frame under her hut, and, in the same sweep of her hand, took Soeuth's arm and held it up to her face. She then shared an observation.

"She say I've gotten white," Soeuth said, smirking.

"If you're white, what the hell am I?"

He put his arm up to mine to show his aunt that at least he wasn't as white as I.

A little girl in tattered gray sweatpants and no shirt smiled shyly at me from behind a post. *"Sa-at,"* I said.

"She is cute," Soeuth agreed.

Then Him lifted the girl and precipitously plopped her in my lap. She made a motion with one of her hands, as if to suggest an airplane, and sent some serious words in my direction.

"She says you can take her."

"Take her?"

The girl looked at me and then at some sugarcane clenched in her fist.

"Adopt her," Soeuth said. "Take her to America."

I stared at him emptily.

"You can't," he finally said.

"I know."

Him sat next to me and stroked the girl's hair and explained to Soeuth other things about the girl.

"This girl orphan," Soeuth said. "Her father shot somebody and ran away to Thailand. Her mother chase after him. Her grandmother here, but she's old, can't take care of her forever."

"What's her name?"

Soeuth asked Him; Him wiped something off the girl's face, looked at me levelly and said: "Siem."

Siem glanced up at the sound of her name and, when she saw a multitude of concerned adult expressions, smiled self-consciously and pulled at the rubber band around her wrist.

"You shouldn't do it, man," Soeuth said. "You can't afford a kid." He paused. "But prob'ly nobody care if you take her."

Siem appeared content to sit in my lap all day, gnawing on her stump of sugarcane, testing the elasticity of her rubber band, idly swinging her feet. The girl was like a marionette's puppet: she never made a sound; and you could shift her in your lap, and she would sit however you had put her, no squirming, no complaints. In the next few days, although I had decided not to "adopt" her, it would become quite clear that she had adopted me. When I awoke in the morning and stumbled onto the porch for a cigarette, she would be waiting for me down below, pulling at her rubber band, and for the rest of the day she would follow me almost wherever I went.

When two young, brightly smiling women came down the steps of Him's hut to greet us, I put Siem on her feet. "These are Him's daughters," Soeuth said. "Rem and Reup. They're my cousins."

Rem, the older of the two, who had the graceful poise of an *apsara* dancer, sat next to me, opposite Siem, and handed me a photo of an emaciated man. She said something to me in Khmer that Soeuth overheard.

"That's her husband," Soeuth said. "He died last year of some sickness. Nobody know what."

Him pointed at me and shouted something at Soeuth and laughed.

"She say she's single now," Soeuth said.

Rem smiled, prettily, ruddy-faced and embarrassed.

I smiled, too; my face hurt from smiling.

"You think she's pretty?" Soeuth asked me right in front of her, because she didn't know what he was saying.

I glanced at Rem, but before I could answer, Soeuth added:

"She loved her husband a lot when I came last time, and she always talk about him after he died. She would be a good wife."

"I . . . I don't know, man," I stammered, looking at Rem, then at Siem, then at Soeuth. "I don't know. I mean, yeah, she's really pretty, but I . . ."

"Don't worry about it," he said.

During the time we would spend with his family in their village, sharing their food, the sleeping space in their hut and the rough rhythms of their lives, I would scrutinize my older brother's countenance, trying to find out if he was ashamed or proud of my presence. I knew he was never fully comfortable with my being there. Sometimes I would ask him what something meant, and he would explain it with animated pride; other times he would say, "Nothing, man; you don't need to know."

I was determined to be on my best behavior, eating whatever was given to me—whether pig intestines or chicken-feet salad or dried catfish (which I liked); smiling whenever anyone else smiled; never refusing cigarettes (I found myself smoking up to two packs a day, the village standard); snapping people's photos whenever they were requested; not drinking too much bottled water, because they drank rainwater out of the ground or clay bins; helping out whenever it was appropriate. Once after dinner, I collected plates off the floor of the hut, and Soeuth's aunt waved her hands frantically and motioned for me to sit down. Soeuth shook his head. "Listen, man," he said. "You don't need to help them. They don't like you to help them. Let them do it."

I also made the mistake of bringing up politics. We were eating lunch in his brother Su's hut one afternoon. I was asking questions; Soeuth was translating. When I asked whom people had voted for in the 1993 elections, everyone in the hut lowered his head and no one answered.

"They're afraid," Soeuth said. "They don't like to talk about it."

Keeping silent was a means of survival in Cambodia. During the Pol Pot Time, an expression of political views could be cause for execution. The people of Kompong Chhlang had learned long ago that offering opinions on such things as elections was unwise.

I soon learned that I wasn't merely an inconvenience for my brother and his family; I was a liability. My conspicuous presence—a tall white man, surrounded by screeching children, stumbling down the village road, a tall white man who was certain to have money—could put his family in physical danger.

Soeuth's father told us one night about the mugging in 1993, after Soeuth's visit. He said he had been awakened by noises in the hut. Someone had shined a flashlight in his face, and someone else had said, "Let's tie him up." He had fled the hut and run down the road. Six men had chased him and, when they had caught up to him, had kicked him to the ground. When he had tried to get up, one of them had struck him in the head with the butt of a rifle. The bandits had returned to the hut and stolen all the gold they could find. Since then, his father hasn't been able to think straight and has trouble finishing sentences.

After telling us this story while we sat on the floor of the hut, Soeuth's father gripped my hand and moved my fingers into a notch in his left temple where the rifle butt had left its mark. It was about half an inch deep.

"Jesus!" I barked reflexively. "Soeuth, I think they cracked his skull . . . do you want to feel it?"

Soeuth shook his head, looking away. He was haunted by the events following his visit in 1992, knowing that not only had he made his family richer—he had made them a target. He had told me many times that he had considered hiring someone to kill the thugs who had done this. Even though he had, in the end, decided not to—an assassination could trigger other assassinations— he had explained to me that if there was any justice in Cambodia, if there was any justice in his family's village, it was swift, personal and usually involved someone being killed. Soeuth's father told us that last year a man who had robbed several families in the village was ambushed one night by the village leader's posse. They took him out to the fields, gagged him, put him on his knees and doused him with gasoline. Then they lit him on fire and watched him burn to death.

It was risky enough that Soeuth himself had come back, that the thugs who had robbed and terrorized his family could get word of his visit. But this time he had brought me with him. I had to be careful, Soeuth said, not to be seen by too many people, not to venture off by myself in daylight.

But the threat of violence, like disease, was something the inhabitants of Kompong Chhlang had never lived without. As recently as 1994, more than a dozen Khmer Rouge guerrillas had raided the village, looting peoples' huts and letting livestock loose to devour crops. They had abducted the village leader, burned down his hut, dragged him out to the fields and shot him in the back of the head. The Khmer Rouge were less of a threat now, since over half of their members had surrendered to the government, but just the mention of their name here still elicited darkened glances.

All of these things had happened more than two years ago, but Soeuth didn't want to take any chances with our own safety while we were here. He had told me before the trip that we would need bodyguards. When he was here in 1992, he had hired five bodyguards, but since neither of us had enough money for five, we hired two. He said they would each cost about $50 a week. They showed up around 6 P.M. on our first night in the village, when the sky shimmered folds of dark silver. They were father and son, both friends of Soeuth's father. The father looked to be in his late forties, and the son no older than thirty, with a boyish face. They each had an AK-47 slung over their shoulder and were both wiry and slight of frame. They rested their guns against the porch railing and drank with us, taking hearty swigs of rice whisky out of a Sprite bottle that was going around.

The son's name was Chut. I sat with him on the bamboo bed frame in front of the hut as the darkness thickened and the chirping of crickets swelled. A fluorescent light that Soeuth had rigged to a generator hung from the porch, making everything on the ground a bright gray and sending a mean glint down the barrel of Chut's AK-47. We leafed through my Cambodian-English dictionary, while the children flocked around us and taught each other token words from our respective languages. We lit our cigarettes, and he held up his, between his thumb and forefinger, and announced crisply: *"Ba-ray."*

"Ba-ray," I repeated.

"Anglais, ta make?" he asked eagerly, setting his gun against the bed frame next to Siem, whose eyes squarely met the top of the barrel.

"Cigarette," I said.

"See-ga-rette," he repeated attentively, a French pronunciation furling his tongue. The children, all except for Siem, repeated in enthusiastic unison: "See-ga-rette!"

He pointed to oxen lying in the road. *"Goa,"* he said.

"Goa," I repeated. *"Anglais,* we say ox."

"We say ox," he said; "We say ox!" the children said.

"No." I laughed. "Just ox."

"Just ox," he said; "Just ox!" the children screamed.

I pointed to the oxen in the road. "Ox."

"Ox," he said; "Ox," the children said.

I flipped through the dictionary, and when I looked up Chut had suddenly grabbed his gun. My heart jumped. He hoisted the rifle up so that it was horizontal, displaying it as though he were selling it at an auction.

"Gum-plerng," he said.

"Gum-plerng," I repeated.

"Anglais, ta make?"

I looked at the long black military rifle, wondering if it had killed anybody. "Gun," I said.

"Gun," he said slowly, as if in a trance.

"Gun!" the children shouted with more enthusiasm than before and tumbled off the bed frame to shoot at each other with make-believe rifles.

Chut rose and paced toward the road, holding his gun out in front of him. "Gun," he said again, like the word had suddenly invested new power and potential in his weapon.

As I picked my teeth after our rice-and-chicken breakfast, I noticed a framed photo of Soeuth on the wall, hanging crookedly, green splotches mottling its surface. It was the same photo that had, at one time, hung on the wall of our parents' room. In it, Soeuth was wearing a heavy wool sweater, camouflage pants, and smiling awkwardly. After he noticed me studying it, he rose and removed it from the wall. "They waste my photo," he said.

On the porch, Soeuth's mother and father and aunt Him were poring over the photo album he had brought with pictures of him and his new wife. Other people leaned over their shoulders to see this pale Vietnamese woman who was now an in-law of theirs.

Him laughed and shouted something at Soeuth.

"What did she say?" I asked.

"She say, 'Your wife is Vietnamese, she must not be good.'" But he was smiling after she said it, so I assumed he assumed it was a joke.

Then Him said, "Oh . . . *sa-at*," when she came across one of the wedding photos and seemed to redeem herself.

"She say she's pretty," he said.

"Thank God."

Then I asked Soeuth's mother: "*Roop taut* Soeun?" She nodded and quietly went inside. She emerged with three photos and passed them to me.

Soeun stood in a simple yellow dress in front of a few rows

of corn and smiled modestly. She looked less like Soeuth than Korng did, but had the same defined cheekbones, the same defiant eyes. I asked Soeuth to ask his mother what Soeun's symptoms were. She said Soeun had been emaciated, had suffered from stomach pains and had had a lump in her stomach. She had taken sick just after Korng's wedding in March of 1995. Three months later, she was dead. She had been admitted to the hospital, his mother said, but no one knew who her doctor was. Are there medical records? I asked. No, his mother said, no records.

I studied her photo for more clues. But all I saw was a healthy, strong and vibrant young woman who didn't like having her picture taken. I turned to hand the photos back to Soeuth's mother, but she had gone inside the hut. I stepped inside, and she, Soeuth and Soeuth's father were sitting in a circle on the floor, their heads bowed. Soeuth raised his head, and for the first time in more than twelve years, I saw tears in his eyes.

We went for a walk that afternoon, Soeuth, I and his younger brother Su. Su was austere and soft-spoken. He was married and had a two-year-old daughter who was usually dressed in frilly pink and blue jumpsuits and could easily have won a village cuteness competition. The day before, I had given Su my old Barlow jackknife—it was one of my first jackknives, handed down from Grandpa Ken—since all I really used it for was slicing through the occasional heavily taped parcel. He had clasped the knife in both hands and then had prayed his thanks at me solemnly.

Su led us on a tour of the family's fields. They owned a modest grove of orange trees, a few rows of banana trees, an acre of cassava, an acre or two of corn and, of course, rice paddies. They still didn't harvest enough crops to sell any of them; it was all for their own consumption.

As we reached the edge of the orange grove and walked along a crude fence made of bamboo and thorn stock, I remembered reading that Battambang Province was the most heavily landmined region of Cambodia. I asked if we should be worried about land mines, and both Su and Soeuth laughed. *"Kroa-up meen . . . ah dtey,"* replied Su dismissively. He pointed at the edge of the rice field where the rice stems grew erect from the shallow water like antennae of something lurking beneath the surface. He then made his hand into a claw and said forcefully: *"Bpoo-ah bpor-bplay-uk!"*

"Land mines no problem," said Soeuth. "Cobras the problem."

Su halted suddenly, knelt down and rubbed his leg, while chattering at Soeuth.

"He says a cobra bit him one day about three months ago," Soeuth told me. "His leg swell up big. He had to take medicine to make him throw up the poison."

After the fence ended, we treaded a narrow path that cut through the tall rice grass, and Soeuth looked as though he were walking along a narrow beam, placing one foot diplomatically in front of the other. I remembered then what he had confided several months earlier about the snake dreams. One night, at his apartment in Malden, Massachusetts, he and his wife and I were watching a Discovery Channel special on the cobras of India. Mai had protested that she was scared and had asked Soeuth to change the channel. He had shaken his head, muttering, "One minute, one minute," his eyes locked onto the screen. Three or four Indian children were stabbing a stick into a hole in the ground, taunting a mother cobra to come out so they could capture her babies. "The Indians, they not afraid of anything," Soeuth had said, awestruck.

Giggling, Mai had pulled at my sleeve and whispered: "One time, middle night, Soeuth wake up very scared, and tell me, 'Get out of bed, honey! Get out of bed now!' He jump up, very scared, and pull off all blankets, very scared! He think a snake crawling in the bed!"

Soeuth's snake dreams had been recurring for the past several years. They weren't like other dreams, he said, they were sharp, vivid. He would feel the snake sliding up his leg, stealing toward his throat, and he would startle himself awake. After he had jumped out of bed and turned on the light, he would snatch a broom, a belt, anything, and scour the room for the serpentine intruder, and when he couldn't find it, he would return to bed, wrapping the blankets around him tight.

He had told me that one day in a Khmer Rouge slave camp, when he was planting alongside another boy, a cobra had sprung out of the benign, lime-green grass, spitting venom in the boy's face. After his face had reddened and swelled, the boy was escorted by Khmer Rouge guards to the camp hospital—a place where everyone knew you did not go to get better, but, rather, to die. Although the boy had somehow survived, his face deflating eventually back to normal size, Soeuth had learned to fear snakes almost as much as he had feared his captors. That didn't stop him, however, from making dinner out of poisonous serpents. He would wade into the river at dusk, when the Khmer Rouge weren't watching, and stand still until he saw an oily form shivering across the water's surface. He would grab the tail and then whip the snake in circles above his head, like a lasso, until its bones were separated. Then he would smash it three or four times on the hard clay of the riverbank, until it went limp. One night after he had eaten his latest catch, some other children in the camp informed him that the snake he had caught that night was a deadly one, and that he was lucky the snake did not strike him first.

"Don't worry," he assured me as we continued along the path. "The snake that bit my brother wasn't in this area." But his sharp eyes, probing the wall of grass, trying to weed out the rustle of a fanged threat, betrayed his words.

The path ended in an open field overspread by fist-sized clumps of dirt that had been scorched gray by the sun. Three women, in bright yellow and red shawls, were hacking away at the clumps with hoes.

"Those are my cousins," Soeuth said.

"The soil is really dry," I said.

"They have no machines," he replied. "Do everything, pour water by hand."

As the afternoon sun seethed out a dizzying heat, Soeuth and I joined his cousins in the field. They laughed at us at first, me in particular, knowing that I was pink-palmed and soft. But as the afternoon wore on, they worked alongside us, telling us they could use our help, that this dry season had been a hard one so far, and they didn't know if the crops would survive.

Soeuth went to work on the hard dirt, throwing the hoe down and snapping it back up, his shoulder blades grinding under his shirt with an almost mechanical intensity. As I took a break to sip some water, I thought about offering some to him, but when I noticed he was working, I knew he wouldn't have heard me. Soeuth was a good worker, always had been. But today he was working harder than anybody. His cousins had learned, after breaking the earth day after day in the insistent sun, to work alongside each other with a methodical symmetry. Soeuth was not part of that symmetry; he struck the earth like a man out for revenge, perhaps trying to force a week's work into one afternoon. We stood still in our own rows, his cousins and I, and watched him. I imagined that he was taken by a similar rhythm to the one that had taken him when he was a child slave, when he had to work for food, when he had to work for his life. But now he was working for his family, not for Pol Pot, and he seemed to believe then, as he hammered the field, that he could save the crops, that he could till all of Cambodia, slamming his hoe endlessly into the soil, until all of the land sprang forth with corn and cassava and the promise that his people would never have to suffer again.

As I worked on my row, alongside the women whose hands were as tough as any Vermont farmer's, everything that separated me from them evaporated for a brief moment, and I knew that the gift they were giving me was the illusion that I was a part of their struggle.

After a break for a late-afternoon lunch of dried fish, Soeuth's brother Wuy trotted over to us with an armful of coconuts. I had seen him earlier, shimmying up a coconut tree, a scarf tethering his feet to its skinny trunk. He set the coconuts down, and hacked them open with a machete. We sprawled on the ground, imbibing the cool coconut juice, and Wuy returned to the field where his father was carrying two large buckets of water, suspended from a bowed stick perched on his shoulders. His father set down the buckets at the field's edge, and they each took up hoes.

Soeuth sat next to me, exhausted, the empty coconut in his lap. "Wuy is seventeen," he said. "He'll be doing this for the rest of his life."

He set his coconut down. "I used to think I was the unlucky one," he said. "They separated me from the family and put me in Vermont." He rose. "But now I know. I'm the lucky one."

Soeuth's cousin Pake invited us that evening to relax in his hammocks. A well-muscled man with an infectious goofiness, Pake was easily the most gregarious of Soeuth's relatives. He tended his own rice fields and raised roosters for cockfighting and caught catfish with his hands in a nearby lake (his forearms were embedded with bits of fin from wrestling with the stubborn fish). He smoked his own tobacco and marijuana, which he grew in small, neat rows behind his hut.

As his two-year-old son wailed over by the cooking pot, Pake climbed up the steps into the darkness of his hut and quickly emerged with a giant bamboo bong and a Sprite bottle full of rice whisky. He handed the whisky to Soeuth, and then lit up the bong and passed it to me. I sucked in the smoke of whatever he had in there, coughed violently, and Pake laughed. After a few swigs of the whisky, I felt suddenly deprived of any sense of balance or motor control. I collapsed into a nearby hammock. The thatched roof of Pake's hut swung to and fro above me, and I closed my eyes. I listened to the pigs; they were making obscene sexual noises and asking me to take their photo. A few of them converged on my hammock, snorting, *"roop taut! roop taut!"*— photo! photo!—and I fumbled for my camera bag, because I didn't want to offend them. I carefully lowered myself out of the hammock, hands first, onto the oak-hard dirt. Steadying on my knees, I removed my camera and fixed a snout in my viewfinder.

Pake lit the bong again, and I waved my hands, no, and glanced up at Soeuth and noticed he had opted not to partake.

A coconut, like a hacked-open skull, had suddenly been thrust before me, and my eyes followed the fingers that were wrapped like spider legs around it to the arms from which the fingers had grown to Wuy's widely grinning face. "Thanks," I said and realized I had to put my camera down before I could accept the coconut. Wuy laughed and took my camera and replaced it with the scalped, head-heavy coconut. I held it close to my lips and tipped it back; juice streamed into my beard, and everyone laughed.

It was a slow, halting, one-and-a-half-hour trip into the city. My motorbike wiped out on the red clay roads, Soeuth's ran out of gas and the one Pake and Su were sharing broke down several times. At one point the road developed a series of consecutive humps in its center the size of pitchers' mounds that made the bikes seesaw noticeably.

After we bought some gas for Soeuth's bike at a roadside fruit stand, we proceeded at about fifteen miles an hour, hoping our decreased speed would improve our motorbike karma. My bike was the last in the three-bike cortege, and when my driver and I rounded a bend and saw Soeuth, Pake, Su and their drivers standing in the road, their bikes leaning up against trees, we both sighed and muttered expletives in our respective languages. When we pulled up alongside Soeuth, I had expected his familiar, self-effacing, this-sucks-doesn't-it? grin, but he didn't even turn to acknowledge me. He slouched, hands in his pockets, peering into the yard of what appeared to be a temple. I dismounted the bike and walked over to stand next to him but did not look at him, not even out of the corner of my eye; we could have been two men in some wistful Winslow Homer painting, staring out to sea.

"This place," he said. "I was here before."

There were two utilitarian buildings with bolted shutters, one with wooden latticed roof rails. The sharp, jagged upper half of a pagoda rose up behind the building on the left. An orange-

robed monk eyed us as he shuffled along a gravel walkway connecting the two buildings.

"Is this a temple you went to?" I asked.

"No." Soeuth inhaled stiffly. "This was a temple before the
Khmer Rouge took it over. This is Wat Slar Gram. This is the place
they took me when they first took me away. You see the cement here?"

"Yeah."

"That's where we slept. Outside."

My eyes scanned the courtyard; it had suffered cracks in its
cement from which weeds and tufts of yellowed grass now
sprouted. A bright-red-and-blue children's tricycle had been left
in the far corner of the courtyard, overturned and resting on its
plastic handlebars.

"How far is this from the village?" I asked.

He didn't answer.

"Not far, I guess," I mumbled to myself.

He kicked a pebble across the road. "A few miles," he finally
said. "Seemed farther then. When it was a Khmer Rouge camp."
He then pointed with his face to a sign secured above the gateway
entrance that I had so far failed to notice. The sign read in Khmer
and English: "Wat Slar Gram School."

As if on cue, the doors of one of the buildings were flung
open and a stream of children in blue uniforms spilled precipitously onto the courtyard.

"Let's get going," Soeuth said.

When we finally arrived in the city, we stopped at the central
market to buy a couple dozen mangoes and some grapes.

The four of us sat on the floor of the hotel room, messily
gnawing on mangoes and watching CNN. Pake and Su were
staring at the TV like children on their first visit to an aquarium.

When I procured myself another mango from the plastic
shopping bag that sat on the floor, Pake was indicating me and
talking to Soeuth.

"He say he like drinking coconuts with us," Soeuth said. "He

said we welcome any time to come to his house and drink coconuts and smoke with him."

"Tell him thank you."

Soeuth did; Pake raised his mango like a mug of mead and
winked.

I unfolded my map of Cambodia and spread it across the
floor. As Soeuth and I inspected the map, both Pake and Su
stared at it blankly. The town and province names were printed
in Vietnamese, and at first, I thought that was why they didn't
recognize anything.

"Battambang," I said and pointed to the city on the map.

They nodded slowly. "Kompong Chhlang?" Su asked.

"I can't find it on here," I said; Soeuth translated.

They were running their fingers haphazardly across the map,
veering at times into Laos and Thailand, before Pake asked me:
"Phnom Penh?"

"Down here," I said, pressing my thumb on the crayon-yellow
splotch that signified Phnom Penh.

They both nodded.

"They don't know," Soeuth said. (Pake had been to Phnom
Penh twice, once with Soeuth, but had probably never seen it on
a map; Su had never been.)

That evening we returned to the Neak Poan restaurant, the
open-air place at which Soeuth and I had dined a week or so
earlier. We were seated at the same table and the same bevy of
beer girls engulfed us. Pake, who sat next to me, stared incredulously at the beer girls, who were shouting out their brands in
English. He glanced at me, wordlessly asking for an explanation.

"Beer," I said and mimed sipping.

Pake squinted at me and continued studying the beer girls.

"They don't drink beer," Soeuth said.

I tapped Pake on the shoulder and growled: "Whisky!"

"Wi-skee!" he agreed and winked.

But they didn't have whisky, so we all drank beer. I stuck to
Heineken, and Soeuth, Pake and Su drank Tigers. Soeuth informed his cousin and brother that these young girls were, sadly,

on sale for $20 a night. Pake and Su, both fathers, grimaced upon hearing this, timidly sipping at their beers.

When I asked for a pair of chopsticks, Soeuth reminded me that only city folks use chopsticks. Soeuth ordered for all of us, because I couldn't speak Khmer, and because the last time Pake and Su had been to a restaurant was probably when Soeuth brought them to one in 1992. They had both been to school for a few years, but there were many words on the menu, printed in Khmer and English, that they couldn't read. Su smiled tentatively when the waitress brought our food and made sure not to begin eating before Soeuth had. Soeuth leaned over at this point and explained to me again that Pake and Su were country people. He sat between Su and me, his two brothers, and at that moment he was the cultural mediator for us both.

After dinner, we smoked and Soeuth made a toast. He raised his Tiger can and said: "This is for good luck." We knocked our cans together, and then Pake belched, and so ensued a belching contest. Pake would swig half a can of beer before demonstrating his gastrointestinal prowess. After he had clearly won, he patted me on the back, and I belched obligingly and then bowed my head before him to concede defeat.

As we left the restaurant, Pake slung his arm around my shoulder, and we stumbled back to the car like two soldiers on the last night of R and R. The taxi we had hired was waiting for us.

At the hotel, we crashed on the beds, and Soeuth turned on the TV. There was a porno movie playing, two fat blond Americans going at each other like animals in danger of extinction. Pake and Su were mesmerized. Soeuth rubbed his eyes.

As the porno's moans and sighs filled the room, Soeuth and I slipped out to the balcony for a cigarette.

"Oh, man," he said, shaking his head. "These guys never seen a porno before."

"Cross-cultural experience," I said.

"Maybe they know what to do with their wives now," he joked.

"Oh God . . ." I laughed.

"Yeah . . ." His voice trailed off. Then his tone assumed a parental concern: "I don't know, man, what do you think? Do you think it's okay?"

I shrugged. "They'll probably never see one again."

While Soeuth and I tried to sleep, Pake and Su watched pornos through the night, sprawled on the floor like kids at a slumber party. I don't think they were even aroused. It was simply something they had never seen before. These two men who supported their families off the land, who had faced hardships I would never know, sat there regarding naked bodies contorted on the TV screen with the raptness of astronomers peering up for the first time at a newly discovered constellation.

Before heading back to the village, we stopped at the market to replenish our bottled water supply, and I bought a couple of bags of toffee candy for the kids and a shirt with a teddy bear on it that said "Happy Time!" for Siem. When we returned and I produced the candy, a sea of children enclosed. Soeuth cautioned: "You got to make sure everybody gets some."

We stationed ourselves on the bamboo bed frame outside Aunt Him's hut and parceled out candy.

Siem didn't hold out her hand, so I folded a few candies into her palm. I found the shirt I had bought, and Him pulled it over her head. Him then lifted Siem into the air, announcing: "Oh, sa-at! Sa-at!"—pretty, pretty—and for the first time, I saw Siem smile. At the end of the day, after all the candy had been dispensed and consumed, I saw Siem walking proudly down the village road by herself in her new shirt, a dozen or so candy wrappers clenched in a tight fist.

One afternoon several days later, as Soeuth and I napped on Him's bamboo bed frame, Him roused us, shaking our shoulders. She was grinning ardently. We sat up. Siem was standing before us, hair combed, wearing a new purple dress. Two women flanked her. The older one was talking to Him, smiling, and indicating me. The younger one, wearing jeans, kept shifting her stance and looking anywhere but at Soeuth and me.

"That's her mother," Soeuth said.

"The one in blue jeans?"

"She came back for her."

"I guess that's good."

The older woman, Siem's grandmother, whose eyes hovered warmly in her loose face, took Siem's hand and led her over to me. She pressed Siem's hands together, and gently folded the girl into a bow.

"*Lee-a-hai*, Siem," Him said.

I prayed my hands at her. "*Lee-a-hai*, Siem," I said. "Bye-bye."

"Bye-bye," all the women repeated.

"Bye-bye," Soeuth said.

Siem regarded me quietly. Then she whispered, "Bye-bye," the first words, Khmer or English, I had ever heard her say.

Then her mother led Siem by the hand away to her new life.

"She be okay," Soeuth assured me. "She live in Thailand now—probably a lot better than here."

Most everyone had dressed up in a multicolored sarong or a best long-sleeved shirt for the festival. I wore jeans and a T-shirt. Crossing the Sangker in the sampan, we could see the strings of lights and hear the thumping and wailing of Khmer music.

Our bodyguard, Chut, who had left his gun back at the hut, led the way. He grasped my hand and pulled me through a crowd of staring people to the brightly lit, sandy dance space behind the temple. "*Rao-um!*" he shouted and joined the undulating mass of dancers, all of them men, and beckoned me to follow. I looked back and noticed Soeuth smirking. I shrugged and timidly trailed Chut.

The dancers were circling a tree in the center of the space. I stayed behind Chut, repeating his steps. But the song was slippery, and the moves snakelike, and my attempt at imitating them resulted in a pseudo–Mick Jagger chicken dance. At some point, Chut glanced back at me and barked out cackles and the guy in front of him laughed, too, and soon big waves of contagious laughter rippled all around. I surveyed the periphery of the dance space to see a crowd of two hundred people or more suddenly staring and pointing at me. I was the only white person present, and figuring that these Cambodians had never seen a white man dance, I went nuts. People clapped and cheered. Soeuth and Pake lingered on the fringe of the crowd, howling along.

After a few songs, I stumbled over to Soeuth. I was exhausted and soaked in sweat. I collapsed, and the crowd enclosed. Soeuth extended his hand and pulled me up. "Follow me." He led me to a table where a young woman was selling drinks and fruit. She was smiling and looking at the ground and stealing brief glimpses of me and Soeuth. Soeuth said something to her and turned to me.

"Get down on your knees."

I squinted at him.

"Just do it," he said. "She wants to feed you oats. It means she likes you. Just eat from her hand."

I sank to my knees, and the girl, whose eyes gleamed fiercely in the low light, lifted her hand, full of oats, to my face. My eyes met hers, and she giggled, gently slipping the oats into my mouth.

As I stood up, Soeuth informed me I was obliged to do the same with her. I scooped some oats of a bag on the table. Then Soeuth said, "Hey, man, look," and I glanced up to see a line of four very pretty girls, giggling and waiting to feed me oats.

As we left the festival, two boys grabbed my hands and tugged me toward the river. I realized then that more than two hundred people had witnessed me make a very conspicuous fool of myself. Even though Soeuth didn't seem too worried about it, I started to feel ill at ease when we boarded the sampan. I quickly assured myself that Soeuth's parents had not accompanied us to the festival and that, hopefully, no one would know whose guest I was. But as the boat slid quietly onto the bank of the opposite shore, I knew I could never be sure: news in Kompong Chhlang and the surrounding villages traveled quickly and infectiously, and since I was probably the first white man ever to have spent a night here, most everyone would probably find out in whose hut I was sleeping.

After Soeuth combed his hair and before we ate breakfast, he lit my cigarette and then lit his, and I said, "We can't put it off much longer."

He nodded. "Okay." He stepped on a water bug that was scrambling toward a crack in the floor. "We do it tonight."

After dinner, Soeuth, his mother and father and I convened around a kerosene lamp on the floor of the hut. We sat in a perfect square, and everybody but me held his hands in his lap. A pack of Victory cigarettes lay next to the lamp, for anyone who would need one. Soeuth's father and mother were smiling faintly while I fumbled with my tape recorder. Soeuth was not smiling. I was nervous, but not possibly as nervous as he was. We were about to open up some old, still sore wounds.

I turned on the tape recorder. "Okay." I cleared my throat. "Tell me what Soeuth was like as a kid."

Soeuth translated the question. His mother and father both chuckled. Then his father answered, not sure whether to look at Soeuth or at me.

"They say that when I was younger . . ." Soeuth was smiling now, though not comfortably. " 'Cause we were poor, mostly I was stealing stuff from the family. When I was at the camp, I came home and stole stuff."

His mother then offered her answer.

"She say that when I was in the camp, I came home. I stole

the cassava. My grandmother said, 'Somebody take all the cassava!'—and it was me. I stole a lot."

"You were hungry," I said.

"Yeah," he said nonchalantly. "They don't give us food.
When I come from the camp, I don't want to go back—so I have
to survive."

I asked his father about life before the Khmer Rouge, if
Soeuth had worked a lot in the fields with him and what kind of
work he did.

"A little bit," Soeuth translated. "They can't really put me
to work."

His father continued, his raspy voice floating across the room.

"He said when I was young, I don't like to work. I like to
lie." All three of them laughed.

"Did they know what happened to you in the Khmer
Rouge camps?"

Soeuth posed the question. His mother answered.

"Sometimes somebody else say they beat me or they tied me
up," he said. "They were sad, you know, always talking about
me, if I'm dead."

"What happened to them during the Khmer Rouge?" I asked.

His father answered with a story about giving an orange to a
little boy who was starving. A Khmer Rouge leader, after retrieving the boy's orange and interrogating him, had detained Soeuth's
father for questions but had released him. On another occasion,
when the rice house he was charged with watching had been
raided, he had again been detained and had been told he would
be killed. A high-ranking leader had intervened, sparing his life.

Then I asked the question we were all dreading.

"Does your father remember the day in 1976 when you were
taken away?"

Soeuth cleared his throat and then mumbled the question at
his father. *"Taer loak oa-bpOOk mien jum barn t'ngai dael Khmer
Gra-horm yoak k'nyom dtou?"*

His father swallowed slowly and nodded.

The kerosene lamp throbbed and painted the room with flickering shadows. Soeuth looked at me, and our eyes locked.

Finally, I said, "You wrote in your journal that he let them take you."

Soeuth lowered his face. "Do you want to ask him if that's what happened?" he whispered.

"I want to ask him why."

Soeuth was silent for a good half minute. His father had raised this matter himself twice before. The first time was in the fall of 1976, when Soeuth had first run home from the slave camp. Two weeks, his father had said, two weeks—I thought they would only keep you for two weeks. It was a brief comment, and since Soeuth was afraid of his father, he had not replied. The second time the issue was brought up was during Soeuth's visit in 1992. His father had admitted that what he had done on that fateful spring day was wrong, but then, immediately after Soeuth had shrugged it off, had artlessly begged his son for money. He had never said he was sorry, and Soeuth never knew if the reason his father had mentioned it at all was because he had been genuinely remorseful or because he had wanted something from him. The two hadn't spoken more than a few mumbled words about it, and Soeuth had ended the conversation. Now his American brother was confronting his father, and Soeuth found himself between us, the translator, the apex of an awkward triangle.

Soeuth inhaled deeply and then stuttered the question at his father.

His father nodded as his son's soft, embarrassed words filled the dim room. He lit a cigarette. He answered in stilted fragments, while looking up at the ceiling, and when he had finished, he sighed and sat back against the wall.

"What happened . . ." Soeuth began. "I was fighting, take the rice . . . hungry, take more rice . . ."

"You were fighting with Soeun—"

"Yes," he said, averting his gaze. "He say they let me go to that camp for study. He don't know. They thought that they brought me to study, exercise. It's not like working or starving—

they had no idea . . . He said the kids really went through a tough time, that they treat us bad . . . He feels bad."

During the early and mid 1970s, the Khmer Rouge, in the years preceding their takeover, had cultivated support in the Cambodian hinterland, repairing peasants' damaged houses, helping them build irrigation systems and promising revenge against the Americans, whose bombing campaign had decimated the countryside. Soeuth's father might have been one of the many who believed in their promises, but that didn't change the fact that he had handed his son over to revolutionaries wielding AK-47s. We all understood, I think, that the underlying reality was even more vexing. During the Pol Pot Time, the Khmer Rouge had favored peasant families, like Soeuth's, over city families. Peasant children had sometimes been allowed to remain with their parents longer than city children. Soeuth's cousin, Khan, for instance, had never been separated from his parents. Soeuth had also been several years younger than the vast majority of children collected by the Khmer Rouge. Had his father not willingly given him to the black-suited soldiers, it is likely they would never have taken him.

Soeuth's father sat in a cloud of smoke, humiliated and hunched over like a shrunken doll. I felt sad but also satisfied at the sight. For once in my life I had been able to do something for my big brother. I had been able to ask the question he couldn't or wouldn't ask—and to get an answer, an answer acknowledging remorse.

I said, "That's it . . ."

Soeuth let out a deep breath, and when he did, it seemed the room was relieved of a stifling humidity. "Okay," he said. "That's over."

I asked then about their lives in the past couple of years, and Soeuth's father started telling a story.

"It was a rainy day," Soeuth began. "Somebody shoot from over there." He waved his hand behind him, in a northward direction. "Far away. They didn't aim at him. But the bullet travel so far and hit him. It went through here." He indicated his left cheek. "The bullet go into his mouth, and then he spit it out. It hit the floor and come back up and hit him. There's a bullet hole right there." He pointed toward the porch.

I asked his father if he lost any teeth, and he said, no, they were gone already.

As if to punctuate this story, a gunshot suddenly rang out in the near distance. I jumped. A baby started wailing. Soeuth's father chuckled.

"Wild West, man," Soeuth said, chuckling also.

"Are our bodyguards out there?"

"Yeah."

As I rewound my tape, Soeuth's father took my arm and squeezed lightly, as if to tell me, it's okay, I forgive you.

It was only a few days before we were set to leave that I took sick. One afternoon at Pake's, I rose and was sharply punished by a sawing pain in my gut. Rifling through my bag for our roll of toilet paper, I was nearly felled by a dizzying head rush. I grabbed a shovel and stumbled off in search of a private, shaded place. At the edge of a rice field, where a few banana trees offered a spotty shade, I began, furiously, to dig a hole. I almost passed out before it was all done.

The next day Soeuth came down with whatever I had, except he had it worse. He could hardly walk and shook from chills, even though it was between ninety-five and one hundred degrees. He wrapped himself in three wool blankets, shivering on the bamboo bed frame under Him's hut. I began to panic as names of various diseases ran through my head—dysentery, giardiasis, Japanese encephalitis, cholera. I had to get him out of here.

That night, under our mosquito net, neither Soeuth nor I could sleep for several hours. When he shivered, it looked as though an electrical current were running through him. He had curled into the fetal position, perhaps in an attempt to keep from shaking. At one point in the night, when sleep and consciousness had reached a stalemate, I saw a shadow moving across the far wall. It turned to regard me once, fleetingly, and at first, I was sure it had the face of a skeleton; but then the kerosene lantern it was clutching filled in the gaping holes in its face, and I could see it was Soeuth's father. He seemed to be squinting at me, but I remembered then that I had never really seen him not squinting. He padded out to the porch, and sleep put a sudden stranglehold on consciousness, and I dreamed of thousands of bullets chasing me through the village like a swarm of bees, and Soeuth's father was running ahead of me, daylight pouring through the holes in his body.

Within two or three days, we both started feeling better. We were still making half-hourly trips to Su's outhouse, a squat box made of leaves and grass, which was situated in an arbor of banana leaves across the path in front of his hut and used by half a dozen different families. Soeuth told me Aunt Him had dug a convenient shitting hole for us right next to her husband's grave, which sat, surrounded by flowers, fifteen feet from her hut. When Rem heard this, she joked to Soeuth, when you go to the bathroom, watch out, our father might reach up and grab you.

One morning as I stumbled toward the outhouse, a soggy roll of toilet paper tucked under my arm, an old woman with black teeth, a neighbor of Soeuth's family, stopped me and began praying her hands. She was muttering Khmer words I didn't understand, waving her prayed hands up and down. Then she said a word I knew: *"Loo-ee"*—money. I pointed to the toilet paper and explained apologetically, *"Meun sroo-ul kloo-un"*—sick—and she let me pass.

Soeuth had cautioned me when we first arrived in the village not to hand money to anyone. We could give some money to members of his family, he said, but not until the day before we left. It wasn't until our last few days in the village that the pleas for money became regular and insistent. One afternoon four or five people convened around me on the floor of Soeuth's family's hut, rubbing their fingers together and barking, *"Loo-ee! Loo-ee!"* Their requests were quickly morphing into demands. I felt myself torn between loving these people and being repulsed by their constant pleading.

One night while we stood under his parents' hut, where we hoped no one could hear us, Soeuth said that if I wanted to give people money, these were the rules: never count the money in view of other villagers, hand it palm to palm inside huts or behind sheds or under the cover of night, don't give money to kids and okay everybody to whom I wanted to give money with him first. In 1992, Soeuth had given money to too many people. Physical danger aside, we didn't want to sow acrimony into the fabric of this village by making anyone feel slighted.

Soeuth gave his parents $500; Korng, $50; and Su, $50. I handed his father a $50 bill, and he thanked me abstractedly, saying, *"Au khun, au khun,"* to the wall. I gave $50 each to Su and Korng; $25 each to Rem and Reup, who had done our laundry and taken care of us when we were sick; $25 to Aunt Him and $50 to Pake, who thanked me effusively.

After all the dollars had been allotted, Soeuth and I sat on the bamboo bed frame outside his family's hut.

"I think this village could be a better place," he said, his head hanging low between his shoulders. "Maybe someday, if I have money, I can hire somebody to bring electricity here, maybe hire some people to be police, maybe hire people to dig more wells so the water is good, maybe . . ."

"That's a lot, old man."

He sat up straight and a little boy climbed into his lap and he steadied the boy on his knee. "I know," he said.

My brother saw this village, in a way, as his responsibility. He knew that he couldn't provide exclusively for his family, because that would make others jealous and would once again single out his family as a target; if he was going to do anything, he had to do it for everybody.

He set the boy on his feet and lit a cigarette. He rubbed a circle in the dirt with the toe of his sneaker. "I can't stand this," he said. "I love them, but I can't stand this."

Finally, he added: "You are my brother. We stick together."

The next day we had packed all our luggage and the motorbikes were waiting out front, and it had started to rain. Everyone stood outside watching the sky. Children scurried out from under the huts and ran down the street screaming in excitement, because even they knew the rain meant that Buddha had brought luck to their village.

Soeuth walked to the fields to say good-bye to all his relatives. When he returned, there was a small, easy smile on his face.

"What's up, old man?" I was lacing my shoes.

"They say I'm the Rain King."

"The Rain King?"

"The God King of Rain," he said. "They say I brought them rain."

It was pouring now.

We lugged our bags down the steps, and Soeuth's father was waiting there for us. He seized my hands and whispered something to Soeuth.

"He says you are his family," Soeuth translated.

Holding my hands firmly, he regarded me squarely, his eyes shining bright blackness. I don't know what else he wanted to say to me—maybe "Thank you," or "Damn you," or "I'm sorry." In his face, in its weathered, worried contours, I saw everything that had been lost. I saw that he knew his son had died many years ago, and that his spirit had been brought back in the man who now stood between us.

Soeuth rested a hand on each of our shoulders and bowed his head. We stood like that in the rain for a long time, the three of us, watching the water bead on the clay of the road. I couldn't see my brother's face, but I knew somehow that he was smiling, knew that, as of this moment, his search was over. He had reached his good soil, that place apart from most of the rest of us, where ghosts return finally into the earth, where new life grows from the old, and where you know unequivocally, for once, that you are complete.

We strapped our packs to our backs. The entire village had gathered around us, or so it seemed.

"Lee-a-hai," I said to them, praying my hands. "Good-bye."

Aunt Him, Wuy, Woeun, Korng and her husband prayed good-bye. Soeuth's mother, Pake and Su, Rem and Reup, some of his other cousins and some of Su's in-laws had hired extra motorbikes so they could accompany us to the airport. We all climbed on our bikes, and the engines rippled to life. The bikes rolled down the village road and the children screamed "hello!" and, soon, the village was gone.

When we reached the airport, about forty-five minutes early, it wasn't raining anymore. No one else was there yet. I snapped photos of everyone sitting on the front steps of the terminal. Rem and Reup had me take special portraits of them, posing for me, their hands demurely folded beneath their chins. I took a photo of Soeuth and Pake, Soeuth giving Pake the bunny ears.

Other people soon arrived for the same flight we were scheduled to take to Siem Reap, hauling their baggage up the steps. As I knelt on the ground to put my camera away, Soeuth hoisted his duffel bag over his shoulder. He said, "Let's go."

"We still have a few minutes."

"No," he said. "We should go."

We made our way up the steps of the terminal, Pake and Su helping us with our bags, and before I realized it, Soeuth and I were inside the building and his family was outside, unable to enter, peering at us through a window.

Soeuth fished out his wallet to pay the airport tax, and I said, "Hey, old man, we didn't really say good-bye."

"We did," he said. "Outside."

His family waited there on the tarmac, waving to us, until our plane was in the air. As the airport became a white dot swallowed in green through the window, Soeuth said, "Good-bye."

On our last day in Phnom Penh, we visited Wat Phnom to have our fortunes read. The temple, an imposing bell-shaped stupa, was perched atop Phnom Mountain, a ninety-foot-high, tree-crowded knoll—the city's only official "mountain." Little girls selling individual sticks of gum and boys offering tours scampered among the discarded cigarette boxes and coconut husks at the base of the hill, latching onto the rare and coveted American, Australian or Japanese tourists. Some boys toted cages with spar-rows or other small birds and were charging one dollar to let you hold a bird and release it and watch it fly into the cloudless blue sky (the birds, however, had been trained to return to their young masters once they had completed their well-rehearsed perfor-mance). The fortune-tellers sat beneath Mild Seven and Tiger Beer table umbrellas that dotted the hill's knuckled, shady slope.

Soeuth's fortune was read by a diminutive, enthusiastically gesturing woman whose table sat in a flat patch of dirt near the winding set of steps leading to the temple. I waited near the street, watching as she whispered his fate to him and he nodded eagerly like a child receiving instructions for some great chore. As a school of templegoers spilled down the steps, Soeuth's fortune-teller stood up and shook his hand in a very official man-ner, and I knew that it was my turn.

I stumbled up the hill, my eyes swimming amongst the table umbrellas. An avuncular Chinese man wearing half-rimmed glasses beckoned me over to his foldout card table, which was shaded by a small palm tree. I sat down in front of his table, and he lit an incense stick for me and slipped it into his vase, which was crammed with the burned stubs of several dozen dispensed fortunes. I was very nervous. Soeuth was standing behind me.

"My name Mr. Turtle," the man said tersely and sniffed several times and then indicated a small tortoiseshell lying overturned on his table. "Give me your hand," he said.

He held the palm of my left hand close to his face and studied it while muttering to himself in Chinese. "Okay." He gripped my wrist and twisted my arm around so that we could both see the face of my palm. "You have two lifeline," he said. "Your life will be long."

He let go of my arm, scooped up his tortoiseshell, slipped a coin inside it and shook it so that the coin rattled like a die. Listening, he plucked a pen from his shirt pocket and noted his findings on a sheaf of graph paper he had torn from his swollen, sepia-colored notebook. He then consulted his cards, fanning them carefully on his table and squinting at them through a magnifying glass. After scanning the cards for several minutes, he set down the magnifying glass, steadied his pen over the paper and drew a nearly straight line. At the beginning of the line he wrote the word "car." Above the center of the line he wrote "way." And beneath the line he wrote "life" and drew a little box around it. He held up the sheaf of paper and said somberly, "This is your destiny." Pointing to the line he had drawn, he pronounced: "This is the way—the car will take you."

Grimacing, concentrating, he opened his notebook and flipped a few pages and then pinned one page with his thumb. He brought his magnifying glass close to the page, which bore a jumble of scribbled Chinese characters, to inspect my fate.

I looked over at Soeuth, who shrugged.

Mr. Turtle soon sniffed a few more times, cleared his throat and said: "You are a noble man. Your life will be prosperous. You will have a good wife. She will be loyal, will take care of you and listen to you."

When Mr. Turtle paused, Soeuth whispered to me, "Ask him where your wife will be from."

Mr. Turtle, overhearing this, said: "She will not be from your province."

Soeuth nodded thoughtfully.

"You are clever and good at your job," Mr. Turtle continued. "You work with your head, not your hand. Most your life bring you great happiness, but you must be careful in the years end with eight . . . when you are twenty-eight, thirty-eight, so on. These years half good, half bad."

Mr. Turtle sat back and drew in air through his nostrils, smacked his lips and brandished his right index finger. "There is one more thing," he said. "The twenty-ninth day of this month, you must be careful. There will be highwaymen waiting for you on this day."

Soeuth took this premonition seriously. "Stay home that day," he said. "Stay with me."

Mr. Turtle closed his notebook with a sudden slap, stood up and extended his hand. "Congratulations," he said. "Your fortune is good. And since you are a noble and generous man, you must give your fortune-teller at least five dollar."

I stood up and fished out a five-dollar bill and two ones and handed them to Mr. Turtle. Soeuth and I walked back down the hill.

"Not bad," Soeuth said.

"I guess not," I said. "How 'bout yours?"

"I think my fortune pretty good. She said right now I don't have a lot of money, but after New Year's and in the next year, I'm gonna have some money, but in the future I'm gonna have a lot of money. She said I don't get along with my wife's family. She said that my wife is hard but loyal to me. She said my wife will have a baby next year. She said me and my wife will be together forever, but that I will have two wives—that the only part that can't be true, 'cause I love my wife, stay with her. She said I'm clever and always thinking about work. She said my wife is clever, too, always thinking about getting different jobs. She said I too easily believe people—luckily, people doesn't rip me off. She said I'm kind, generous. She said if I love somebody, I love them for life; I didn't say nothing."

"She was pretty close."

"Yeah," he said. "Close enough."